THE HERITAGE ARENA

Food, Nutrition, and Culture

Series Editors: Rachel Black, Boston University
Leslie Carlin, University of Toronto

Published by Berghahn Books in Association with the Society for the Anthropology of Food and Nutrition (SAFN).

While eating is a biological necessity, the production, distribution, preparation, and consumption of food are all deeply culturally inscribed activities. Taking an anthropological perspective, this book series provides a forum for thought-provoking work on the bio-cultural, cultural, and social aspects of human nutrition and food habits. The books in this series bring timely food-related scholarship to the graduate and upper-division undergraduate classroom, to a research-focused academic audience, and to those involved in food policy.

Volume 1
GREEK WHISKY
The Localization of a Global Commodity
Tryfon Bampilis

Volume 2
RECONSTRUCTING OBESITY
The Meaning of Measures and the Measure of Meanings
Edited by Megan B. McCullough and Jessica A. Hardin

Volume 3
RE-ORIENTING CUISINE
East Asian Foodways in the Twenty-First Century
Edited by Kwang Ok Kim

Volume 4
FROM VIRTUE TO VICE
Negotiating Anorexia
Richard A. O'Connor and Penny Van Esterik

Volume 5
THE HERITAGE ARENA
Reinventing Cheese in the Italian Alps
Cristina Grasseni

The Heritage Arena

Reinventing Cheese in the Italian Alps

By Cristina Grasseni

berghahn
NEW YORK • OXFORD
www.berghahnbooks.com

Published in 2017

Berghahn Books

www.berghahnbooks.com

Library of Congress Cataloging-in-Publication Data

Names: Grasseni, Cristina, author.
Title: The heritage arena : reinventing cheese in the Italian Alps / by Cristina Grasseni.
Description: New York : Berghahn Books, 2016. | Series: Food, nutrition, and culture ; v. 8 | Includes bibliographical references and index.
Identifiers: LCCN 2016025397 | ISBN 9781785332944 (hardback : alk. paper)
Subjects: LCSH: Cheesemaking--Social aspects--Italy--Bergamo Region. | Cheese industry--Italy--Bergamo Region. | Cheesemakers--Italy--Bergamo Region. | Cheese--Varieties--Italy--Bergamo Region. | Slow food movement--Italy--Bergamo Region. | Food law and legislation—European Union countries. | Bergamo Region (Italy)--Social life and customs.
Classification: LCC SF274.I8 G73 2016 | DDC 637/.3--dc23
LC record available at hjps://lccn.loc.gov/2016025397

British Library Cataloguing in Publication Data

A catalogue record for this book is available from the British Library.

ISBN 978-1-78533-294-4 (hardback)
EISBN 978-1-78533-295-1 (ebook)

To Jonathan,

With whom life is worth living

Contents

List of Tables, Figures and Maps

Tables

Figures

Maps

Acknowledgments

I am indebted to many scholars who generously shared insightful discussion and work-in-progress research: the *Cheese Scholars Collective* convened in Devon in 2010 by Heather Paxson and Harry West; the participants and discussants in the Exploratory Seminar on *The Reinvention of Food* that Heather Paxson and I co-convened at the Radcliffe Institute for Advanced Study at Harvard University in 2012; Carole Counihan and Rachel Black, with whom I had the pleasure of working at Boston University's Gastronomy Program in 2013; the participants in the *Edible Identities* panels at the 2013 AAA Meeting in Chicago co-convened by Ronda Brulotte and Michael Di Giovine; and finally the SOAS network on Food and Heritage convened by Harry West in September 2014. The work with the international research team of PATRIRUR led by Xavier Roigé at the University of Barcelona (Patrimonialization and Redefinition of Rurality. New Uses of Local Heritage, 2012–14) allowed me to deepen my critical look at practices and discourses of heritage, especially thanks to conversations and conference panels shared with Letizia Bindi, Camila del Marmol and Ismael Vaccaro in Barcelona and Montreal. Finally I owe many dinners—never cheesy!—to Michael and Nea Herzfeld, and much more.

I wish to thank the Radcliffe Institute for Advanced Study at Harvard University for offering a one-year Fellowship and the Department of Anthropology at Harvard University for affiliating me as Visiting Scholar for two years—a safe haven during which I developed a number of research projects, including this one. At Bergamo University I wish to thank the co-directors and research partners of CORES LAB, particularly Francesca Forno, Silvana Signori, Silvia Contessi and Federico de Musso for the enthusiasm with which they study food production and consumption as significant sites of sustainable economies. With my colleagues at Utrecht University I share an interest in discourses and practices of sovereignty and social contestation as well as in sustainable citizenship.

One particular thanks to the indefatigable Michele Corti who never fails to share ideas and projects. In Val Taleggio, Arrigo Arrigoni is perhaps the most knowledgeable connoisseur of the extant historical documentation. I wish to thank the many 'informants' who appear under pseudonyms in this book, for their generous help and enduring friendship. I continue here a convention that I began in my book *Beyond Alternative Food Networks. Italy's Solidarity Purchase Groups* (2013), namely, to use pseudonyms for people who are probably easily identifiable locally, but whose privacy can still be protected from a wider readership. Thus, unless I quote public documents by public figures, or media that identify individuals by name and surname, I use pseudonyms throughout the book.

Abbreviations

AIA	Associazione Italiana Allevatori
ANARB	Associazione Nazionale Allevatori Razza Bruna Italiana
AOC	Appellation d'Origine Controllée
APA	Associazione Provinciale Allevatori (a section of AIA)
DOC	Denominazione di Origine Controllata
DOP	Denominazione di Origine Protetta (in English: PDO)
HACCP	Hazard Analysis and Critical Control Points
IGP	Indicazione Geografica Protetta (in English: PGI)
ONAF	Organizzazione Nazionale Assaggiatori di Formaggi
PDO	Protected Designation of Origin
PGI	Protected Geographical Indication
STG	Specialità Tradizionale Garantita (in English: TSG)
TSG	Traditional Speciality Guaranteed

Introduction

Why Cheese?

I do not often eat cheese; I simply do not like it. How I came to earn a diploma as cheese-taster in 2006 and became a member of ONAF (the Italian Organization of Cheese Tasters, Organizzazione Nazionale Assaggiatori di Formaggio) is part of my intoxicating engagement with cheese-making as a bittersweet by-product of studying dairy-farming, and with dairy-farming in the first place as a fundamental alley to complicating the self-image (and stereotype) of *bergamaschi* – people from Bergamo – as being 'mountain people'. I pursued this interrogation for some time with particular zest, being *bergamasca* myself.[1] When I started doing fieldwork in the valleys north of Bergamo in 1997, I found that my hosts – then supporters, among many other things they did and said, of the infamous Lega Nord[2] – were actually talking mostly about cows, mostly in dialect. I understood them because these people talked my own dialect, *Bergamasco*, from which I had been actively alienated by my own parents in fear of the social stigma that it still bears.[3] Since then, I have been following the cows, so to speak.

I coined the notion of 'skilled vision' in order to make sense of how cow-talk seemed to be an encompassing way of articulating presumptions about animal beauty, moral integrity, economic savviness, and feeling 'at home' in the world (Grasseni 2004). In a book entitled *The Reinvention of Food* (in Italian, 2007a), I focused on the meaning of 'reinvention' for the social actors engaged in transforming local foods into heritage foods. I suggested that reinventing local foods is a process of 'calibration': redefining and interpreting tradition in the face of multiple pressures and encroachments – from mutually entrenched technologies and audit cultures, as well as from a globalizing market that encourages branding. More recently, I have worked with alternative food provisioners in northern Italy, analysing their networks and their relationship with local producers, including cheese-makers (Grasseni 2014a).

What does all this mean to someone who does not even like cheese? To begin with, I can claim the privilege of an alien point of view coupled with intimate participation. As events unfolded that momentously changed the fortunes and fame of the families and friends who hosted me as a student at the end of the 1990s, I could focus not only on the sensory substances and textures that were pivotal to them, but also on their representations and their logics. Eventually, this gave me the gut feeling that the reinvention of food is actually something hardly palatable: perhaps this ultimate sense of alienation filtered the lyrical but hard-nosed clinging of people, politics and very real interests to something we can call 'our own' – something that, were we not in ever-campanilistic Italy, one could call a national consciousness.[4]

My first visit to Val Taleggio as an ethnographer dates back to the summer of 1997 as part of my Ph.D. in anthropology at Manchester University. As 'pre-fieldwork', I spent three months with a family of dairy farmers on the upper pastures of their mountain community. In 1998, as part of my training at the Granada Centre for Visual Anthropology, I went back to repeat the experience and produced a film about mountain dairy-farming, *Those Who Don't Work Don't Make Love*. Living together with one family of mountain dairy breeders for six months during two consecutive summers, I personally experienced their work routines, struggles and joys both in their village family house and in their mountain lodgings. During my summer stays I took part in and filmed milking and cheese-making in both the village stable and the stations on the high pastures. I filmed the daily toil with the cows in the shed, I took part in hay-making on the fields around the village and on the high pastures, I shared and prepared meals, made beds and played with the children, helped leading the cows uphill to the next station . . . After this intense acquaintance with the daily and seasonal practices of just one family – and their socio-professional network of visitors, clients, friends, consultants, customers and apprentices – for another six winter months between 1998 and 1999 I took up residency in the village of Vedeseta and met the other breeders and cheese-makers of the valley, whose farms and enterprises I visited. I also met the rest of the population – Vedeseta then counted about 250 inhabitants and Val Taleggio as a whole about 800. It would have been impossible not getting to know practically everyone: ageing pensioners and school kids, teachers and housewives, clerks, builders, lumberjacks and factory workers. I frequented the very active parish church, the municipality, the dairy co-operative and the marching band.

At this stage I also conducted 'shadowing' observation with technicians of the agricultural trade union (Coldiretti), the breeders' association (APA) and the experts of the breeders' association of the Italian Brown Breed (ANARB). In other words, instead of conducting interviews or visits by appointment, I took part, as an observer, in some of their routine tasks. Accessing farms and cheese-making facilities together with the relevant professionals meant observing farmers' interactions with them, witnessing debates, negotiations, complaints and gossip. While APA and ANARB technicians were mostly interested in animal husbandry, Coldiretti offered ampler consultancy, including on how to improve or set up farmers' cheese-making facilities and practices. I recorded some of the conversations for later analysis and filmed their working environments for my record. During my shadowing of experts I was then given detailed explanations, for example on the rationale of breed 'improvement' for an intensified but 'quality' milk production that would favour the national cheese-making economy. What is most relevant, I also listened to the explanations they gave to farmers. Residential fieldwork in the village resulted in my Ph.D. thesis and monograph (2009). This book builds on these previous insights but moves beyond them.

From 2002 to 2011 I was based at Bergamo University and the geographical proximity to my fieldsite facilitated continuous updates, correspondence and feedback visits to the cheese-makers of Val Taleggio. Taking a four-month cheese-tasting course organized by the chamber of commerce in 2006 – professional training for practicing cheese-makers – allowed me to reconnect with or meet new contacts, sharing with them a classroom experience that was at once relevant to and removed from their practice. I participated as guest speaker in 2006 in the valley's cheese festival, the Sagra dello Strachitunt, and collaborated with the nascent Ecomuseum of Val Taleggio. Through engagement with the Lombard Ecomuseums network, I visited similar projects in other valleys in Piedmont and Lombardy. I participated in the Slow Food international biennial food fair, the Salone del Gusto, of 2004 and 2010, first as ethnographer (videoing the Strachitunt presentation) and then as member (participating in the farmers' happening Terra Madre, visiting the valleys' Ecomuseum exhibit and actually selling the newly established Slow Food *stracchino all'antica*). Locally, I updated myself with yearly visits to the valley cattle fair and with follow-up conversations, emails and dinners with long-standing cheese-operators in the valley (entrepreneurs, cheese-makers, refiners, technical advisors, cooperative members and their families, buyers and market-stall vendors). Some of these conversations were recorded and transcribed, some were annotated in my fieldnotes.

In the meantime I had two children. I found myself breast-feeding at book presentations of local historians, attending community feasts and religious commemorations, or simply visiting families at home, exchanging experiences and views on entrepreneurship and motherhood. At some point I stopped counting the days and months, events attended and press clippings accumulated, as well as the hours of footage, interviews and soundscape – not to speak of the photographs and emails received and sent, particularly while I began spending most of my time abroad again in 2011. I was no longer thinking in terms of amassing data, of carefully selecting information to craft an article or book chapter. My ethnography ceased to be extractive. I was following events as they unfolded, trying to distil a logic, keeping a record of illuminating anecdotes – moments of insight – waiting for some kind of closure. The EU concession of the Protected Designation of Origin (PDO) to Strachitunt in March 2014 is the end point that I artificially chose for events and agencies that still laboriously unfold, with no lack of dramatic turns as people continue to fight with by now old enmities.

What I offer is an ethnographic investigation of ordinary activities and discourse both back- and frontstage of this arena. Cheese is here the chosen pivot of broader epistemologies that are acted on the ground, mediating personal, local and scalar levels of agency. The protagonists' enterprise is both heroic and banal. It is eventually about making a living and celebrating this fact *as if* it made sense. The concepts they mobilize – *patrimonio, tipicità, eccellenza* – speak to cheese as they could speak to other foods, to food heritage as to other heritage items. It is cheese in this case, because cheese is a marker of cultural heritage in these mountains. By making it, tasting it, naming it, selling it, eating it and celebrating it, the entrepreneurs, farmers and administrators of Val Taleggio found a way of talking about their valley as a community, and to lay claim to cheese denominations as a form of cultural property. Cheese is therefore here eminently a political conduit.

It is also of course so much more than that. The nitty-gritty of hygiene regulations and animal husbandry form the normative, milky and environmental substance of cheese-making. As we will see, for local cheese-makers it is important to determine the pedigree of their cheeses, including which Bergamasque valley produced which cheese in the sixteenth century. The convivial significance of sharing a plate of polenta and hunted birds is a multi-layered social performance. All of these topics and moments make up the ethnographic substance and the unruly detail of what people do for, about, and through cheese.

To make sense of it all, I use here two main metaphors, one of drama and one of war, conflated in one conceptual image, that of the arena. The war metaphor underlines how the reinvention of cheese as a heritage item is a process to which many competing actors concur: key local producers, influential food activism groups, local and regional decision-makers, and media figures. The drama metaphor highlights how the power relations and the strategic interactions among them are played out as political and cultural performances, which allows them to claim moral representation and political responsibility for an entire community. The war of the cheeses is certainly opportunistic and strategic like all wars, but, as any drama, it unfolds through powerful symbolic moments – both individual and choral – at once orchestrated and heartfelt by all involved. Precisely because of its intrinsically strategic character, however, the reinvention of cheese as heritage is an ongoing and dynamic process: it is constantly repitched and reperformed in relation to the actors' reciprocal repositioning.

"Positions and position-takings" (Bourdieu 1993: 30) happen within 'fields of heritage production' (Di Giovine 2014: 89) which juggle the social production of recognition with the very serious business of making a living, namely the social reproduction of the relevant actors, *qua* protagonists in the commodity arena. The concept of the arena indicates 'either a battleground or a stage or theatre' (Buijtin et al. 2013: 16). Through the trope of the drama, the book lingers on the linguistic and symbolic practices that turn a 'community of practice' into an 'imagined community', the subject and owner of heritage food as a patrimony, and of its *tipicità*. Recent heritage studies analyse the transition, in the language and practice of the heritage complex, from an expectation of communities 'bearing' cultural heritage to one of 'participating' in it (Adell et al. 2015: 8). Quite the other way round, here I unveil 'the mercurial, idiosyncratic processes of identification experienced by individuals in a mobile, globalized and uncertain world' (Adell et al. 2015: 9) as they become implicated in 'the intricacies of heritage governance at different levels of agency' (Adell et al. 2015: 14). The war trope allows me to dwell precisely on the 'arena of everyday life', on the idiosyncrasy of individual and collective engagements, and on the rhetorical and practical ways in which people balance pragmatically authenticity and anachronism, opportunism and sincere identification in food as a repository of their identity. Appadurai has taught that the politics of authenticity and the politics of connoisseurship are but some of the forms that 'politics', understood as 'the link between regimes of value and specific flows of commodities', can take (1986: 57). His use of the word 'arena' pertains specifically to how 'large scale exchanges' interact with 'more humble flows of things': 'in the politics of reputation, gains in the larger arena have implications for the smaller ones' (Appadurai 1986: 20). I approach the production of value for heritage cheese as a pivotal moment that brings politics to the fore and aligns social actors in relevant ways.

I am humbled by the task of bringing to synthesis over fifteen years of evolving scenarios. I have opted for an experimental narrative structure: the book is divided in three parts, each pivoting around key ethnographic scenes: a public speech given in 2006 by a local cheese entrepreneur, the official 'audition' for the concession of the PDO geographic indication to Strachitunt cheese in 2010, and a convivial meal in a mountain retreat involving Slow Food activists, myself and a local cheese-maker in 2013. The ethnographic settings will bring to relief the personal dilemmas and collective vicissitudes that unfolded over time. Each event marks a significant passage in the political and cultural dynamics that allowed a limited number of breeders, cheese-makers and refiners of a small mountain enclosure to obtain a PDO for their valley, namely for Strachitunt cheese. This is the story of how Val Taleggio lost cultural ownership of its Taleggio cheese, fought for a cheese of its own, and won Strachitunt (while rediscovering *strachì* – a humble transhumant cheese – in the process).

The goal of the book is to investigate the discourse and practices that turn food into heritage. By highlighting the key interpretations and performances of cheese as patrimony (*patrimonio*) and as a bearer of *tipicità*, I offer an ethnographically grounded theory of how cheese is reinvented, namely used as 'heritage' to leverage the glocally induced plight of local cheese-makers and mountain communities. The book shows how turning cheese into heritage (in other words, reinventing it) only works as a result of active and continuous intervention, including commercial tactics, symbolic politics and the pervasive performance of a culture of gastronomic discernment (gustatory, sensorial, historical, genealogical, geographic, agronomic and culinary).

Part 1, *The War of the Cheeses*, elaborates on the joined aspects of guardianship and reinvention, in the cultural mobilization of food as heritage. Economic rivalries, moral manoeuvring and political alliances are the protagonists of the intertwined histories of neighbouring mountain communities whose entrepreneurs and administrators choose divergent paths to 'valorize' their cheeses as 'patrimony'. Small and fiercely territorial PDO geographic indications coexist with other forms of self-safeguarding of other niche productions in the same area. Some opt for the distinction of hard-core authenticity, with marketing support of associations such as Slow Food. Others make use of more malleable quality certifications such as the commercial trademarks bestowed by local chambers of commerce. Others linger between quantity and quality, caught in the chasm. Each agenda is pursued by local politicians, entrepreneurs and activists who skilfully trade in the most viable currency of the moment (PDOs, Presidia Slow Food or chambers of commerce protocols) to articulate and claim their perceived right to the cultural ownership of 'their own' product. Chapter 1 explains how claiming control of a cheese as patrimony of a locality falls nothing short of advocating sovereignty for it. Chapter 2 in particular introduces and compares the cases of three significant neighbours of Val Taleggio's Strachitunt: Bitto, Branzi and Formai de Mut. Partly or entirely produced in the Bergamasque mountains, the destinies of these cheeses intertwine with those of Strachitunt, Taleggio and *stracchino*, tracing a complex geography of strategic choices, commercial alliances and political skill.

In Part 2, *We the People of Val Taleggio*, I shift focus from upland cheeses to transhumant ones. It is in the context of transhumance that the cheese called *strachì* in Bergamasque dialect by Bergamasque transhumant herders originates and eventually translates into *stracchino* and achieves the distinction of the PDO as 'Taleggio'. I will explain how Taleggio cheese failed its valley of origin – Val Taleggio – in the eyes of its residents and entrepreneurs. An unexploited 'patrimony', a lost 'typicity', Taleggio cheese looms large in the resentment of the people of Val Taleggio, who feel forgotten by history and marginalized by the current economy. Caught in the chasm between the 'quantity economy' of cheap lowland cheeses and the 'quality economy' of exclusive upland cheeses, the cheese-makers of Val Taleggio tried everything, from renaming the valley's cheese as 'Taleggio of Val Taleggio' – which they were prevented from doing – to reinventing Strachitunt as the valley's own cheese and claiming a PDO for it. A consortium of dairy-farmers and cheese merchants was established as early as October 2002 to request a PDO for Strachitunt. It took them more than eleven years to obtain it, as it was registered as an EU-wide PDO trademark in March 2014.

In Chapter 3 I provide an explanation of why Strachitunt can be considered a post-transhumant reinvention of a cheese-making tradition that historically connected alpine pastures and lowlands, providing an ethnographic contextualization of the historical evidence provided by local researchers. In Chapter 4 I comment on the peculiarities of Italian food politics and the key role played by geographic indications – and especially PDO – in supporting food economies. The ethnographic scene with which I close, the public audition for a PDO Strachitunt held in Val Taleggio in October 2010, shows how local and political actors compete and sometimes converge to define heritage food in the contemporary market, speaking at once to national and European regulators, as well as to potentially global competition. Cast as distant and inscrutable, these agencies nevertheless magnify and heighten very local but very real animosities.

In Part 3, *Dulcamara's Senses*, I plunge into the sensorium of cheese, analysing the performance of locality and the language of its consumption. I look at the cultural meaning of cheese through the performance of those who make and sell it and the showcasing of its consumption in tourist venues, professional fairs and ecomuseum installations. In the description of a single moment of elaborate conviviality, I convey the ritual and symbolic value of food beyond exchange, to decipher how food is used politically even at the table. I use the name of an opera character in Donizetti's *L'Elisir d'Amore* to obliquely point at the bittersweet aftertaste of the reinvention of cheese – indeed, of the taste of heritage. Dulcamara is a charlatan, selling his love potions to 'rustic' peasants. His own name – Dulc-amara, the bittersweet poison – betrays the contradictory sensorium of the potions whose virtues he extols to the populace.

In the case of Strachitunt, both the actual cheese and the long-drawn sagas of their makers are double-layered, sweet and sour at once. Heralded as the dairy 'excellence' of Val Taleggio with both gustatory and moral suasion from a number of paladins (initially Slow Food, then the valley's own Ecomuseum), Strachitunt delivers its PDO perhaps too late, leaving the unsurpassed protagonists of its reinvention as veritable kings of a ghost valley. Both chapters show ethnographically how the performance of authenticity is elicited and extracted. In Chapter 5 I revisit my own apprenticeship as a cheese-taster alongside the valleys cheesemakers, and I follow the performance of street theatre and interactive video-installation that were set up in the Ecomuseum Valtaleggio as part of its effort to boost tourism and the cheese-making industry in the valley. In Chapter 6, the discourses and practices of relocalization will be analysed from the point of view of the actors themselves: I recall and comment on an elaborate lunch with Slow Food activists, cheese makers and local tourist entrepreneurs, during which some key political struggles around the reinvention of a potentially competing Slow Food presidium for *stracchino* are voiced, performed and negotiated. Performance is fundamental to the reinvention of cheese both in closed-door negotiations and in strategies for public communication: I use my involvement in the local Ecomuseum and participant observation at fairs and educational presentations of Strachitunt to highlight the ambivalent and prescriptive nature of the roles of those involved: tourists, residents and cheese-makers alike.

Calibrating Cheese

In *Developing Skill, Developing Vision* (2009), I maintained that, among the dairy smallholders of the Lombard mountains, skill and 'practices of locality' are mutually co-constitutive. I described how their skilled practice of animal husbandry is not ahistorical but rather intimately connected with a regime of agricultural counselling, hence with local and translocal politics of food. I initially focused on how this translates into local and translocal 'skilled visions', prescribing and enacting certain ways of looking at cattle (Grasseni 2007b). Following the cows, and their milk, I turned to investigate the transformation of cheese-making – particularly its spaces and timescapes – in my fieldsite. During several years of observation, I witness how upland cheese-making was driven from high-pasture domestic mountain huts to HACCP-run creameries. Hazard analysis critical control point (HACCP) is a self-monitoring method employed in food production protocols to enforce hygiene and safety requirements at every stage of the process. It is a management tool visualized in a flowchart that assesses and monitors the risk of occurrence of specific hazards during the production cycle (Grasseni 2009: 145). Mandatory HACCP was introduced with Directive 43 of the European Economic Community for all European commercial food producers in 1993, as a precursor to the establishment of a European Food Safety Authority in 2002 (with Regulation n. 178), to guarantee the free circulation of safe food within the European Union. The introduction of HACCP was but one of the many ways in which artisan cheese was being repositioned within the global forces of a 'field of production' (Bourdieu 1993). This entailed a potent incept of 'audit cultures' (Strathern 2000), which had momentous effects on high-pasture cheese-making. I began to observe its effects at the end of the 1990s and I referred to the consequent adjustments of local cheese-making as a process of *calibration* (Grasseni 2007a: 61–90).[5]

Reinventing cheese means calibrating its 'ecology of production', an apt phrase which I adopt from Paxson (2012), to the increasing pressures to standardize procedures, environments and operations. But it also entails a symbolic calibration, namely its transformation from a perceived 'traditional' yet everyday foodstuff to a distinctive item of 'food heritage' (Grasseni 2011; Di Giovine 2014). Further, it means that production systems must be *calibrated* to normative and commercial expectations that have purchase both on international economic circuits and on very local arrangements. This does not mean that the alpine cheeses I am talking about have suddenly begun to sell on international markets – though some of them do, and have done for some time. Rather, it means that they have to be entirely refashioned *as if* such potentiality was at hand. The arena they choose as audience, although in practice very local, is symbolically, rhetorically and normatively global.

Moreover, the expectation that tradition has unexploited potential, that it is a resource deserving of development, calls for added value to be made evident and relevant not only to consumers, but to 'communities' at large. Entire localities are thus called into play in the moral labour of identifying with, and properly exploiting, one's 'heritage' (*patrimonio*). In Italian this process goes under the name of *patrimonializzazione* (roughly translatable as 'heritagization'). 'Patrimonializing' alpine cheese entails that a number of social actors (not only dairy farmers, cheese-makers or refiners but also public administrators, consumers' associations and tourist entrepreneurs, for instance) cooperate to identify, describe, study, safeguard, extol, reproduce and market specific items of tangible and intangible heritage. *Patrimonio* is often described as a common wealth – a patrimony in fact, which is handed down (patrilinearly, presumably) from generation to generation. It thus pertains to autochthonous residents or at least to a community that identifies itself as largely unchanged over time. To the risky rhetoric of autochthony (Kalb 2004; Geschiere 2011), patrimonialization adds a 'metaphysics of sedentarism' (Malkki 1992) that, even in a realm that is not usually considered 'political', introduces some serious frictions and dilemmas. For example, it requires the identification of *borders* for specific production areas of as many traditional products.

This runs counter the very tradition that is being invoked in the making of mountain cheese as an item of food heritage: the *alpeggio*. *Alpeggio* or *monticazione* is connected to though not identical with cattle transhumance. Transhumant trails could extend over hundreds of kilometres and be used in a seasonal cycle. Transhumance has evolved over time and it is now virtually extinct in northern Italy – at least in the form described by historian Fernand Braudel (1995) in his *The Mediterranean at the Age of Philip II.*[6] Nowadays only very few herders move all the way from peaks to lowlands and these tend to be mostly sheep-flocks. Transhumance was only one of often highly professionalized forms of seasonal migration that could integrate the income of alpine families: for example male-only winter migration would be based on exercising salaried professions in urban areas, including the development of guilds of carpenters, lumberjacks, smithies, builders, decorators, stonemasons and carriers (Viazzo 1989).

In Val Taleggio, practices that were historically a ticket for the outside world are currently a powerful symbolic device for marketing *locality*. The Republic of Venice's governor Antonio da Lezze desolately observed in the sixteenth century how

> these valleys don't enjoy revenue of any sort . . . They do not reap wheat nor corn, but most of these people travel the world, to Italy, mostly to Rome and Venice, keeping themselves busy trading goods, working in inns, or as coppersmiths, tinkers etc. They do not return to their homeland but once every two or three years, staying only for six months . . . . (da Lezze [1596] 1988: 508)

Among such itinerant crafts were metal-working, logging and carpentry, which made their bearers professional seasonal migrants. Cheese-making and dairy-farming were residual, subsistence activities unless mobilized for transhumance. Connecting with the outside world, for example in the form of transhumant farming, was part of the local repertoire. Only the clueless stayed behind, firmly rooted in their turf, as the normative imaginary of geographical indications currently prescribes. So goes da Lezze: 'Those who stay in the village are poor people, and tend their own cattle, the richest having up to 25 cows. These, at winter, descend to the Milanese plains. . . . In Taleggio there are 500 cattle, 100 among horses and mules, 200 sheep' (da Lezze [1596] 1988: 510, 512).

Now that local cattle are few, there is no need to descend to the Milanese plains to feed them. By converse, *alpeggio* is the summer grazing season spent by cattle (and occasionally goat) herds on the high pastures, which are covered by snow during the harsh mountain winters. Often the word 'transhumant', referring to cattle, is used for the *alpeggio*, even though this generates confusion, as cow breeders take only short summer trips to the closest higher pastures.[7] Notably, *alpeggio* entails more limited cattle movement than original transhumance trails – which took place practically all-year round, following fixed routes and visiting well-stocked stations. The *alpeggiatori* are mostly mountain farmers who drive herds from the village stables to the upper pastures, while they make hay in the meadows around the village to stock up for winter.

Pastures in the high grounds could be actual collective property of a community, with formal covenants regulating access and obligations to maintenance work. Some of these regulations – *statuti* or *regole* – would be granted to individual communities by a higher authority, for instance a duke or other feudal sovereign.[8] Even when the high pasture land was held as a 'common', access to it is historically highly regulated, as land and grass are key economic and ecological resources (Netting 1981: 89).[9] Crucially, with long-distance dairy transhumance gone, the families of cheese-makers eventually settled down in the richer plains, investing in large-scale dairy creameries, leaving the bothersome business of making upland cheese during the *alpeggio* to the (other) mountain people. This contextualizes Val Taleggio within a complex scenario of competing and partly overlapping cheese productions, each claiming distinction for their tradition, and the urgency of survival for their communities of producers.

In the following chapters, I will speak mostly of Val Taleggio's Strachitunt cheese, but I will also discuss other cheeses, all originating from the same area of northern Italy: the Lombard mountains and plains. These are Bitto, Formai de Mut, Branzi as well as Taleggio and *stracchino* (see Table 1). Their divergent histories and uneven fortune put the uniqueness of Strachitunt in perspective. We should imagine these upland and lowland cheeses as complementing Strachitunt in a geography of opposites: the cooked and the raw, so to speak. All of them originate from a tradition of transhumant cheese-making straddling peaks and plains, summers and winters, fresh grass and hay, craft and industry. Made in the high-altitude summer pastures at the head of the Bergamasque valleys, Bitto, Formai de Mut and Branzi triangulate different versions of one ideal-type upland cheese: cooked, fat, round-shaped, matured, high-prestige, yellowish 10-kilo wheels with a brushed-hardened crust similar to that of Parmesan or Grana. On the other hand, Taleggio and *strachì* are respectively the PDO and non-PDO evolution of fresh, uncooked, square, whitish, soft, flowery-crust slabs of two kilos at most, made for common consumption and cheap markets. *Alpeggio* or upland cheese is for the discerning and the affluent. Lowland cheese by contrast is the unassuming by-product of transhumance: what we know about the origins of Taleggio and *stracchino* is that it was cheese made by transhumant mountain peasants who could not even afford to heat their cows' milk and would curdle it at milking temperature, hastily (*all'infretta*), in their makeshift abodes, on the trail of available grass (Jacini 1882: 27).[10]

Within this geography of opposites, Strachitunt of Val Taleggio marks a veritable shift: technically, it is a raw milk cheese, worked *a munta calda*, namely while still warm immediately after milking. It is a double paste cheese, obtained from layering cold curd from the night before with warm curd freshly renneted. Strachitunt is a blue cheese (*formaggio erborinato*), namely it develops moulds inside the paste, which give it specific aromas and taste. Dry-salted and aged for 75 days, it is pierced twice during maturation, twenty days after casting and again after a fortnight. This allows the development of blue moulds without inoculation, as a result of interaction with the maturing environment. As a raw *strachì*, Strachitunt would belong to the family of lowland cheeses like Taleggio or *stracchino*. But as an aged, cylindrical, and heavy wheel it positions itself among nobler upland cousins. Matured even longer than Bitto PDO (at least 75 days versus the 70 days of Bitto), Strachitunt is produced all year round and not just in *alpeggio*. Triangulating Taleggio and *strachì*, it adds a modern zest for uniqueness to the tectonic of the raw and the cooked, and combines it with the European obsession with pedigree: claimed as an upland, aristocratic precursor of Gorgonzola itself (just as *strachì* of Val Taleggio is claimed to be the precursor of Taleggio), it is the rawest of the raw: *a natural blue cheese*. That is, it is an

Bitto PDO. Author's photograph, Salone del Gusto Slow Food, Turin 2010.

Slow Food Presidium Bitto Storico. Author's photograph, Salone del Gusto Slow Food, Turin 2010.

Formai de Mut dell'Alta Valle Brembana PDO. Courtesy of Associazione Principi delle Orobie.

Formaggio Tipico Branzi. Courtesy of Associazione Principi delle Orobie.

Table 1. Photographs of Bitto PDO and Slow Food Presidium Bitto Storico, Formai de Mut dell'Alta Val Brembana PDO and Branzi.

uncooked cheese made with raw milk and manipulated in such a way as to allow natural moulds to penetrate and nest in the fault lines between two curds from subsequent different milking days, layered like lasagne.

This reinvention is only one, possibly *the* most successful and hard-fought, of many other attempts to achieve the ever-elusive goal of using cheese to leverage systemic issues of local importance: branding, development, ultimately survival. The reinvention of cheese engenders conflicting agendas, which could not easily be comprehended without an understanding of a common terminological choice and its implications, namely that of defining local products as *tipici*. This is a distinctive cultural strategy to claim that certain foods are not only place-based (as

Stracchino all'Antica delle Valli Orobiche, Presidio Slow Food. Courtesy of Slow Food Italia.

Stracchino di Vedeseta, Cooperativa Sant'Antonio di Vedeseta, Val Taleggio. Courtesy of Casarrigoni.

Strachitunt PDO.
Courtesy of Casarrigoni.

Table 1, cont. Photographs of Slow Food Presidium *Stracchino all'Antica delle Valli Orobiche, Stracchino di Vedeseta,* and Strachitunt PDO.

they are claimed to carry 'the taste of place', Trubek 2008), but are also distinctive of specific 'practices of locality' (Grasseni 2009), namely routines, expertise and skills that emerge both as a form of functional adaptation to specific natural and material conditions, and as historical and cultural diversifications: some community of practitioners went one way, others chose differently under slightly different circumstances.

On the one hand this is achieved by marketing an entire sensorium related to cheese: hence not only its taste, but its visual appearance in packaging and commercial documentation. One the other, cheese sells the whole of a locality: the history and the community of practice from which it derives its *tipicità*. With the expression 'authentic anachronism', Guntra Aistara conveys the syncretic coexistence of elements of authenticity, nostalgia and fake in the foodscapes of postsocialist Latvia (2014). In our case a post-transhumant theatre of 'authentic anachronism' is not directly aimed at a tourist audience but rather to a commercial one. Marketing the cheese sensorium entails important processes of *calibration*, not only of the cheese itself – its recipe, working environment and tools, visual identity and organoleptic features – but of its own cultural and natural environment. Landscape and communities are enrolled in a collective effort to communicate the unique and distinctive characteristics of their cheese – and of an entire 'mountain cheese experience', but the calibration of this unique image to a discerning clientele is not exempt from conflicts of interest and petty competition. The result is an extremely diverse scenario of recipes, exceptions and idiosyncrasies.

Post-transhumant Timescapes

Val Taleggio was thinly populated in 1998. It is now alarmingly depopulated. The village of Vedeseta that I describe in *Developing Skill, Developing Vision* (2009) counted 281 inhabitants in 1998, and had 216 residents in 2014, having lost a further 30 per cent. In its golden era – the sixteenth and seventeenth century – Val Taleggio was populated by more than five thousand people (Arrigoni 1983).[11] Val Brembana, the wider mountainous area of which Val Taleggio constitutes a branch, is the Lombard mountain area that has suffered the highest depopulation in the last thirty years – hosting nowadays a population of 43,000 scattered over 38 municipalities: 29 of them count less than 1,000 inhabitants; 19 are under 500 residents each (Comunità Montana Valle Brembana 2000, 2006).

Consequently, Val Brembana recently featured as the recipient of an EU intervention, project PADIMA, 'Policies against Depopulation in Mountain Areas', together with analogous areas in France, Norway, Spain and Sweden. The main measure suggested as 'strategy to increase the attractiveness of mountain areas' was to develop an integrated 'new economy'. 'Marketing the territory' (*marketing territoriale*)[12] should mean promoting a 'patrimony' that so far has failed to perform: the alpine landscape, the 'strong local cultures', but especially its *prodotti tipici*.[13] The idea of branding heritage is of course not new, and in the rest of this book I explain how rethinking the economy in the Italian mountains today is not just a question of marketing but of political imagination. The promotion of regional food economies involves business entrepreneurs, area administrators and local notables, and includes the collaboration (and sometimes competition) with relatively new social actors: most notably in this case the Slow Food association but also more or less participated institutional projects for local development such as ecomuseums.

Europe-wide, heritage foods are at the centre of active strategies of territorialization, locating gastronomic knowledge in as many distinct practices of locality (Bowen 2011; Chrzan 2007; West 2013b). Heather Paxson's book on the renaissance of artisanal cheese in the United States argues that American cheese-makers live by 'a tradition of invention' – echoing Hobsbawm and Ranger's 'invention of tradition'. This book articulates a different thesis, which pertains to Italy and to European ethnographies of food more specifically, namely that the politics of food designations is neither an invention of tradition nor a tradition of invention, but a reinvention of food within a specific 'field of production' that includes heritage and place-based names as major force fields. These articulate and shape both the marketability and political capacity of food to mobilize resources and passions, to foster conflict and suggest alliances. Their outcome, in the marginal rural areas of the northern Italian Alps, may determine the very serious business of economic viability and even demographic survival for a whole mountain community.

Crucial to the field of production is the issue of standardization. How much diversity is allowed in contemporary global food systems? How should it be measured, monitored and valued? What are the accountability tools for it? Calibrating cheese to a 'global hierarchy of value' (Herzfeld 2004) means negotiating and enforcing protocols of production. They will feature heavily in the debates and diatribes analysed in this book. One of the most contested issues regards their area of pertinence – the geographical boundaries within which protocols should be enforced. The other regards the matter of cheese-making, milk: its treatment, quality and provenance.

The work of Bruno Latour has eloquently connected the history of microbes with the disciplining of the French public and the establishment of hygiene as an issue of public safety (1987). In the United States, Heather Paxson has identified the current 'renaissance' of artisanal craft cheeses as a 'post-Pasteurian' phenomenon (2012). A post-Pasteurian stance, she explains, is not 'anti-Pasteurian'. For the cheese-makers, it means allying oneselves with microbes to cultivate ad-hoc ecologies of practice: the cheese-maker tries to actively select and cultivate benign microbic strands. Possibly, these will enhance the cheese taste as much as its safety.

However, if American practitioners weave together artisanship and a discourse of skilled coexistence with tricky natural organisms (Paxson 2008), especially in the United States there is heightened awareness of the risks involved, both in terms of food contamination and of the economic ruin that would strike craft dairies, should they release dangerous microbes in their inventory. As Paxson (2012) contends, after having coined the 'assistance to comply' line of self-monitoring for industrial concerns, the Food and Drug Administration in particular has developed a peculiarly watchful attention on the risky business of consuming and transforming raw-milk cheese, which is somewhat contradictory. In Ireland, Colin Sage has eloquently remarked the disproportion of attention to risk factors in the case of raw milk and cheese, compared with the neo-liberal attitude of encouraging 'self-monitoring' on the part of large agribusiness concerns (2011). In this political and economic context which straightforwardly privileges industrial food production and takes it as a golden standard against which to assess artisanal workshop practices, 'post-Pasteurian' cheese cultures move beyond the Pasteurian hygienist agenda of microbes' eradication, and articulate a stance of subtle if marginal resistance to the accompanying agenda of social sanitation.

In Europe, hygiene regulations are also a pressing matter for artisanal cheese-makers, especially in the mountains. Raw milk's characteristics are variable. They depend on climate conditions, on the environment of the animals producing it, and on their nourishment. Gambera and Surra (2003) specify that while there are exceptions allowed for matured cheese (aged for over sixty days), European regulation does create problems for artisanal producers of fresh cheese, because pasteurization does alter the dairy properties of milk, as it reduces its natural bacterial flora and destroys some enzymes and proteins. It thus inevitably alters the final organoleptic of the product, as well as obviously introducing costs and logistic issues, especially to mountain cheese-makers.[14]

Despite these difficulties, the 'reinvented' cheeses covered in this book are raw milk cheeses. This is especially pertinent to Strachitunt, the main protagonist, and to the *stracchino* of which I talk in Part 3 – while the upland cheeses are cooked – not only because of their organoleptic qualities, believed to be superior, but as a sure means to limit the range at which milk can travel. Raw milk Strachitunt, and raw milk *stracchino*, are curdled *a munta calda*, namely while still warm from the milked cows. The imperative to make cheese with warm milk without reheating it determines per se the very short distances it can travel. It can move from a shed to a creamery, even from a village to another within the same valley, but it cannot travel afar. In the present conditions of compliance with strict regulations about the hygiene of the creameries, raw milk cheese is sedentary by definition – an ironic result, considering that *stracchino* is a trans-humant cheese. As noted before, in 1882 Stefano Jacini in his parliamentary investigation on 'the state of the art of Italian agriculture and the conditions of the rural class', states that 'the word *stracchino* derives from the small soft cheeses produced during the journey from the mountain to the lowland and vice versa. These *malghesi* make it swiftly in their resting stations, with milk from tired cows after their long journey'. *Stràc* means 'tired' in Bergamasque dialect, hence *strachì*, the Bergamasque word for *stracchino.*

I watch my 1998 film *Those Who Don't Work, Don't Make Love* and see my host Guglielmo, born 1932, plunge his hairy arms elbow-deep in the curd he is cutting. Both cauldron and curd-slayer are made of copper – and they are unchanged since I witnessed him brushing them daily and covering until next use for the first time, at the end of the 1990s. In the film, he is working in an unpaved mountain abode – kids, tourists and myself walking in and out of the dairy without much care for changing out footwear . . . I ask myself: Is the raw-milk *stracchino* and Strachitunt cheese made by Guglielmo's ungloved hands 'post-Pasteurian'? Or is it rather, quite honestly, pre-Pasteurian?

Asking this question is a risky move. It may be read as simplistic, or as yet another way of casting rural cheese-makers as backward inhabitants of ahistoric eras. Tourist brochures systematically do so: presenting them as authentic specimens of timeless tradition. Less benignly, agricultural consultants also argue that family-run businesses with just a few cows and goats are remnants of preindustrial times and should be encouraged to die out. And they routinely are, either through unsustainable requests for audit paperwork and structural requirements, or by monetary incentives to cull small herds and pack up business: a practice infamously known as *abbattimento* – culling – as productive livestock are sent to the abattoir because their husbandry is uneconomical or simply uncompetitive.

John Agnew has noted how certain geographical areas become associated with essential attributes of time, relative to other geographical 'blocks': thus 'modernity, confused by some with the United States, becomes a social model to which other 'less developed' societies can aspire' (1996: 31). Within a stereotypically 'backward' Italy, hence, Alpine dairy farmers would appear even more exotic and 'primitive'. Marginal cheese-makers and family farmers feel that they are indeed the survivors of an era: prematurely culled, persuaded into bankruptcy or cornered into foreclosure.

When I first began to do fieldwork on alpine dairy-farming at the end of the 1990s, the newly ratified EU hygiene standards for cheese-making on the upper pastures were a hot topic. In Lombardy, the latest hygiene regulations about milk and cheese production was the regional decree (DPR) number 54 of 14 January 1997, which established stringent conditions for the kind of mountain infrastructure where upper-pasture grazing takes place. Cheese-making should take place in tiled environments with running water, toilets and hot-water showering facilities. At the time, data presented by the Region admitted that 72 per cent of the active mountain structures used for making cheese upland did not have toilets. Only 28 per cent had running water and in 48 per cent of cases, by-products such as whey were dispersed in the surrounding environment. This was also possible because the *alpeggio* was a residual practice, only kept alive by small herders transforming less than 300 litres of milk a day in 38 per cent of cases, and between 300 and 600 in 47 per cent of cases. Only 11 per cent of *alpeggiatori* transformed more than 1,000 litres per day and only in 45 per cent of cases was milking carried out with mechanical means, while only in 51 per cent of structures there were separate rooms for conserving and maturing cheese.[15]

I was present when these data were announced on 16 March 1999 in Lecco at the Chamber of Commerce Auditorium. The open debate was aimed at creating consensus among farmers, union operators and local administrations on the regional guidelines for the application of European regulations in dairy-farming and especially cheese-making. At the conference, everyone was well aware that traditional *alpeggio* did not abide by the ideal conditions of DPR 54/97 – which simply ratified, with delay, the 1992 EU regulations 92/46 and 92/47 which established the use of HACCP self-control protocols, laboratory analysis of milk for somatic cell counts and bacterial content, and the minimum structural pre-conditions of cheese-making workshops. These had to be abided by to authorize the direct sale of cheese – an authorization that cheese-makers usually referred to as obtaining 'the blue stamp' (*il bollino blu*), an identification code for product traceability.[16]

Some operators of the farmers union and technical advisors would confide to me that they were expecting these measures to expedite a 'cull' and a 'pruning' that was long due, in the interest of 'natural selection', to finally drive out of business those stingy old herders who would not fit a bathroom in their *baita*[17] or, worse, would have it fitted with funding aid and then not use it! Fifteen years later, the 'natural selection' seems to have largely taken place, and most of the active cheese-makers have a 'blue stamp' for selling their production. In the year 2000, the total number of farms with cattle stock in Lombardy was 19,704 with 1,610,678 livestock units; in 1990 it was 34,920 with 1,960,565 units and in 1982 49,832 farms with 2,082,665 cattle. In the 2010 agricultural census, the number of farms with cattle was down to 14,718 with 1,484,991 cattle.[18] Since cattle herding in Lombardy is prevailingly a dairy-farming activity, I would confidently take this as an indication of a consistent trend to consolidate farms, decreasing the number of businesses and increasing the herds. At the same time the number of cattle also decreased altogether since, thanks to 'genetic improvement', a dairy cow nowadays produces more than double the amount of milk she could produce in the 1980s (cf. Grasseni 2007c).

The ageing president of the Associazione per la Valorizzazione degli Alpeggi gave a heartfelt speech at the 1999 conference, ending up in tears but eliciting little sympathy and quite a few sniggering comments from an overly male, working-age and practically minded audience. He denounced the context-blindness of the regulation of food production and its structural requirements, predicting that it would lead to the outright extinction of the few traditional practitioners left in business: milking their cows by hand under the rain directly in the mountain meadows. He made a plea for the goodness of sterilizing cheese-making tools in boiling whey as it is customary practice in those stations that do not have running water facilities. Very few listeners felt that those practices had intrinsic value and deserved special concessions. His younger colleagues were figuring out how the new legislation would impact their businesses, computing the costs, networking and lobbying on the spot to receive funding aid with the help of unions and public administrations.

The majority expected that a number of concessions would be made to allow for time to implement these ameliorations, and major exceptions (*deroghe*) were indeed made for dairy stations in the upper mountain pastures. The regional government followed up with a number of extensions (regional government decree DGR n. VI-42036 of 19 March 1999). Concessions included untiled concrete floors and walls (as long as they would be washable), doors and windows in the workshop (as long as they could be protected by nets and robust enough to impede the access of animals), and non-stainless steel tools (as long as easily washable and noncorrodible). The regional government also introduced the regulation of maturing cheese for a minimum of 60 days for cheese made in *alpeggio*, specifically as one additional concession to DPR 54/1997, as a measure to naturally ensure that cheese maturation would lower its pH and thus set in an antibacterial self-cleansing. The same concession is made to cheese made with milk whose bacterial charge is higher than 100,000 units per millilitre, as well as for milk with high somatic cell counts (more than 400,000 per ml – a usual indicator of ongoing inflammations or infections, typically mastitis). Despite the lenient regulation and accommodating for exceptions and delays, the widespread feeling among mountain smallholders was and remains that of being a population on the brink of extinction. Some used the expression of being 'Indians without reservations' to capture the essence of feeling left behind and at the margins of a society striding forth on an accelerated path.

Marginality itself can be harnessed as a cultural resource through the poetics of heritage, recasting animal husbandry and cheese-making in the mountains as much more than a residual practice. At the public presentation of the oral history book *Bergamini* (Carminati and Locatelli 2004), roughly translatable as 'The Cheese Makers', the local entrepreneur and leader of the Consortium for Strachitunt cheese of Val Taleggio also broke down. He was perhaps overcome by the enormity and rapidity of the transition from the lifestyle of his parents-in-law, who stored cheeses in stone huts astride a stream to keep them fresh in the summer, to his own, a 'modern' business man negotiating with international buyers, producing innovative hybrids such as *stracchino* marinated in Sicilian wines, and winning prizes at national events such as Cheese at Bra, the Slow Food Salone del Gusto, or the Cibus International Food Exhibition in Parma. All the more though, he was claiming 'tradition' as the repository of skill and legitimacy to be 'reinventing' it.

Bergamini is the name historically given in Lombardy to transhumant dairy farmers – allegedly, as the name goes, mostly coming from the mountains of Bergamo. Transhumant herders were necessarily also skilled cheese-makers, as they would transform their milk in their seasonal stations, taking their herds from the upper pastures in the Lombard Alps for the summer grazing season to their lower reaches along the rivers Ticino and Adda. *Bergamino* in Italian means cheese-maker. To be a *bergamì*, in the local dialect, in Val Taleggio means not just being a cheese-maker, but crucially to be someone on the move with one's herd. Long-range transhumance being practically extinct, shorter-term, shorter-distance summer stays on an alp or high pasture – namely the *alpeggio* – are increasingly rediscovered as mountain practices that add value to upland cheese, which can claim the 'taste of mountain grass' (Huseby 2012).

Alpeggio is often claimed as the common heritage of the dairy breeders of the Bergamasque valleys and proudly celebrated by local historians and research centres (*centri studio*) such as the one that published *Bergamini*, the above-mentioned volume with testimonies from the twenty-one last witnesses of this way of life in Val Taleggio. This calls for a different timescape altogether, neither pre- nor post-Pasteurian, but rather one of 'structural nostalgia' (Herzfeld 2005: 147): a lost time of plenty of which successive generations reminisce. While we do not have evidence here that the previous generation in turn had been reminiscent of a more wholesome era before themselves, the reference is granted because of the collective performance of present witnesses as relics of pristine times, and of modern entrepreneurs as true heirs to those. This is after all precisely the cultural work of heritage as harnessing history (in particular, a nostalgic perception of history as natural repository of lost values) as a form of value-addition.

To instruct a case for a very small PDO for Strachitunt cheese involving only four municipalities, and to preside over it for eleven years could look like megalomania. But the arguments between neighbouring villages and competing family enterprises look different, in the realization of the gravity of their local effects. This book shows how, for the few hundred people involved, the cause of obtaining a Europe-wide protected denomination for Strachitunt was believed to make the difference between becoming a dying valley or following in the footprints of other niche producers, such as the 'Bitto rebels' (Corti 2012), namely heritage cheese-makers who had fought bitterly, and commercially won, against larger consortia. As we shall see in Part 1, the Bitto diatribe illuminates the politics of large geographic indications favouring industrial concerns and intensive dairy-farming, a style of animal husbandry that has determined the demise of dairy-breeders in Val Taleggio. This was a veritable war, a war of the cheeses, and each economic actor involved fought for their livelihoods with the resentment that only history's losers can have.[19]

Memory of course plays an important part in imagining futures – both collective and individual, both real and fictional, both resistant and hegemonic. In no case does the anthropologist simply voice the underdog. I am aware that I played a part in these processes, for example when I was called upon to draw a community map for the newly established Ecomuseum of the valley. More importantly, my own conversations and interactions with local actors, including publications in Italian that were read and presented in the valley, probably contributed to the local reflections on the meaning and implications of 'reinventing' Strachitunt. This book offers an ethnographic long-take of the sometimes conflicting voices and agendas that contributed to determine which strategies of reinvention and icons of locality became in turn viable: supportive local administrations, well-established entrepreneurs, food activists, international buyers, local historians, social workers with political ambitions . . . The overall result is a skilful and precarious reinvention of the everyday, often dependent on selling ambivalent notions, including the very concept of community. Within a 'food heritage' framework, some ambitious local administrators and entrepreneurs, far from solving local conflicts, have succeeded in using the language of dairy 'excellence' as a springboard, hopefully for the valley and certainly for their own political careers and economic viability. However, reading the Strachitunt PDO story as a mere social construction of a geographical indication would be diminutive of the 'ecologies of sentiment' (Paxson 2012) that underwrote this epic. Similarly, it would be misleading to read the struggle of the Val Taleggio producers to obtain a prestigious geographical designation as a mere result of neoliberal governmentality exercised through the food heritage complex: as we shall see, neoliberal accountabilities can be readily embraced by enthusiastic actors.

I will now present the reader with a palette of six cheeses, six cases of which Strachitunt is one: Bitto, Formai de Mut, Branzi, Taleggio, *stracchino* and Strachitunt. Each represents a peculiar arrangement of institutional alliances, tactics and tools that were variously assembled and harnessed to validate some aspect or dismiss some other, within an ongoing politics of distinction that is key to market survival. Their value is articulated in the language of *patrimonio* and *tipicità* and is consistently applied to upland cheese as opposed to lowland cheese.

Notes

1. For ethnographic analyses of the self-stereotypization of mountain people as 'hard', in the Italian Alps, see the monographs *The Hard People* by Patrick Heady (1999) and *The Bounded Field* by Jaro Stacul (2003).
2. Lega Nord is a political party, especially popular in northern Italy since the 1990s, which participated in the Berlusconi-led coalition governments. On the racist and xenophobic rhetoric of Lega Nord see the work of Lynda Dematteo (2007), who has notably also worked on northern Italian entrepreneurs and their expansion in Romania in the 1990s (2009: 68–72). The rhetoric of sovereignty and autochthony of Lega Nord and the economic imaginary of northern Italian small and medium enterprises are closely tied with each other, but beyond the scope of this work. On northern Italian political subcultures and their fundamental link to economic practice and institutional tactics see the work of political scientist Patrizia Messina (2006).
3. On the renaissance of Bergamasco dialect in the town of Bergamo see the monograph *Living Memory* by Jillian Cavanaugh (2009). My book focusses on the valleys and plains just north and south of the town of Bergamo. A note on language: Cavanaugh opts to use *bergamasco* as an adjective, as in '*bergamasco* women'. I prefer to use the gender-neutral 'Bergamasque' as an adjective, to refer to people, valleys, cheese, etc. So for example I will refer to the Alpi Orobie as 'the Bergamasque Alps'. I only use *bergamasco* as a noun, for the dialect, and *bergamaschi* as a plural noun for the population of the province of Bergamo, thus maintaining the original uses for *bergamasco* and *bergamaschi* as in the native language.

4. On the symbolic discourse of national identity in relation to folklore in Greece, see Herzfeld (1986) and, by converse, Herzfeld (2009) on the social construction of locality in Rome. On the politics of naming cheese in Greece, see Petridou (2012).
5. I derive the notion of calibration from the science-historical work of Otto Sibum on Joule's experimental definition of the mechanical equivalent of heat (Sibum 2003). Sibum shows how mastering the use of the period's thermometers to achieve a precise measurement of temperature was a craft, rather than a black-boxed procedure. This art was mastered, in the Northwest of England where Joule was operating, by brewers like himself.
6. Braudel (1995), vol. 1, pp. 85–99. See especially the map of European transhumant trails on page 98, which involves the southern ridge of the Italian Alps.
7. On the distinction between *alpage* and transhumance see Jones (2005).
8. See for example the fourteenth-century 'Statutes and Ordinances' of Val Taleggio and Averara in Upper Val Brembana, of 1358: Lions Club Valle Brembana 1980.
9. The *magnifica comunità* (magnificent community) of Fiemme, in Trentino, boasts one of the most ancient statutes for the collective self-management of the local forests. The *comunità*'s website publishes the current regulation, which absorbs and adapts the 'privileges' of the 'neighbours' that were first conceded by the local bishop with a 'pact' in 1110 (http://www.mcfiemme.eu/).
10. 'I malghesi producono caci di mediocre qualità, ma sanno confezionarli mercantili, e li smerciano facilmente quasi tutti in prossimità dei luoghi di produzione. Il vocabolo *stracchino*, che oggi ha ricevuto un'applicazione molto estesa, deriva dai piccoli formaggi teneri che quei malghesi, nel loro viaggio dalla montagna alla pianura e viceversa, sogliono confezionare all'infretta nelle stazioni di riposo, col latte delle mucche *stracche* per il lungo viaggio' (Jacini 1882: 27).
11. *Val* or *valle* means 'valley', and I prefer to use the autochthonous names Val Taleggio, Val Brembana etc. rather than resorting to inversions (Taleggio valley, Brembana valley). This will only be done occasionally for added emphasis or to clarify a point.
12. See http://www.euromontana.org/en/project/padima-policies-against-depopulation-in-mountain-areas/, last accessed 15 January 2015.
13. Maria Grazia Pedrana, project PI for IREEAALP (Istituto di Ricerca per l'Ecologia e l'Economia Applicata alle Aree Alpine), quoted in Fabio Paravisi, 'Fuga dalla Val Brembana. L'Europa studia il caso', *Corriere della Sera* 8 August 2012.
14. Pasteurization is a thermic treatment aimed at destroying pathogens. According to Gambera and Surra 2003: 147, the thermic treatment of milk regulated by Directive EEC n. 46 of 1992 (acquired in Italy as DPR 54 of 1997) ranges between pasteurization at 63°C for at least 30 minutes or instant pasteurization at 95°C, but other combinations of temperature and length are also used (the most common is 72°C for 15 seconds, or 'flash pasteurization' for 4 seconds at 85°C).
15. Conference: I prodotti caseari d'alpeggio. Convegno-esposizione linee guida della Regione Lombardia per l'applicazione della normativa nazionale (DPR 54/97). Lecco, 16 March 1999.
16. As per law 283 of 30 April 1962 and decree 155 of 26 May 1997.
17. *Baita* is the name commonly used in Lombardy to define a stone mountain abode, nowadays used exclusively during the *alpeggio* (summer grazing season), but previously commonly used for hay barns, cow-sheds and human habitation.

18. Quinto Censimento dell'Agricoltura Italiana, ISTAT 2002: Tavola 1.7 – Aziende con allevamenti secondo le principali specie di bestiame: http://www.census.istat.it/index_agricoltura.htm. Sesto Censimento dell'Agricoltura Italiana, ISTAT, 2012: 'Censimento dell'Agricoltura in Breve' http://censimentoagricoltura.istat.it/inbreve/?QueryId=675&lang=it&graph=&subtheme=5&cube=DICA_ALLEVAMENTI#.
19. In *Il mondo dei vinti*, a collection of 270 interviews gathered in the mountains of Piedmont, historian Nuto Revelli gives a vivid portrait of the demise of the mountains – 'the world of the losers' – losing out both to intensive agriculture and to invasive tourism, both to the ills of modernization and to the assumption that casts them as marginal and residual to growth and progress (Revelli 1977).

PART

I

The War of the Cheeses

CHAPTER 1

Patrimonio and *Tipicità*

Patrimonio and *tipicità* are the words with which Italians express the closest native concepts to the English-language *heritage*, and the French notion of *terroir*. Unsurprisingly, they do not mean exactly the same as *heritage* and *terroir*. In particular, *patrimonio* does different cultural work than the language of heritage. It constitutes a 'patrimony' that requires custodians and guardians. The lucid reflections of Val Taleggio's food heritage entrepreneurs on *patrimonio* and *tipicità* clarify how these notions are performed in the processes of food reinvention. In their own words, we will find an ethnographic distinction between invention and reinvention. Naturally, these actors are not unscathed by the 'heritage complex' and its language – in fact they appropriate it as a toolbox to rethink their local food systems as heritage items (Bendix et al. 2007).

Hobsbawm and Ranger's call to appreciate and study the actual historical circumstances in which national and hegemonic institutions perpetrated the 'inventions of tradition' (1983) has been widely appropriated in current scholarship. Initially iconoclastic, the idea of exposing traditions as 'invented' has nevertheless been critiqued, for positing an underlying distinction between supposedly 'authentic' and allegedly 'fake' traditions (Bendix 1997).[1] Heritage studies show, on the contrary, how the notion of tradition mobilizes a veritable theatre of authenticity whose 'audience anticipates and participates in the performance' (Halbertsma 2011: 3). This is a complex and fluid dynamic that pertains to food no less than to other items of heritage (May 2013).

In Italy there is a specific way of conceptualizing culinary or gastronomic heritage (*patrimonio culinario* or *patrimonio eno-gastronomico*), namely the notion of *tipicità*. Understanding how this is employed and made relevant to very local economies, histories and animosities means gaining specific regional insights into the global phenomenon of food reinvention. After devoting some space to each concept (firstly *patrimonio*, then *tipicità*), I will show how the Bergamasque valleys constitute a unique cultural and historical environment that has been enrolled in a 'heritage theatre' (Halbertsma 2011).

Tipicità is variously translated as 'typicity' or 'typicality'. In brochures or commercial materials aimed at international buyers, more often than not 'typicity' translates *tipicità* (while *terroir* is never used in the documentation I gathered). The authors of *Typicality in History* (Ceccarelli et al. 2013) opt for 'typicality', asking how *tipicità* accrues value in significant ways in specific historical circumstances for local and regional economies. While I address a similar issue here, I also raise a wider question, regarding how *tipicità* is socially constructed as *patrimonio*. This brings about a veritable 'reinvention of food' by activating specific networks, local connections and mediations – both through discourse and through practical arrangements (Grasseni and Paxson 2014).

There are divergent ways of appropriating the concept and practice of *patrimonio*, and regions differ widely for institutional organization and political practice. Regina Bendix refers to national ratifications of UNESCO determinations as coining different 'heritage regimes' (Bendix et al. 2012: 11). In the case of food, this is in line with the comparative findings of Jacinthe Bessière and Laurence Tibère (2011): even though collectivities identify and perceive food cultures as 'héritage partagé' (common patrimony). Crucially, the politics of food heritage is made in as large a measure by economic actors as by bureaucracies: 'innovations are driven by agribusiness players large and small' who 'reinvent their relationship with tradition' (Bessière and Tibère 2011: 1). These local players are active both in public performances and private negotiations: in this book we will see local entrepreneurs educating the public to understand what 'reinvention' means in the case of Strachitunt; fuelling a choral manifestation of resentment and avenge, pivoted around the name of a cheese; scheming and mediating across parochial conflicts of interest, played out through logos, packaging paper and competing denominations.

The social sustainability of marketing traditional cheese as a heritage commodity is questionable as it engenders heightened competition and ambivalent outcomes in local communities (Leitch 2003; Markowitz 2012). Each municipality is striving to gourmet-profile their own 'basket of products' (*paniere di prodotti tipici*) to the point that it seems impossible in Italy to find foodstuffs that do *not* claim to be 'typical'. These strategies of cultural conservation are pragmatically dependent on the possibility to strike a fair price for local goods – something that in turn depends on their visibility on the market rather than on the work of 'commoning' collective resources such as nature, history and culture. Indeed, not everyone is equally successful in 'adding value' to one's produce.

Conversely, locating value in a geographical interpretation of *tipicità* alone would be a myopic strategy for local entrepreneurs and communities (for a similar argument on *terroir*, see Paxson 2010 and Vitrolles 2011). As we shall see, the same economic and social actors show the capacity to pick and choose among different possible denominations and certifications, enrolling or discarding alliances with the very same institutional or NGO actors such as the chamber of commerce or Slow Food, according to what they feel is the most appropriate and effective strategy to support the pedigree of one or another product.

The high stakes and moral suasion of the stakeholders involved are conveyed through a discourse of *tipicità*. In this and the following chapter, we witness the rhetoric and political performance of *patrimonializzazione* for the valley's cheese, first of all at the Sagra dello Strachitunt (Val Taleggio's cheese festival dedicated to celebrate Strachitunt). In Chapter 2, to contextualize the Strachitunt saga, I introduce Bitto, Formai de Mut and Branzi as examples of the many possible triangulations over the quality, value and authenticity of 'typical mountain cheese'. I use a recent thesis from local historians, who fundamentally claim that one single 'upland cheese' evolved over time in a region straddling the north and south ridges of the Bergamasque Alps (the *Alpi Orobie* or *Alpi Orobiche*). This thesis becomes significant to the Strachitunt *querelle*, as it shows how the very same basic substance accrued different names and prestige according to the more or less fortunate strategies of their promoters.

Claiming sovereignty over cheese means first and foremost advocating the right to name it and the right to police its boundaries. The strategies to achieve this goal may include introducing variations in the cheese-making or refining technique, enrolling documentary evidence from published sources or oral history, enlarging production areas, or vice versa 'presiding' over niche productions. Long-time enmities and tactic coalitions are implicated in how cheese-scapes are differently put to work by competing communities of upland and lowland cheese-makers.

The Entrepreneur as Sovereign

On 20 October 2006 the president of the Consorzio di Tutela dello Strachitunt[2] addressed the participants of the valley's first Sagra dello Strachitunt. This is a food festival organized by the local tourist association (Pro Loco Val Taleggio), featuring popularly priced Strachitunt-based meals. The highlight of the day was a panel of speakers, to assess the progress made by the Strachitunt Consortium, whose name is translatable as 'Consortium for the Protection of Strachitunt Cheese'. *Tutela* though deserves a more complex definition than 'protection'. *Tutela* includes safeguard from corruption or misuse, presiding over the future, and actively promoting something or someone's flourishing. Tellingly, *tutela* is the same word used in Italian for the custody of minors: it is the duty and privilege of a parent or guardian. The same word is used for the protection of natural, artistic, architectural and intangible heritage (*tutela del patrimonio naturale, artistico, architettonico e immateriale*). Slow Food shares this language of defence, salvage and tutelage with its own system of Presidia and the 'Ark' of taste (Sardo 2004). At the Sagra of Strachitunt, the president of the consortium advocated this role of guardianship while squarely addressing the issue that had already been raised several times in gossip, altercations and several press articles, documenting the struggle of Val Taleggio to obtain 'a PDO of their own'.

> What is a consortium? It is a group of entrepreneurs that represent the entire value and supply chain of one product. These entrepreneurs have realized that they own a product, which has been handed down to them from previous generations and that they can make. They consider this product unique, and in danger of being imitated. A consortium is an institution that preserves something that can be *reinvented*. Those who make this product somewhere else, in a different guise, under different conditions, *invent* it. This is a fundamental distinction. *We* can do a few things to make our product in slightly updated ways, with new tools and everything that innovation has offered us in the latest decades. But we are not *inventing* anything. We are *reinventing* something that already existed, maybe dwindling, but continuously. We give it a new image, new clothes, and a tipicity [*una tipicità*]. *If* we'll be able to do so, we'll make it *consistent,* and we'll put it back on the market. (Sagra dello Strachitunt, Pizzino di Val Taleggio. 20 October 2006, audio-recorded public speech)

In this complex passage, Anchise (a pseudonym) achieves a complex conceptual and linguistic work: he advocates the role of guardian – of a cheese and of an entire valley and its community – for the Strachitunt consortium; he uses the established notion of *tipicità* to refer to the value, rootedness and marketability of (one of) the valley's cheeses; he explains, in his own words, how to distinguish between an (illegitimate) 'invention' and a (legitimate) 'reinvention' of a local, traditional food. We will elaborate on the notion of *tipicità* in the next section. Here, I dwell on the aspects of guardianship and reinvention as significant cultural aspects of the mobilization of food as heritage – indeed as patrimony (*patrimonio*) of a community. By assuming custodianship of the valley's 'patrimony', the entrepreneur claims nothing short of sovereignty of such community, territory and boundaries.

A philosophy graduate as well as a shrewd entrepreneur with decades of business experience, Anchise played a vocal part in articulating the mission of his own family enterprise as well as that of the entire valley. He had authored the motto for his firm's commercial: 'Tradition as a principle, progress as a vocation'.[3] What then did he mean by *reinvention*? With this speech, he clearly demarcates pure 'invention' from the reinvention of a dairy production that already exists, however tenuously, but continuously. The temporal dimension of such production, its permanence over generations, and its material 'circumstances' are clearly evoked as *traditional* here: the producers of Val Taleggio have the right to call their cheese Strachitunt because they own it, because its recipe was passed down from their ancestors, because they have learnt to make it and *still can make it* there, in the same 'circumstances'. When spelled out, such circumstances mean:

> First, respect for an area of production [*territorio di produzione*] which has its historicity [*che ha la sua storicità*], namely we can demonstrate that this product, here, was made 20, 50, 100 years ago. It is irrelevant if this is a big or small area. We are making the product of this area [*zona*]. Second, the technology of production. Strachitunt must be made with milk from two consecutive milkings: evening and morning. This is not what our lowland competitors do. Third: forage must be prevalently produced in the valley [*prevalentemente foraggio del luogo*]. Fourth: milk must be made by cows of Brown breed: our cows. These are the characteristics that cannot be reproduced outside of our typical area [*zona tipica*], Val Taleggio. (Sagra dello Strachitunt, Pizzino di Val Taleggio. 20 October 2006, audio-recorded public speech)

What defines the 'expectations and perceptions of authenticity' (Di Giovine 2009: 2) in the case of Strachitunt is thus the history of a bounded territory, the vision of a certain landscape and flora, the continuity of a specific production technique, and investment on a specific type of breed – the Brown cow. However, Anchise also stresses how this core identity is necessarily reinvented:

> A consortium should represent the entire production chain and it does in our case: we have dairy farms, cheese-makers, and cheese-maturing facilities. Our production protocol spells out how our cheese should be made in the closest way possible to how it was made once upon a time [*come si faceva una volta*]. These are serious, fair and stringent rules. But they also need to be applicable rules. There's no point saying that we should make Strachitunt keeping our cows grazing on the pastures at 1,500 meters altitude only, because this is no longer the case. We need a constructive compromise between how we made it once upon a time [*come si faceva una volta*] and how we have to make it today. (Sagra dello Strachitunt, Pizzino di Val Taleggio. 20 October 2006, audio-recorded public speech)

With these considerations, tradition is recontextualized within a dynamic frame of value-addition and realistic assessments. As Barbara Kirshenblatt-Gimblett has spelled out, 'heritage is a value-added industry'; 'heritage is a new mode of cultural production in the present that has recourse to the past' (1995: 369–70). 'The value of past-ness' is added to a commodity, for example food, which makes it suitable for multiple and global markets: 'Heritage produces the local for export' (1995: 373). While Kirshenblatt-Gimblett had especially the tourist industry in mind, here I focus on the reinvention of food not so much to stress its dependence from and functionality to culinary tourism (as in Long 2004), but rather on the preliminary and often fraught processes of identification and localization of specific forms of 'food heritage' (see Bessiére and Tibére 2011).

As Anchise so clearly articulates, certain foods (in this case Strachitunt) are singled out for promotion over others because they better respond to very specific and contextual circumstances that allow their *valorizzazione*, namely their repositioning in a system of recognition (Bourdieu's 'field of production', 1993) by which they accrue a higher value. Regina Bendix has underlined how selectively choosing specific elements of a cultural complex is problematic. While underlining how cultural heritage *becomes*, rather than *is* ('Kulturerbe is nicht, es wirdt': Bendix 2007: 340), she proposes the working concept of 'heritagification' (*Heritage-ifizierung*) to pinpoint the political processes that educate people to recognize something as heritage and as their own patrimony 'reframing their relationships to habitat and habitus in terms of heritage' (Bendix and Hafstein 2009: 7). In the case of food heritage, Bérard and Marchenay observe that denominations of origin offer 'a selective reading of the past that keeps the evolution of custom in perspective, as well as their transmission' (1995: 162). Consequently, idiosyncrasies, conflict and negotiations are necessarily back-staged.

Marketing and communications strategies construct 'territorial systems' (*sistemi territoriali*) such as wine – and culinary districts (*distretto eno-gastronomico*) as marketable configurations of gastronomic, natural and cultural patrimony. While this creates real economic opportunities in some localities, it also mobilizes a localist rhetoric that is entrenched in the poetics of *campanilismo*: the often folklorized competition and animosity between neighbouring localities of comparable size and importance, such as cities, towns or villages.[4] The *campanile* is the bell-tower, standing for the identity of those who look up at it and recognize a familiar feature. It marks the most important feature in an ecology of belonging. Ernesto de Martino (1977) has famously described the sense of panic and disorientation that losing sight of one's *campanile* had induced in a villager accompanying him on one of his 'expeditions' in Calabria. While localism is certainly paramount to any understanding of Italian cultures (in the plural), it has been noted how the pressure to territorialize foodstuffs may lead to conflicts between communities, or may empower specific social actors and agendas within communities, thus widening power imbalances between winning strategists and less resourceful smallholders.[5]

Following Karpik (2007), Siniscalchi (2009) argues that heritage foods respond to regimes of 'singularity'. In order to be 'typical', they presume the repeatability of their production. However, these practices are held as unique and distinctive of specific communities and localities, even of their identities. Similarly, in tourism and heritage studies localities have to be unique, yet standardized (Di Giovine 2009). Such logic of singularity is also applied to the much wider national discourse, for instance for UNESCO intangible cultural heritage recognition. Marketing culinary objects as 'ancestral, ongoing community culture' (UNESCO 2010) follows (or indeed sometimes precedes) registration in UNESCO's List of Intangible Cultural Heritage (*patrimoine culturel immatériel*). Beginning with the Mediterranean, French, Mexican, Japanese and Korean reinventions of 'culinary patrimonies', the list of nation-states that are actively engaged in 'gastrodiplomacy' is lengthening – one more proof that candidating food to heritage status is little short of an active exercise of sovereignty.[6]

Naturally 'There is, really, no such thing as heritage'; Laurajane Smith reminds us to retrieve the intellectual awareness that heritage is not a thing but a process, and an 'inherently political and discordant' cultural work (Smith 2006: 11). That culinary heritage is considered intangible is also debatable, since it is difficult to think of what we ingest and the way we do it as something different than *both* a cultural *and* material practice at once. However, Smith and Akagawa rebut that 'all heritage is intangible, not only because of the values we give to heritage, but because of the cultural work that heritage does in any society' (Smith and Akagawa 2009: 6).

In Italy, both native and foreign anthropologists have worked on and with heritage as a conflictual site of cultural production, where stakeholders' interests and agendas are deliberately and sometimes aggressively played out in relation to art-historical, architectural or devotional practices and preferences (Di Giovine 2009). Anne Meneley, on the basis of comparative fieldwork with Italian and Palestinian olive growers, has shown how criteria for food 'quality', in the case of olive oil, are culturally scoped and privilege the established traditions of politically strong and commercially represented countries (2011). Cristina Papa observes that olive oil protocols of production mostly underline 'physical, climatic or soil conditions relative to the area of production' and this 'brings territory to the fore at the expense of the human factors that create it' (Papa 1999: 165–67). Foodstuffs, foodscapes and foodways are icons of locality tout court on Italian media since the inception of television; and this media tradition has roots in radio programming too (Bindi and Grasseni 2014).

While case studies abound (for example Scholliers and Geyzen 2010; West and Domingos 2012; May 2013), we lack longitudinal, critical ethnographies of the making of food heritage: what this process entails and what it brings about in social, cultural, relational and political terms. Appadurai reminds us that 'the semiotic virtuosity' of food, a 'powerful semiotic device', 'takes particularly intense forms in the context of gastro-politics – where food is the medium, and sometimes the message, of conflict' (1981: 494). As noted by Rodney Harrison, 'once heritage moves into the political arena it becomes a symbol of something else – nationalism, culture, class – a touchstone around which people can muster their arguments and thoughts' (2010: 191). The same can be claimed of food heritage, in the sense that the notion of *patrimonio* is invoked largely to heal a perceived wound to the valley's sovereignty over their own cheese, as it will become clearer in Part II. In fact, as I have also discussed elsewhere in the case of Bitto cheese, *tipicità* is not an inherent *quality*, but a *strategy* to demarcate and defend boundaries (Grasseni 2012). Understanding the politics of food heritage in Italy cannot then dispense with an ethnographic appreciation of the meaning, practice and performance of *patrimonio* and *tipicità*.

As Bessiére and Tibère suggest (2011), a definition of food heritage (*patrimoine alimentaire*) is difficult to convey in just a few words because several disciplines have developed distinct and sometimes conflicting approaches: the socio-historical deconstruction of heritage (Ulin 1996; Terrio 2000) but also its ethnological inventory (Papa 1992); the ethnography of local cultures of food quality and taste (Counihan 2004; Harper and Faccioli 2010) or the critical contextualization of specific culinary items in socio-economic and historical terms (Meneley 2007 and 2011; Kulick and Meneley 2005; Black and Ulin 2013; Paxson and West 2012). Moreover, there persists a substantial divide and even a certain incommensurability between the concepts and usage of 'heritage' and 'patrimony' between scholarship in English (see Kirshenblatt-Gimblett 2004) and scholarship in Latin languages (notably French, Spanish and Italian: see Chastel and Babelon 1994; Desvallées 1998; Fournier et al. 2012). This, *despite* the fact that one can peruse the UNESCO site and leisurely transition from English definitions of cultural heritage and French canons for *patrimoine culturel*.

Patrimonio, rather than a process of value-addition, spells out a claim to ownership and the symbolic and material wealth that accompanies it – with the concomitant competition and eventual impoverishment of those who are excluded from it. A number of authors have highlighted the entrenchment of cultural strategies with commercial and political agendas in the 're-evaluation' of landscapes, foodstuffs and cultural traditions (Roigé and Frigolé 2012; Del Marmol et al. 2015; Vaccaro and Beltran 2007). 'Appropriative' language is to be found across a wide spectrum of social actors, from political speeches to participatory development initiatives with varying degrees of actual involvement by local actors.[7] That *patrimony* (*patrimoine* in French) stands for 'possessive individualism' has already being remarked by Handler (1985) and Herzfeld (1992: 104), in the case of nationalist rhetoric. Contemporary heritage discourse may obscure the social dynamics of sovereignty that come to the fore in ethnographic observation, and of which the social actors involved demonstrate to be eloquently aware.

Local cheese-making traditions are often referred to as forms of patrimony. For example, in Anchise's speech the meaning of *patrimonio* is clearly connected with the 'wealth' and the 'riches' of the community, as something *both* material and immaterial that was handed down from previous generations at the cost of toil and labour, and has to be appropriately preserved and handed down to future generations. Just as a form of inheritance in the case of *patrimonio* 'property is ideally held in trust for all future generations' (Herzfeld 1992: 138). The fact that local cheese, as patrimony of previous generations, is not generating revenue and a future for the valley feeds on the feeling of dispossession that its inhabitants – not only the cheese-makers – resent:

> Let me spell out things for those who may be unaware of our plight. I am talking about a product made in the lowlands, which is not the same as our product. These lowland producers and some important institutions at the province level say that we are not capable of managing our product [*dicono che noi non siamo in grado di gestire questo prodotto*], which has a much wider value than Val Taleggio alone, and that this production should be brought out of our valley. But this product is maybe one of the last riches of our valley, together with its landscape and its rural architecture. To these people, who talk about safeguarding the mountains, I want to say that we have enough of being considered custodians on behalf of others. We are custodians of our own wealth and of our own people. Above all we are not *stupid* custodians, who let thieves take away our riches without noticing. If this wealth of ours is needed to be distributed more widely, to guarantee a future to more people, then write this down to us, and pay for it in advance. Not as you did with our Taleggio cheese, of which we pocketed nothing! *We* are the owners! Lowland dairies are badly imitating a product that they do not know how to make. We will decide, consciously, democratically and intelligently what to do with our *own* product. (Sagra dello Strachitunt, Pizzino di Val Taleggio. 20 October 2006, audio-recorded public speech)

In times of more enthusiastic collective political engagement, this could have been a party rally, both for the lively rhetoric and for the heartfelt attendance of at least a couple of hundred people, which in a valley of 800 is a veritable mob. Anchise skilfully appropriated the idea of patrimony as community-owned *despite* everyone's awareness that only some individuals in the valley would benefit in varying degrees from a cheese PDO. Herzfeld has underlined how the idea of patrimony emphasizes 'the congruence of familial metaphors with the interests of the state' (1992: 141). In this case, cheese is evoked as patrimony in order to advocate *local* sovereignty, for and in the name of the 'imagined community' of Val Taleggio. What I mean by sovereignty here is exactly 'responsibility for local practice in matters relating to inheritance and property ownership' (Herzfeld 1992: 154). Cheese being patrimony, it symbolically embodies a form of collective inheritance: 'the territorial expression of social relations' (Herzfeld 1992: 154).

The tirade delivered by a local notable, a leading entrepreneur, in his role of president of the cheese consortium, places the reinvention of cheese squarely within competitive economic and institutional dynamics that are often rightly perceived as intrinsically damaging of community needs. Especially the recurrent reference to riches, wealth and custodianship reveals how Strachitunt cheese is not imagined here as a simple commodity, but as a more complex 'product', which embodies a system of local value and stands for a regional economy. Mountain cheeses struggling for distinction such as Strachitunt are not just reinvented to invest them with added exchange value. They are not just commodities. Their regional economies and environment are implicated through their communities of practitioners and stakeholders. Their mode of existence in time, their temporal agency is at stake: ownership of history, present predicaments and capacities of future-making. Those who take it upon themselves to preside, lead and represent these material, emotional and political interests assume a huge social responsibility – whether consciously or not – sometimes greater than that of elected representatives or public administrators – and will be judged by it.

With this speech, the Strachitunt consortium president takes responsibility for interpreting and 'managing' a traditional production practice, which implies landscape conservation, breed improvement, the definition and innovation of specific production techniques, and above all the drawing and policing of clear-cut geographical boundaries. Through legitimate custodianship of the valley's patrimony – a legitimation that comes from the economic interest at stake – nothing short of sovereignty is claimed. In this case sovereignty is claimed *through* a political performance by economic actors – in a reversal of the customary 'metacultural operations that constitute heritage' when heritage conventions are ratified by the state, with the following 'host of regulatory steps, actors and institutions that transform a cultural monument, a landscape or an intangible cultural practice into certified heritage' (Bendix et al. 2012: 11). In this case the local arena of heritage governance is directly shaped by the 'field of forces' that is located at the level of commodity production: once established that food, *qua* patrimony of a community, deserves guardianship, its candidate guardian is the local entrepreneur who controls its supply chain.

This process does not pertain to Val Taleggio alone (and could explain the political success of more infamous 'national' entrepreneurs). However, Anchise's eloquence spoke to a local plight: that of having failed to harness political control of an economically important geographical denomination, the PDO for Taleggio cheese, *despite* that fact that the valley bears its very name. I will return to the historical details of this lost battle in Part II. For now, let me stress how cheese is a pivotal resource in the political performance of heritage in the Alps today – both in Italy and across the border, in Austria, Switzerland, Germany and France (Kah and Weixlbaumer 2013; Burigana 2013). In light of its significance in the Alpine peasant diet, subsistence agriculture and merchant economy, it is no surprise that cheese is recognized as a potential protagonist of *patrimonializzazione* in the alpine regional economy. LEADER, LEADER2 and LEADER+ European funding rounds supported the establishment of so-called Local Action Groups – committees of local entrepreneurs, administrators and local stakeholders who would draft, bid for and manage EU-funded projects. This opened the path to conceiving of *patrimonio* as a broader field of production and political forces than entrepreneurship. For example, 'cheese-paths' (*Käsestrassen*) were the novelty of local development plans in the 1990s, promoting cheese as a cultural symbol and a tourist attraction alongside viewing it as a commodity.

In Anchise's speech the Strachitunt consortium was being presented as a similar institution – not just an alliance of business partners but a political and moral institution for the valley's development, with its president as its guardian. Everyone was called upon in his speech: for example the local competitor who subscribed to the consortium but matured the cheese of the lowland 'enemy' from outside the consortium ('Either we are in or we stay out!'), or the restaurant manager catering for vegan bikers and advertising his hotel in German, who does not buy his cheese locally ('We should sell our cheese and our cheese only!'). Things did get personal, for all those present who could understand the precise references made in Anchise's speech. For all intents and purposes, he was 'naming and shaming'. This self-appointed role of public chastiser was not just an emotional outpour from a frustrated businessman, seeing a long and torturous path ahead to keep the consortium together and obtain the PDO. It was also the performance of moral *auctoritas* that he was expected to assume, being in charge of an economic concern that has obvious strategic and social impact on the community's future.

The Language of *Tipicità*

Anchise – the cheese entrepreneur who explained in his own words the difference between inventing and reinventing a cheese – is probably the main commercial stakeholder in this enterprise, though he casts his argument in terms of the wealth of the community, its future prospects and its capacity for collective future-making. In the previous section I explained how by advocating the role of custodian of the valley's patrimony he effectively claimed sovereignty – for the valley, the consortium and eventually for his family enterprise – over the reinvention of Strachitunt.

We focus in this section on the discourse of *tipicità*, which is the main conduit of that claim. We have seen in his speech how the usage of the word *tipicità* both evokes a traditional status quo, specifically the *auctoritas* of 'what it was like once upon a time' (*come si faceva una volta*), and invokes substantial margins of intervention, innovation and discretionary choices: *tipicità* can and must be 'given' to a product (*gli diamo una tipicità*). Actually being able to do this is the question (*se siamo capaci*). *Tipicità* is both a quality, a characteristic, a state of things that is claimed as demonstrable and incontrovertible, and a dynamic process of reinvention, which requires skill that must be proven. How is this apparent self-contradiction spelled out and acted upon?

Elsewhere I talked about how, in the eyes of many agricultural consultants and according to a number of strategic actions plans for alpine marginal rural areas, the mountains need 'developing': cow breeds need improving, new skills need to be acquired, a new vision of local resources needs implementing (Grasseni 2009). As Anchise stresses when he talks about 'giving a product its typicity' (*gli diamo una tipicità*), it is cheese itself that needs 'developing'. Developing cheese means securing, branding and expanding very local and often microscopic productions. It means establishing production protocols and tallying viable normative and commercial ways to enforce them: whether by European law through a Protected Denomination of Origin, or through Slow Food–presided niche productions (*Presidia*) or through trademarks and brands granted by the chamber of commerce (such as the one mentioned by Cavanaugh 2005). Developing cheese means reinventing it, not simply as a commodity but as *patrimonio*.

Cheese is imagined as embodied in a cultural landscape that has been shaped by generations of dairy-farming and the related activities of wood-keeping and hay-making in the pastures. In the heritage imaginary, such landscape nourishes not only the grazing cattle (which in turns yields quality milk) but also the artisanal crafts and skills of curdling and maturing cheese. This explicit (and sometimes implicit) symbolic enrolment of the skill of a bounded community of practitioners translates in its value. In the informants' own words, the notion of *tipicità*, sometimes in conjunction with *territorio* – never with *terroir* – refers to the unique emplacement of cheese in a locality. Here are some examples of how the notion of *tipicità* was used by different people, active in the cheese-refining industry of Val Taleggio, over a time span of fifteen years:

> 'Taleggio's taste is getting lost because it is suffering a lot on the market, and it sells for very low prices, so they make it with cheap stuff, such as freeze-dried yeast, and its *tipicità* is getting lost . . .'
>
> 'Our idea was to bring an important incentive to Val Taleggio: we asked the Taleggio consortium to have number one of their production registry for the valley's cheese-making cooperative – an entirely symbolic acknowledgement. We offered to host the consortium seat in the valley. We asked to develop a production protocol for a more typical cheese [*un formaggio più tipico*] within the consortium, as they do with Camembert, so we could produce a typical Taleggio cheese of Val Taleggio [*un taleggio tipico della Val Taleggio*] . . .'
>
> 'Our producers turned down a Slow Food presidium for Strachitunt because Slow Food does not accept silage as fodder. Our dairy farmers don't understand they we need a strongly typical milk [*un latte fortemente tipico*].' (1 September 2006, dinner with entrepreneurs and administrators of the valley)

Seven years before:

> Our *tipicità*, bound to our territory is lost . . . We missed our chance thirty years ago, when we could have fought for a Taleggio DOC within the DOP, tied to our territory, instead our Taleggio is just as DOP as that of Treviso. It could have been a flagship production, it could have distinguished our local production, based on our *tipicità* . . . Our smallholders continue to make their Taleggio but cannot call it Taleggio and brand it as such because they are not members of the consortium, hence they cannot sell it because they do not have a hygiene authorization, et cetera. (Director of Arrigoni Valtaleggio, 12 March 1999, audio-recorded interview on the premises of the valley's main cheese-refining industry)

And seven years later, at the 2013 Sagra dello Strachitunt:

> We have volunteers coming from Lecco, Como, Gorgonzola to support us in the effort of organizing this feast. This is in connection with the history of our mountain people who descended from the mountains and established themselves in the lowlands. Those who live in the mountains have to face quotidian sacrifices and problems: think about our students who get up at 5 am to take a bus and travel downhill to secondary school and only come back in the late afternoon. (President of Pro Loco Val Taleggio, 27 October 2013, Sagra dello Strachitunt, audio-recorded inaugural speech)

> To defend life in the mountains, to defend the *prodotti tipici* means not only to create added value for the local population but also for the public administration. Mountain economy, the *alpeggio* and the protagonists of the *alpeggio*, the Bergamini, have been discussed in our regional government committees on health and on the environment. Huge expenses go to intervene after landslides and hydro-geological damage in the mountains, and one of the causes is the abandonment of pastureland. I was mayor in Alta Val Seriana; to live and to do business in an eco-compatible logic is not done with words but with the reality of Val Taleggio, which in this last few weeks has achieved important objectives such as the transitory European concession of nationwide PDO. (Angelo Capelli, elected representative to the Regional Council of Lombardy, guest speaker at Sagra dello Strachitunt, 27 October 2013. Audio-recorded)

As we can see from these quotes, *tipicità* is a multifaceted concept, very much alive and longitudinally employed by politicians, community activists, entrepreneurs, administrators and historians. *Tipicità* (translatable in French as *typicité*, in Spanish as *tipicidad*, but difficult to pinpoint in English. It allows active agency on the part of the speaker, who is free to select specific elements and hold them up as relevant: locality, landscape and community are all implicated in the semantic construction of worth. Consequently, there does not exist one textbook definition of it; however, uniqueness, value and emplacement play a ubiquitous role in the way it is used by speakers. A *prodotto tipico* of a certain locality is singled out and rewarded by the market as being at once unique and representative of that locality.

In Southern Europe, entire regions struggling with industrial stagnation have invested in 'typical' products (*prodotti tipici, productos tìpicos*) – an expression usually translated in English as 'local products'. However this expression misses many nuances of the original phrase (Ceccarelli et al. 2013). In Italy, a *prodotto tipico* is not just local, stemming from a specific locality, but is considered representative of its distinctive soil, fauna, flora, exposure, historically documented techniques and material culture, tools, rural architecture, terminology and prescribed usage – including associated festivities, folklore, religiosity and seasonality. 'Typical' betrays this paradoxical nature in the English language too: something is typical if it is of average expectancy for a certain phenomenon, process or material. But the median sample is also expected to stand up to the ideal type. *Tipico* thus means to be unique in its instantiation, but representative of a reliable average that is associated with a specific state of things (historical and geographical), in ways that introduce an expectation of invariance – similarly to the much-debated notion of 'tradition'.[8] '*Tipico*' is the expression used to define place-based foods as pertaining to distinct environments *in a historical dimension*. Hence *tipicità* may be predicated upon specific ecological niches that could *in principle* be found elsewhere (soil, specific anthropic landscapes and the agro-economic practices that shape them) but do not, in actual temporal and cultural terms.

Perhaps as a result of this, *tipicità* is often discussed in relation to a spatial dimension: is this product typical of *this area*? Does it pertain to *this zone of production*? These questions are never asked neutrally or disinterestedly. If it is, it must be possible to exhibit historical documentation of the continuous and relevant existence of that production *in that area*. *Tipicità* can thus be predicated of milk and cheese, but also of an area of production (*zona tipica di produzione*) or even of a landscape, a way of life. The language of *tipicità* does not pertain exclusively to food practices such as cheese-making. *Tipico* sets a claim on the landscape itself, as belonging 'to those born and raised in a specific locale, namely, those who have a long-standing working relationship with territory' (Stacul 2010: 231). This is true not only of place-based foods, but also of forestry or hunting (see Stacul 2003) – in other words, of a way of life.[9] Consistently with this, as we will see in Part III, when the two new mayors of the administrations of Val Taleggio chose a name to establish an eco-museum in Val Taleggio in 2006, they chose to call it Civiltà del Taleggio e delle Baite Tipiche.[10]

The equation between *tipicità* and locality, and its rooting in geographically detectable boundaries, dominates PDO protocols of production and their national precedents in European legislation. For the dairy trade, these have a long history. In 1951 the Stresa Convention, established between ten European countries, acknowledged the need for an international system of geographical denomination. Italian law then distinguished between Denominations of Origin and Denomination of Typicity of Cheeses (*Denominazioni di origine e tipiche dei formaggi*). Law number 125 of 10 April 1954 ascribed the 'Denomination of Origin' (DO) to cheese produced in specified geographical areas, making use of 'local and constant custom', and whose commercial characteristics derive mostly from the environment of production. A 'Typical Denomination' (DT) would instead denote cheese produced anywhere in the country, 'made observing fair and constant custom', and whose commercial characteristics derive mostly from 'methods and techniques of production'.[11]

Already then, a DO was considered superior to a DT, since a DO would somewhat encompass DT requirements but with the additional quality of associating them to a specific territory. Since 1992, European Regulation n. 2081 certifies two denominations under the names of PDO and PGI (Protected Designation of Origin and Protected Geographical Indication).[12] They follow an analogous logic: a PDO is a place-name (which can be as wide as a country), designating a product originating from that place, whose quality or characteristics are 'essentially or exclusively' originating from the 'geographic environment of that place, inclusive of the human and natural factors' and *whose production, transformation and refinement take place within* that locality. A PGI is still a place name, but only one that defines the product qualities (including its reputation!) that are associated to such locality. Any (but not necessarily all) of the phases of production, transformation or refinement take place in that locality. Making a case for a PDO by converse *requires* producing historical documentation of actual geographical *origin*, *continuity* of local tradition, and local provenance of the *ingredients* – all of them in the same locality (Bérard and Marchenay 1995).

Notably, the same European regulation also allows for a Traditional Speciality Guaranteed (*Specialità Tradizionale Garantita*, STG), which is *not* place-bound at all, but this is seldom used for cheese, at least in Italy. The language of *tipicità* somehow requires territoriality. This fact, however, is not enforced by Brussels bureaucrats or national experts. *Tipicità* expresses an eminently cultural notion rather than simply a spatial one. In the language of both consumers and producers, *tipicità* is broadly associated with phenomenological and affective experiences, almost as a synonym for 'sense of place' (Trubek 2008). While *terroir* is also being increasingly used in food studies to define this concept, *tipicità* and *terroir* are not the same: they do not do the same cultural work. Macro-environmental factors are traditionally played up in the understanding of *terroir*: soil, climate, air and the conditions of the anthropic landscape that sustain traditions of cultivation. Naturally it would be difficult to elide the cultural aspect altogether (the Latin *colere*, from which we derive 'culture', means to cultivate). However in Italian one would translate *produits de terroir* as *prodotti del territorio*. But one says instead *prodotti tipici*. The prevalent metaphor evoked is thus not one of soil (best translated as *terrain* in French), or even locality-bound climatic and agronomic characteristics (such the quality of pasture grass, or of a maturing cave). These alone are never held as sufficient definitions of *tipicità*. Even though there is ready recourse to the phrase that 'mountain cheese should taste of mountain grass' (Huseby 2012), the peculiarities of the landscape must be matched by the skill of operators, who know how to handle a very specific raw material in a very specific environment, resulting in a unique end product.[13] The place-name of a *prodotto tipico* stands for the skill to tackle local diversity, in a conceptual short-circuit between *tipicità* and *territorio*, which nevertheless does not assume *territorio* to be a matter of mere geography.

This is an important nuance. Foods that carry no notion of their provenance rate very low in Italian taste, *not* because they are not associated to a specific *place*, but because their disassociation from a locality, with its properties and idiosyncrasies, is a sure sign of the deskilling of the manufacturing process, which in fact can take place *anywhere*. Hence the perceived low quality of the final product, which is 'standard', 'mass-produced', 'all the same' (*tutto uguale*). It is unlikely that place-name connections will be dropped, even if scientific evidence could potentially be harnessed to link micro-cultures to taste, in a much more defining way than previously considered. In Europe, and in Italy especially, the question 'is there a relevant and possibly even vital connection to be made between food and place?' (Trubek 2008: xiii), which American scholars increasingly ask and eloquently answer (see Weiss 2011; Belasco 2006), finds answer in common sense: yes! In Italy as well as in France, this is in fact 'a culture's common sense' (Trubek 2008: 210) and one of the many symptoms of the charged discontinuities between European and American food cultures.

I was witness to such cultural disjuncture at an event about the 'local food movement' held at Tufts University: one of the questions asked was precisely whether recent research in microbiology could establish that the microbic cultures of cheese are place-based in a much different way than what the European regime of protected designation of origin assumes.[14] Could the fact that the same models of microbic culture can essentially be found in a pedigree French cheese, or in a neorural establishment in Wisconsin, finally convince Europeans to drop their unreasonable claims to label foods for provenance, as if they had to be named after specific, non-replicable localities? The question, cast by an expert in rural development and farm management, was based on recent mycology research currently conducted at Harvard University. Such research shows that the microbial communities that populate the rind of different types of cheese are universally dispersed, thriving in ecologic niches that, crucially, seem to be equally developed on either side of the Atlantic. Of course this takes into consideration *only* the crust of cheese, not its paste – or its taste. But findings about the cheese rind were sufficient to trigger the question: won't the EU drop their claim to a commercial superiority of say, PDO Parmigiano Reggiano over Parmesan – if such findings are confirmed?

The obvious answer (no) is unlikely to be dictated by syllogism or laboratory protocol, since it carries obvious commercial and strategic interests. In general, no universal consequence could easily be derived from such a partial premise. However, there is more to the European attachment to place-names than mere marketing strategies. An anthropological understanding of such attachment should take the language of *tipicità* into consideration. That anything like *tipicità* exists is actually a commonly accepted platitude, whose longevity transpires from the national and European laws that elaborate, articulate and wield it for the protection of food quality and commercial interests alike. This notion was used and debated well before GMO crops – perceived as the embodiment of 'American' capitalist encroachments on local, regional and national(ist) foodscapes – made organic agriculture or the local food movement relevant to the general public in Europe. The notion was well established before a handful of wine-loving communists from Piedmont had the seminal idea of transforming what was ARCI GOLA in the 1980s (literally the 'gluttony' section of the Association for Recreation of Italy's Communist Workers) into an association that became known as Slow Food. Naturally, the contemporary social, political and economic constructions of food's *tipicità* are ongoing, but the notion has a pedigree in and of itself.

The 'vital connection' between food and place is both historical and cultural; as such, it can be activated, performed or even negated. For example, as we shall see in Part II there obviously *is* a vital connection between *stracchino* and the economic, social and environmental history of the northern Italian plains. That connection is transhumant pastoralism and its historical transformations, which have determined at once the unprecedented diffusion *and* the commercial demise of Taleggio cheese as 'too big', 'too common', 'too cheap' to be effectively appropriated as a flagship denomination for Val Taleggio alone. So that vital connection could not be activated in favour of the people of Val Taleggio, who resent it. This is why the battle for the PDO Strachitunt was a veritable saga of self-enfranchisement in the eyes of its protagonists (cooperative farmers, cheese-makers, sellers, cheese matures and exporters) and its reinvention as a traditional cheese was at once authentic and strategic (Hobsbawm and Ranger 1983; Meneley 2007). In the next Chapter, building on the contemporary reconsideration of several artisanal upland cheeses, I will contextualize the reinvention of Strachitunt not only as the attempt to relocalize a specific supply chain, but also to competitively participate in a broader culture of dairy resistance.

Notes

1. Bendix (1997: 253n33) quotes Bausinger (1969) to support her critique of Hobsbawm and Ranger (1983). In her view, they would offer a simplistic analysis of the authenticity of traditions vis-à-vis their 'invention'.
2. See the website http://strachitunt.it/#. Note that 'Strachìtunt' appears with the accented 'i' in the cheese logo and in most documents produced by the consortium. It is obtained by joining the two dialect words *strachì* (*stracchino*) and *tunt* (*tondo*): round *stracchino*. In the official protocol for production, though, the accented 'i' has been dropped creating a neologism: Strachitunt.
3. See www.arrigonivaltaleggio.it (last accessed on 11 January 2011).
4. See for example Silverman (1975) and Stacul (2003).
5. See Leitch (2003) for the case of Slow Food Presidia and Cavanaugh (2007) for IGP productions.
6. UNESCO has so far recognized the 'Gastronomic Meal of the French' (*le repas gastronomique des Français*), 'Traditional Mexican Cuisine,' the 'Mediterranean Diet' (jointly: Spanish, Greek, Italian and Moroccan), 'Washoku, Traditional Dietary Cultures of the Japanese' and 'Kimjang, Making and Sharing Kimchi in the Republic of Korea'. On 'gastrodiplomacy' and the discursive strategies of culinary nationalism and regionalism see Bestor (2014); Kim (2012); Burigana (2013); Brulotte and Starkman (2014).
7. For instance, on the ambivalent premises and outcomes of two eco-museum projects, including the Val Taleggio community map project, see Grasseni (2015, 2011).
8. 'The object and characteristic of 'traditions', including invented ones, is invariance' (Hobsbawm and Ranger 1983: 2).
9. See Bowen (2011) for another example of how imaginaries and strategies of embeddedness and (re) territorialization go hand in hand, in the case of Comté cheese, an origin-labelled cheese produced in eastern France.
10. The *baite* of Val Taleggio and of the neighbouring Valle Imagna are characterized by a distinctive architecture, with a T-shaped door and very thick, sloped walls, supporting a stone roof (*tetto a piöde*) made of overlapping layers of thick slabs of rock from the nearby caves of Valle Imagna. Once crowded, tens of *baite* now lie roofless and abandoned in the upper reaches of the valley, as the dwindling population has abandoned the most isolated hamlets and now resides only in those boroughs that are served by roads.
11. The text of Italian Law 10 April 1954, n. 125, *Tutela delle denominazioni di origine e tipiche dei formaggi* (Protection of denominations of origin and typical denominations of cheeses) is available online on the site of the World Intellectual Property Organization. Here is the original text in Italian: 'Sono riconosciute come denominazioni di origine le denominazioni relative ai formaggi prodotti *in zone geograficamente delimitate* osservando usi locali e costanti e le cui caratteristiche merceologiche derivano *prevalentemente dalle condizioni proprie dell'ambiente di produzione*'. 'Sono riconosciute come denominazioni tipiche quelle relative a formaggi prodotti nel territorio nazionale osservando usi leali e costanti, le cui caratteristiche merceologiche derivano *da particolari metodi della tecnica di riproduzione*' (art. 2). Available at http://www.wipo.int/wipolex/en/text.jsp?file_id=234636. Last accessed 20 January 2015. Italics added by author. See also Gambera and Surra (2003: 216–21) for a commentary of the same law.

12. In English, European Regulation n. 2081 reads like this: 'Article 2. Point 2. For the purposes of this Regulation: (a) designation of origin: means the name of a region, a specific place or, in exceptional cases, a country, used to describe an agricultural product or a foodstuff: – originating in that region, specific place or country, and – the quality or characteristics of which are essentially or exclusively due to a particular geographical environment with its inherent natural and human factors, and the production, processing and preparation of which take place in the defined geographical area; (b) geographical indication: means the name of a region, a specific place or, in exceptional cases, a country, used to describe an agricultural product or a foodstuff: – originating in that region, specific place or country, and – which possesses a specific quality, reputation or other characteristics attributable to that geographical origin and the production and/or processing and/or preparation of which take place in the defined geographical area'. Available at http://eur-lex.europa.eu/legal-content/EN/TXT/?uri=CELEX:31992R2081. Last accessed 20 January 2015.

    In Italian, European Regulation n. 2081 reads like this: 'per denominazione d'origine si intende "il nome di una regione, di un luogo determinato, o in casi eccezionali di un Paese, che serve a designare un prodotto agricolo o alimentare originario di tale regione, di tale luogo determinato o di tale Paese e la cui qualità o le cui caratteristiche siano dovute *essenzialmente o esclusivamente* all'ambiente geografico *comprensivo dei fattori naturali ed umani* e la cui *produzione, trasformazione ed elaborazione* avvengano *nell'area geografica delimitata*". Per indicazione geografica si intende invece "il nome di una regione, di un luogo determinato o, in casi eccezionali, di un Paese, che serve a designare un prodotto agricolo o alimentare originario di tale regione, di tale luogo determinato o di tale paese, e di cui *una* determinata qualità, la reputazione o un'altra caratteristica possa essere attribuita all'origine geografica e la cui produzione *e/o* trasformazione *e/o* elaborazione avvengano nell'area geografica determinata"' (Gambera and Surra 2003: 222–26).
13. For an argument on enskilment regarding gardening vis-à-vis industrial horticulturalism, see Gieser (2014).
14. The event was held at Tufts University on 7 March 2014: 'The Work of Culturing: Labor and Local Food', including a local food production exhibition, featuring sixteen local food organizations, businesses and activist collectives (such as Groundwork Somerville, Food for Thought, the Somerville Mayor's Urban Agriculture Initiative, Union Square Main Streets and M. F. Dulock Pasture-Raised Meats). After a cheese-tasting session including among others some local raw-milk cheeses presented by the Tufts Cheese Club, guest lecturer Heather Paxson gave a talk on 'Raw (Milk) Politics: Safety and Skill in Small-Scale Cheesemaking', followed by discussion with an interdisciplinary panel. Within this framework, the research conducted at the Dutton laboratory of the Center for Systems Biology at Harvard University was discussed. The findings of this laboratory are reviewed, from an anthropological point of view, in Paxson and Helmreich (2014).

CHAPTER 2

Cultures of Resistance

Food is increasingly seen as a significant national resource, often identified with specific territories: *Forbes* recently designated the regional cuisine of Emilia Romagna as one of the country's most valuable assets.[1] Bergamo, as already noted by other anthropologists, does not feature among the Italian culinary Walhalla (Cavanaugh 2005; Castellanos and Bergstresser 2006). However, when it comes to cheese, it can certainly count on a very rich palette of local productions. A province of about 1 million within the 10 million inhabitants of the Lombardy region, Bergamo boasts the highest number of PDO cheeses in Italy: there are nine protected denominations of origin for cheese whose area of production falls entirely or partly within the province of Bergamo (Formai de Mut, Strachitunt, Bitto, Taleggio, Gorgonzola, Quartirolo, Salva, Grana Padano, Provolona Val Padana), plus one PDO request pending approval at the regional level (for Branzi) and two Slow Food Presidia (Stracchino all'Antica delle Valli Orobiche and Agrì di Valtorta). Two of the PDO cheeses have very small production areas, practically mapping one single valley: Formai de Mut in the Upper Val Brembana and Strachitunt in Val Taleggio, while Branzi is the name of a village in Val Brembana.

Small PDOs work differently from the large commercial consortia of Gorgonzola, Taleggio or Grana Padano: they involve smallholders or producer-cooperatives of no more than twenty members, sometimes as few as five, and turn over very small quantities: for example Strachitunt makes about twenty-four tons a year, according to the producers' register for 2014.[2] As for Formai de Mut, others have already asked whoever outside of Bergamo could care about a PDO cheese called 'mountain cheese' (Cavanaugh 2007). This is in fact the meaning of '*formai de mut*'. The Formai de Mut and Strachitunt consortia are run by local entrepreneurs who act as community organizers, officiating both public events and hard-nosed business negotiations. In fact, they are similar to Slow Food Presidia for size and membership.[3] Both Slow Food Presidia and what I call here 'community PDOs' function in full awareness that the products they protect would be commercially nonviable without a supported market. This may come in the form of a promotion circuit, which Slow Food engineers around its Presidia for example. Or it may be a premium on price, justified by a protected denomination. Community PDOs are tiny productions but straddle multiple regimes of local relevance from a political point of view, at once addressing procedures of transnational governance (the issuance of PDO designations) and negotiating local power. They produce their socioeconomic and geopolitical locality by the very act of making the case for a local product; they thus embody the practice of locality.

According to the technicians who managed the case for Strachitunt, since the late 1990s PDO certification is encouraged to go small by the very bureaucrats who provide first-time evaluations of PDO submissions, at the regional level. It is not the global marketing potential of the product that is being evaluated, but rather its significance for local economies. This is taken into consideration in the feasibility studies, where aspiring certified food producers are persuaded to go 'typical', locating their value in *tipicità* (Evaristo, 8 August 2006, Arrigoni Valtaleggio).

Community leaders and Slow Food promoters alike risk engaging in long bureaucratic battles with neighbouring competitors. Unsurprisingly, these are keen to file exceptions to slow down the appointment of what is undoubtedly a marketing advantage. As a result, it took Strachitunt over eleven years to obtain its PDO, from the establishment of the consortium in October 2002 to the concession of the PDO in March 2014. The Branzi procedure, to mention another example, was blocked at regional level because of two competiting requests to file the same PDO name.

Community PDO promoters intend to use the market as a way of ensuring the continuity of marginal local productions. The objective of a community PDO is to increase and protect the marketing value of specific commodities without questioning the workings of a potentially global competitive market. At least in the intentions of the Strachitunt consortium, a geographical indication would provide a world-wide competitive edge with a view to preserving very local economies. Part of this strategy is the active deployment of the idea that their cheese is a unique item of food heritage that deserves protection. The tension between the very local scope of the economies and powers that are meant to benefit, and the dynamics of supralocal and at least potentially international market that should create such benefit, underlies this strategy. Furious battles ensue between small producers – who claim the practice of locality – and competitors or institutions that claim the right of free market, or, more convincingly, argue that much larger communities of producers should benefit from such practice. This is the argument adumbrated by Anchise in his resentful plea for Strachitunt. It is also the case of the long-standing controversy around Bitto cheese in Valtellina, just north of Val Taleggio.

What distinguishes craft cheese from industrial cheese, and at which point do the scales tilt? Heather Paxson elaborates on the craft/mass distinction in the case of American artisanal cheese. She analyses the strategies of neo-rural cheese-makers to add value to their production, illustrating the variety of their practices, and their beliefs in the possibility to steer a different course for local development – one that allows for both environmental and economic sustainability. Moreover, this sensibility builds not only on moral economy but on the phenomenological understanding of complex 'ecologies of production' (Paxson 2010), which depend on specific terrain, exposure, pasture, breeds, diet integrators (if any), season, animal health and welfare, as well as techniques and times of milking, curdling agents and tools, working environments, milk heating techniques and implements (if any), and of course maturing environments.

Unlike the craft cheese renaissance of the United States, the specific histories of Alpine cheese constitute their entitlement to claim the privilege of locality. Not because their tradition is any more authentic, or any less 'invented', than any other socially constructed commodity, but because of the extremely differentiated social and economic histories of their contexts of production. The first survey of Italian agriculture commissioned by the government of the unified state (the famous *Jacini Report* on the state of agriculture of the 1880s) and, in the case of Lombardy, earlier governmental reports about the Lombardo-Veneto region of the Austro-Hungarian Empire (from 1815 up until 1860 as well as before the Napoleonic conquest) document how distinct localities were associated with appropriately praised and priced cheeses (see Mitterpacher 1784).

There is a bewildering variety of artisanal cheeses, for cultural as well as ecological reasons (West 2013a). In the Alpine region, one substantial differentiation lies between the fat, matured, heavy cylinders of upland cheese, produced for commercialization over the centuries (Bitto, Branzi or Formai de Mut just to mention the Lombard ones, and certainly Fontina for Val d'Aosta and Asiago in Veneto) and the lean, smaller, freshly consumed lowland cheeses for family subsistence. The former – but also 'well matured *strachì*' – could even be used as cash substitute or for paying tax,[4] while the more modest *strachì*, Taleggio and, in Piedmont, Toma, were made within and for the local economy (Viazzo and Woolf 2002).

In the following sections, I briefly focus on three neighbouring upland cheeses, three 'cousins' whose histories tell of different capacities of place-named cheeses to harness commercial pedigree and political alliances. Their divergent and serendipitous fortunes reveal how place-based cheeses are not by definition tied to a locality: such a link must be woven, argued for and especially made relevant to ad-hoc contexts, where demand may vary, trustworthy partners may be scarce and the value of place-based quality must be restated anew in shifting circumstances. The following sections compare and contrast the different trajectories of Bitto, Formai de Mut and Branzi.

For the Lombard upland communities, making cheese was equivalent to turning the wheels of a not-so-small-world economy. Saffron-stained, multiyear-matured Bitto was traded at the height of the Renaissance along the Roman cart-way Via Priula, coming down from Valtellina through the Bergamasque valley of Formai de Mut, stationing in the trading centre of Branzi, now giving its name to yet another 'mountain cheese' aspiring to PDO certification: Branzi itself (Corti 2011). According to local historical investigations, cheeses such as Bitto, Formai de Mut and Branzi are closely related, but their institutional histories make them today very differently priced merchandise.

Bitto is protected by a PDO, but PDO Bitto is a far larger protected designation of origin than the Bitto valleys themselves. It encompasses the entire administrative unit (province) of Sondrio, including mountain peaks and lower valleys, and also the upper reaches of the Bergamasque valleys. It makes 240 tons of branded cheese per year of which 22 tons come from the upper reaches of the Bergamasque mountains (by itself, this production is almost equivalent to the Strachitunt production in Val Taleggio). By engaging in 'the mother of all battles', the cheese-producers of the Bitto valleys exited the consortium in polemic disagreement with the policy of 'turning Bitto into a lowland cheese'. As a result, they could no longer brand their cheese as Bitto. When they did, their production was seized and the maturing departments closed down by officers of the Ministry for Agriculture. But with the perseverant and vocal protection of Slow Food and of the 'paladins' of heritage Bitto (Bitto Storico) – food journalists, cheese historians and chefs – they carved a profitable niche of the market for highly priced, sought-after cheese that is considered by a discerning demand more 'authentic' than its PDO counterpart (Grasseni 2012). Such a niche, however, is really small: 1,500 wheels of cheese in all, of a weight between 10 and 13 kg, are branded every year. As many wheels are sold 'fresh' directly on farm, when they are not suited for ageing.

Formai de Mut on the other hand was meant to be a community-bound PDO since its inception in the mid-1980s, a veritable exception at the time, within a commercial scenario dominated by the large industrial consortia of Taleggio, Gorgonzola and Parmigiano. It was the first cheese in Lombardy to obtain a PDO.[5] A descriptive brochure that I gathered from the dairy cooperative in Valtorta claims that 'it has represented for centuries the classic type of cheese produced on the *alpeggi* of the Brembo valley'. Formai de Mut paved the way for Strachitunt to defend its reasons for a *small* designation of origin – whose dimensions unsurprisingly coincide with those of the head of a valley, as it is the case with Strachitunt. The production is small: for 2014 according to the producers about 56 tons of cheese was branded, of which about a third came from upper pasture (summer) production and two thirds from village-based (winter) production.

In the village of Branzi in Upper Val Brembana, fairs such as the recently revived Fiera di San Matteo welcome the herds descending the pastures in early fall. Symmetrically, Morbegno at the foot of Val Gerola and Albaredo (known as 'the Bitto valleys') would host the fair of Bitto cheese at the end of the high-pasture *alpeggio* season. Lying respectively south and north of the Alpine ridge of Valtellina, Branzi and Morbegno were the trading centres of upland cheeses that would then follow two different paths. Directly connected to Milan, Morbegno would trade Bitto. At the heart of Venetian-dominated Bergamasque valleys, Branzi would sell a 'Bitto-like' mountain cheese. According to local historians, what came to be called Formai de Mut and Branzi was still called Bitto in the sixteenth century, and would be treated with saffron in preparation of the journey that would take it to the Pope's table (Corti 2006a). Branzi is now commercialized as good quality, nondenomination, fat mature cheese, in yellowish wheels of about 10.5 kg. The cooperative creamery (*latteria sociale*) based in Branzi produces about 26,000 wheels of cheese a year. But it trades for nothing like the collector's-item price of Slow Food Bitto Storico. The following three sections explain the relevance of these three cheeses to the Strachitunt case.

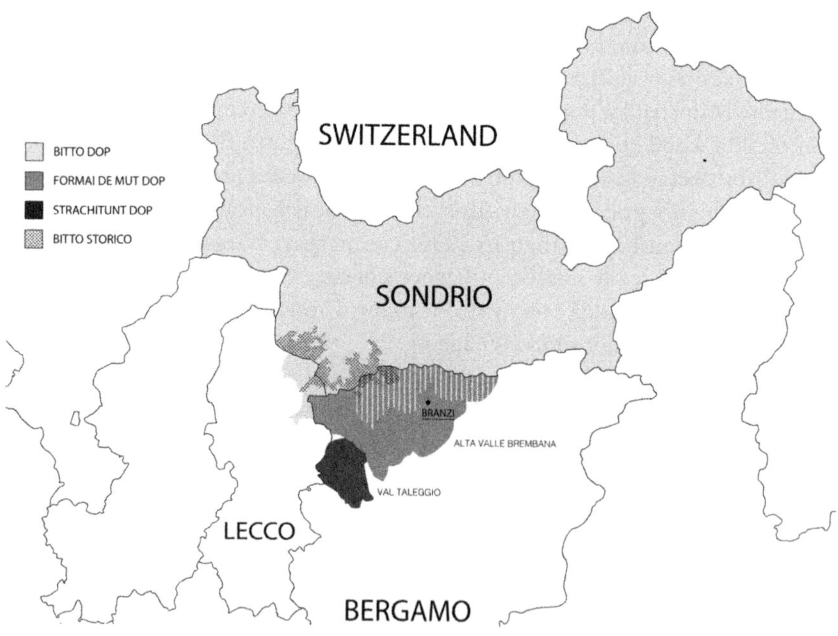

Map 1. Production area for Bitto PDO, Formai de Mut dell'Alta Val Brembana PDO and Strachitunt PDO. The production areas for Formai de Mut dell'Alta Val Brembana PDO and of Bitto PDO overlap (vertical trait). The Slow Food presidium for Bitto Storico enrols 12 producers located at the border between the provinces of Sondrio and Bergamo (dotted area). Branzi cheese is not protected by a geographic indication; therefore only the seat of the consortium is indicated on the map. Map produced by Federico De Musso.

The 'Mother of All Battles': Slow Food's *Storico* versus PDO Bitto

In Valtellina, just north of Bergamo in the province of Sondrio, a tiny Slow Food presidium engaged what Piero Sardo, president of the Slow Food Foundation for Biodiversity, called 'the mother of all battles' against the PDO consortium for the Bitto and Casera cheeses.[6] There were several reasons. Since its inception in 1995, the Bitto and Casera PDO consortium identified the production area of both cheeses as the entire province of Sondrio. This area largely exceeds that of the original consortium that Bitto producers set up in 1970. Moreover, Casera literally means 'creamery': this is cheese made in permanent premises, rather than in makeshift summer arrangements at high altitude (called *calècc*), during the *alpeggio* season. Heritage Bitto makers resented that Bitto could be associated with the not-upland, all-year production of Casera. Non-*alpeggio* production obviously exceeds summer production in the uplands, the latter representing a minority in the consortium. This, and the enlargement of the production area, caused the rebellion of the producers of the Bitto valleys, namely those crossed by the river Bitto. The 'Bitto Rebels' (an expression of Corti 2012) were banned from calling the cheese they make 'Bitto', since they left the consortium that regulates access to that precise denomination. So they called themselves Association of Producers of the Bitto Valleys (Associazione Produttori Valli del Bitto) and formed the Consortium for Heritage Bitto (Consorzio Salvaguardia Bitto Storico), with the protection of a Slow Food presidium for Bitto Storico.[7]

Historical documentation identifies different areas as zones of Bitto production, as surveys, consortia and trademarks succeed to each other since 1902 with shifting boundaries (Corti 2006a). However, as early as 1995, a Denomination of Origin (Denominazione di Origine Controllata, DOC) was unprecedentedly granted to a Consorzio Tutela Valtellina Casera e Bitto with a production area that coincided with the administrative boundaries of the province of Sondrio, plus the high pastures of the Upper Val Brembana just south of it, in the province of Bergamo. Against this enlargement, a committee of producers began to act as early as 1994 as Comitato per la salvaguardia del formaggio Bitto, hence formalized in the Associazione Produttori Valli del Bitto in 1997. These established a Slow Food presidium in 2003 over fourteen high pastures of the valleys Gerola and Albaredo (the Bitto valleys) and upper Val Brembana. Moreover, in 2005, the Slow Food producers left the PDO consortium and established in 2010 a 'Consorzio salvaguardia Bitto Storico'.

These heritage producers had stringent ideas on what makes Bitto. First the season: 'real Bitto' can only be made during the summer *alpeggio* and not throughout the year. Second the goat/cow milk ratio: the Bitto of the Valli del Bitto contains a mandatory 10 to 20 per cent goat milk, to preserve high-pasture goat herding.[8] Third, the area of production: Bitto should only be made in the valleys that can claim pedigree high pasture cheese-making tradition. Fourth, cows (and goats) should only eat grass, without dietary integrations. While the use of corn- or soy-based fodder is commonplace in the dairy industry to favour milk production, upland producers distinguish themselves by marking the *alpeggio* season a 'grass-only' diet.

For the communities of practice that depend on these economies, these are not hair-splitting questions but fundamental regulatory issues, which determine *how* one can make mountain cheese, *what* mountain cheese is and *who* should benefit from it. The Slow Food Presidium Bitto Storico (since 2016 simply 'Storico') and the PDO Consortium Valtellina Casera e Bitto engaged in what commentators called an 'exemplary' conflict. On the one hand, the mission of the Slow Food presidium is to 'safeguard and valorise' (*valorizzare*) food heritage:

> Its members maintain a number of traditional practices: the *alpeggio* itself with the local breed of goats [*capre orobiche*], whose milk makes up 20 to 30% [sic] of the cheese, fencing off daily sections of the pasture for grazing [*pascolo turnato o razionato*], hand-milking, and use of the thousand-old roofless stone stations, the *calècc*, which serve as cheese-making facilities directly on the pastures. (Milano and Ponzio 2004: 173)

On the other hand, the trajectory of 'heritage Bitto', seceding from a larger PDO because a small circle of purist producers found that PDO production had gone too mainstream and had compromised quality for quantity, is similar to that of 'Old Serpa' sheep cheese investigated by Harry West and Nuno Domingos (2012) as they analyse the momentous implications of establishing a Slow Food presidium for 'Serpa Velho'. Similarly to the case of Bitto, one of the issues at stake here is the preservation of landraces – the *capra orobica* (Bergamasque goat) in the case of Bitto and the Merino sheep in the case of the Alentejo in Portugal. Domingos and West are sceptical of the neo-peasant rhetoric of Slow Food and remind us of how meagre the diet of Alentejo sheep cheese-makers was. Similarly, mixing goat and cow milk while on the *alpeggio* was presumably necessitated by pooling together all available milk in one cauldron, rather than by the pursuit of gastronomic excellence. In line with popular agricultural policies, according to conversations I had with representatives of Coldiretti (the largest agricultural trade union of the area), the strategy preferred by the Valtellina Casera and Bitto consortium was to favour as many mountain farmers as possible. Thanks to the premium price of Bitto and its fame on the Milanese market, they professed to make of Bitto a regional economic driver.[9]

The Rebels' divergence from the consortium became so divisive that they left the consortium altogether. The modifications introduced in the PDO protocol allowed fodder (up to 3 kilos of grains) and the use of starter cultures (*fermenti lattici*) for curdling the milk (but only if cultured from autochthonous strands).[10] The issue of starter cultures – as much as that of the inoculation in the curd during maturation – is particularly sensitive in artisanal cheese-making, and remains a topic of heated debate. Milk safety is particularly important to low-acidity cheeses such as young, nonmatured wheels and *formaggelle*. On the other hand, milk that is impoverished of microbic flora as a result of thermic treatment will need starter cultures, which can be either industrially produced or developed from local cultures (Zannoni, Morara and Berozzi 2004: 115–17). Raw milk cheese can boast *not to need* starter cultures in addition to rennet, and to derive their flora from the working environment and surfaces, the cheese-making tools themselves, and microclimatic conditions. Among cheese-lovers, aromatic distinctiveness is appreciated over standardization. It is widely believed that cheese made with local starter cultures or without them altogether displays a richer variety of organoleptic characteristics and a higher variability, thanks to the complexity of the microbic population. Provisions were made for a special sub-branding of specific pastures where cheese is made without ferments and fodder – not exclusively those of the Valli del Bitto though. This specification would then be in the name of the technique used, not a geographical 'subdenomination' as requested by the producers of the Valli del Bitto. Once they left the PDO, though, the Association of Producers of the Valli del Bitto received visits and injunctions from officers of the Ministry for Agriculture for misuse of a PDO name, and had to stop using the name 'Bitto', which they dropped altogether also from their Slow Food Presidium denomination as of July 2016.[11]

At the time of their 'secession' in 2005 the Rebels'production amounted to only 3 per cent of the consortium, which enlisted 110 Bitto producers and 700 Casera producers. The thirteen producers who actually left certainly made a symbolic dent in the consortium, but not an economic one. On the contrary, some commentators interpreted this as elitism, aimed at scoring 'a few Euros more' on the market, as the president of the heritage producers could boast on national press that their cheese sold for €15 a kilo (in 2005) against the €7 per kilo of the rest of the valley.[12] Critics noted that the long-term objective of a consortium should be to guarantee its own longevity, for example by ensuring a wider membership, and not only the preservation of standards of 'quality' abstracted from inevitable technological advancements. Others defended the Bitto Rebels from the start, extolling the choice of using goat milk – thus stimulating the preservation of an autochthonous breed – and of curdling exclusively straight after milking, without refrigerating and reheating the milk as it is standard practice in creameries. Heritage Bitto is also associated with milking by hand (though this is not mandatory), which allows the cheese-makers to reach the herd throughout the pastures, and transforming the milk on the spot in the *calécc*. These are traditional makeshift tents arranged upon pre-existing stone walls, which dot the pastures of this area.[13]

In nearby Val Taleggio, the withdrawal from the PDO consortium was perceived as an inevitable choice for the heritage Bitto producers, dictated by the necessity not to drown quality in quantity. 'Così si perde la tipicità' (this is how you lose typicity) was the comment of Taleggio makers of Val Taleggio, who often expressed a comparison between their own condition within the Taleggio consortium and that of the 'Bitto Rebels': 'It was a mistake to make this political choice, to extend the PDO to the entire Valtellina. Now the presidium of Bitto Storico can sell their own for even up to something like €45 per kilo' (conversation with the president of the dairy cooperative of Val Taleggio, 11 August 2006).

The war of Bitto Storico vs PDO Bitto, in the words of Val Taleggio's cheese refiners, was simple and pragmatic: 'In Val Gerola they say that their Bitto is better than the others' (Ugo, refinery co-owner, 8 August 2006). 'They are the ones who brand most of the wheels actually made in the uplands,' he continued. 'And they have the Slow Food presidium. Once you have that, you can afford to withdraw from the PDO consortium.' On the other hand:

> The PDO consortium fosters a joint management of Bitto (an *alpeggio* cheese) and Casera (a creamery cheese), to increase member numbers and quantities. What does this policy have to offer to the dozen mountain producers of Val Gerola? And vice versa, why should the consortium feel motivated to keep them as members? They hold the knife by the handle because if you are not a member you cannot brand your cheese . . . It is the consortium that owns the name. (Evaristo, dairy technician, 8 August 2006)

Already in 2004 the Fiera del Bitto in Morbegno hosted two different sales stands, one of the PDO consortium and one of the Slow Food presidium (with the Associazione Produttori Valli del Bitto). The Minister of Agriculture visited the former in person, while there was a live demonstration of how Bitto is 'cooked'. In the Valli del Bitto stand on the other hand there were no actual wheels on sale; only tasting slices were offered and cheese had to be booked for the following season or further. Bitto, by definition a seasonal product of the *alpeggio*, is matured for at least seventy days, but selected for much longer maturation. According to the association's spokesperson, it is the only cheese in the world that can be matured up to and beyond ten years. With only a very limited production, it was against the interest of the presidium to use the fair as a sell-out. In October, there was no 'new' cheese available and the best would be matured for several months yet.

Previously, the Bitto delle Valli del Bitto had deserted the competition in 2003. In 2004 a compromise had been reached at the last minute, which established not only one single competition for all Bitto PDO, but also a special prize reserved to the producers of the '*valli storiche*' (the heritage valleys).[14] This precarious coexistence broke up again the following year, when the producers of the Associazione Produttori delle Valli del Bitto withdrew from both the fair and subsequently from the PDO consortium, as reported even on national press (Gilberti 2005).[15] It was a slap in the face of the ninety-eighth edition of the Mostra del Bitto, the yearly fair held in Morbegno since 1907.

One point of difference between the French system and the Italian one is the possibility to distinguish, within one appellation d'origine contrôlée, between industrial and artisanal productions – as it is the case with Camembert. This is hardly an accepted custom in Italy. The entire Bitto controversy could have been avoided if the Casera and Bitto consortium had allowed for a different branding of heritage Bitto from the start, allowing the producers to identify the individual pastures from which each wheel was produced – as it is done in the Slow Food presidium. Precisely because this compromise was rejected, the Bitto Rebels left the consortium altogether and opted for all-out legal and commercial war. One paladin commented on his blog: 'the consortium's version of the facts is hypocritical, since they say that they would be ready to concede subdenominations but the European rules forbid them and the ministry does not want them. One should be incensed! The ministry has always underwritten the desiderata of local lobbies! In the same area, take for instance the case of Formai de Mut . . .'.[16] What does the plight of Bitto Storico have in common with Formai de Mut, an obscure (but PDO) Bergamasque 'mountain cheese', made south of the ridge that divides Bergamo to the South, and Sondrio to the North? The story of Formai de Mut, in fact, is not peripheral to the conflicts surrounding *alpage* cheese.

The Niche PDO: Formai de Mut

Bitto and Formai de Mut share Upper Val Brembana – in the northernmost reaches of the province of Bergamo – as a legitimate area of production for both PDO cheeses (see map 1). Their protocol of production is compatible, too – one distinguishing feature being the goat milk used in Bitto.[17] As a result, dairy farmers in Upper Val Brembana can choose between making Formai de Mut at their local cooperative – a PDO cheese but commercially not extremely rewarding – or making the much-sought-after Bitto cheese. 'Which one would you make?' asks wittily Tito (a pseudonym), the herder who took me to my first trip *in alpeggio* in the summer of 1997. Lucia (a pseudonym), an experienced cheese merchant, adds:

> This year you could find Bitto all year round. Usually they would run out by spring because of high demand. Why? Because in Upper Val Brembana, around St. Mark's pass, people can choose to make either Bitto or Formai de Mut. You sell the latter at €6–7 per kilo, the former for €16! (Lucia, cheese merchant, 8 August 2006)

Tito laughs: 'which one would you make . . . not a difficult choice!' This choice, however, has important historical and economic implications. While the production area for Formai de Mut lies entirely south of the ridge dividing the Alpi Orobie or Bergamasque Alps from Valtellina to the north, the production protocol of PDO Bitto includes the entire province of Sondrio north of the ridge *but also* the upper pastures of Val Brembana, the southern versant of the same ridge.

For the dairy cooperative making Formai de Mut, the Latteria Sociale di Valtorta, the establishment of a Bitto PDO protocol that included part of its own production areas was a real problem. Since 1995, dairy farmers in Valtorta and Foppolo could choose, and the choice was obvious. They could make *another* mountain cheese, and sell it at twice the price. True, Formai de Mut is made entirely from cow milk, while Bitto traditionally contains goat milk. The extra labour entailed in combining goat and cow herds could have deterred one from making Bitto, but the 2009 version of the production protocol registered with the Ministry for Agriculture *limits* the amount of goat milk to *up to, and no more than* 10 per cent. 'Which one would you choose to make?', insists Tito with a grin.

As mentioned in the previous section, according to historical evidence apparently Bitto *never was* exclusively a cheese from Valtellina, namely made north of the ridge of the Alpi Orobie. This documentation is being gathered largely in support of the cause of the Bitto Rebels, but has important consequences for understanding upland cheese economies. According to local historians in fact, up until the early twentieth century Bitto was an upland cheese predominantly commercialized in the upper reaches of the Bergamasque valleys, not in Valtellina (Corti 2011). The ironic twist of Bitto being 'son of the Orobie'[18] is that the Bergamasque breeders of the Upper Val Brembana, depicted by my friends as cunningly profiting from the serendipitous overlap of two PDOs, would be unwittingly replicating a state of affairs that was actually predominant throughout the nineteenth century – and which the paladins of the Bitto Rebels claim as historical truth – namely making Bitto in the mountains of Bergamo. This has important political overtones in the current Bitto querelle and beyond.[19]

Formai de mut means literally ' mountain cheese' in Bergamasco. According to the production protocol of Formai de Mut dell'Alta Val Brembana, it 'designates specifically the prized product of the summer high pastures located between 1,300 and 2,500 meters above sea level on which cattle traditionally graze during the summer'.[20] It was the first 'DOC' cheese of Lombardy, a national denomination of origin conceded in 1985 subsequently equated to PDO in 1996. Its production protocol describes it as 'a semicooked cow-milk cheese with at least 45 per cent fat, cylindrical, weighing between 8 and 12 kilos and straight or slightly convex sides. Matured for at least forty-five days, it can be hardened up to one year and beyond. The crust is thin, yellow and turning to grey. The curd is ivory, compact, elastic and with diffused, "bird's eye" holes. Palatable, not hot, only very slightly salty, it preserves the aroma of mountain grass'.[21]

Unfortunately, the original consortium Formai de Mut went bankrupt. The name of its president, unmistakably not local, still elicits head-shakes, hints to 'political protections in Rome', and the occasional resentful yarn. In an area that has more than once been described as being 'far away from Rome,' both geographically but especially symbolically, Roman affairs are per se questionable. *Far Away from Rome* (*Lontano da Roma*) is the title of Davide Ferrario's damning documentary about early-day Lega Nord militants. Produced in Lombardy in the early 1990s, the film is shot in purely observational style. Without a word of commentary, it vividly depicts the uncouth rallies of the (then) secessionists, highlighting their consumerism, blatant sexism and unfocused resentment against the parasitic state. *Far Away from Rome* is also a collection of essays about Ermanno Olmi's cinema (Masoni 1990). His period fiction *L'Albero degli Zoccoli* (1979) presented the Italian televisual audience of the late 1970s with an elegy of miserable peasant life at the end of the nineteenth century in the Bergamasque lowlands. The film was criticized as nostalgic, but was a landmark breakthrough in monolingual Italian cinema. It was screened in cinema theatres nationwide in Bergamasco with Italian subtitles (but curiously dubbed in Italian for television).

There does not seem to be much reflection among Italian intellectuals about *how* or *why* the starved sharecroppers of the turn of the century might have evolved into the affluent but uneducated bourgeoisie of the northern Italian backwaters. Such questions were raised only in the aftermath of the 1990s electoral success of the Lega Nord, which won plebiscitary in the Bergamasque valleys. Sociologists rushed to produce comprehensive 'identity'-bound explanations. There seemed to be a problem with the identity of northern Italians, nouveaux riches lacking solidarity with the rest of the nation. The so-called northern question inspired books and talk-shows, but is currently no longer mentioned, with 43 per cent youth unemployment nationwide registered in 2014, after Berlusconi's era.[22]

The 1980s and the 1990s, which saw the rise and fall of Formai de Mut, were indeed another century. In 1992, Piazza Brembana, a village of then 1,100 inhabitants, came first for money-saving in a national survey of the Banca Nazionale del Lavoro: apparently each resident averaged the equivalent of (then) €35,000 in the bank. Their DOC cheese allegedly employed 600 people in eighty-seven cheese-making firms. The rest of the working population (probably overlapping with the former) would crowd three commuter buses, leaving at 4 am each day for Milan to work in the Falck steelworks of Sesto San Giovanni, now closed down.[23] Winter tourism was also thriving, especially at the skiing resorts of Foppolo and Piazzatorre. The villages burgeoned with holiday homes for *villeggianti* (second home owners). Everyone felt rich and diligent, perhaps sharing in a naturalized feeling of self-righteousness that is otherwise more typical of northern Europeans.

Twenty years later, a Milanese blogger twice 'names and shames' the local notable (*commendatore*) and the Bergamo-born Minister of Agriculture, who in his opinion fraudulently connived to obtain a DOC that had no reason to exist.[24] According to Corti (2011) in fact, Formai de Mut was the most banal name for the 'Bergamasque Bitto'. Trying to win a premium over the Bitto competitors north of the mountain ridge with a niche PDO could have been a gamble worth taking. But the business went bust because of mismanagement – say my cheese-maker friends in Val Taleggio. They talk about a manager 'immanicato' with the Christian Democracy party, then solidly ruling over the souls and pockets of the 'white' North: being 'up their sleeves', being 'paraded about in the palm of their hands'. Then things got nasty. Some mention a parallel enterprise set up with the consortium's credit; some others talk about simple incompetence, squandering the cooperative means. People point to the location of the vendor's warehouse: '1,500 square meters for one single pallet of cheese – as dry as cement in such a big airy space of course!'. People remember the van and the paid driver who would 'come up to Val Taleggio to pick up two boxes of cheese *only*. And then how do you repay the costs?' (conversations with Lucia, Evaristo and Anchise, 8 August 2006)

With hindsight, these Roman implications were enough to avert trust – not so much of the consumers, but especially of the peer-producers who should find in trust, as well as necessity, the motivation to join a cooperative enterprise. The plight of the consortium's members who were left behind to repay the debts, while the *commendatore* vanished into thin air, painted a no-go sign for similar cooperative projects. Not many would have bet on the new consortium when it reopened in 1997 as 'Consortium of Producers for the Safeguarding and Valorization of Formai de Mut dell'Alta Valle Brembana':

> Guy such and such had his house repossessed, he had to pay back for it, coin upon coin. But they did not give up, Coldiretti [the Catholic farmers' trade union] mediated a bit over the transition, they found some new conferring farmers, now they can afford to pay them decent shares. They diversified production, they also make a winter, less distinctive production of about 2,500 wheels *tipo Branzi*. (conversations with Lucia, Evaristo and Anchise, 8 August 2006)

This was a compromise solution to mitigate competition with Bitto, branding winter production differently but keeping the producers on board. A blue and a red stamp differentiate between the two, so that faithful summer producers can claim higher prices on their upland *cru*, but winter production can still be retained and monitored for quality. Operating from the cooperative dairy of the village of Valtorta, Formai de Mut slowly but steadily rose from its ashes, culminating with the Slow Food prize for a cheese-maker's career, an honorary recognition bestowed in 2010 on the consortium re-founder and head of the Valtorta dairy.

The production of the creamery being largely run by his sons, Formai de Mut dell'Alta Val Brembana PDO, grew to a peak of sixty-two tons a year in five years.[25] According to the manager of Cooperativa Latteria Sociale Valtorta the winter production was around 2,500 wheels in 2006, the main problem still being to convince the consortium's members to confer their cheese to the cooperative not only as a remedial winter outlet, but also and especially during the summers, when upland cheese is in high demand and can be sold directly to travelling tourists in the mountain stations.[26] If in 1998 the summer production gathered milk from about 40 mountains stations between June and October, from 44 members including 2 breeders' cooperatives over 21 municipalities, over 10 years the milking and maturing stations on the upper pastures (*casere d'alta quota*) have shrunk from 40 to about 20, also because of the costs of converting them to authorized cheese-making facilities. The local press estimated in 2006 that the summer production was around 1,500 wheels (*L'Eco di Bergamo* 15 September 2006, 29, confirming the same data of the chamber of commerce of 1998). In 2014, only eleven pastures were listed on the official website of the PDO with as many family enterprises still conducting them. However small in production, though, this 'local' PDO has resisted since its financial re-foundation in 1997, and gained in market appreciation as well as visibility, thanks also to support from professional organizations such as ONAF (the Italian national organization of cheese tasters). With the price of PDO Bitto dropping vis-à-vis heritage Bitto, Formai de Mut tacked its course and gained prestige, at least locally.

Its protocol of production can be consulted online on the site of the Ministry for Agriculture: it is a sixteen-page typescript manuscript produced in the 1980s with subsequent integrations, still featuring the signature of the original *commendatore*. This is a very different document than the slim, three-page technical list of requirements of the Bitto PDO protocol. The former contains first and foremost a number of arguments and information that situate Formai de Mut geographically and historically, thus stating a claim to its *tipicità*, and only in conclusion and almost cursorily describes the technical procedure for production.[27] In the 'DOC' dossier submitted for Formai de Mut in 1985, the history of the Bergamini is quoted as evidence of an autochthonous cheese-making tradition. One reads:

> Formai de Mut is *tipico* because of: a) where it comes from (*per la sua provenienza*); b) the fact that it is made *in alpeggio*, in buildings (*baite*) apt not only to give refuge to the herders but to work and mature the curd: these *baite* are called *casére*; c) the way it is made (*per il tipo di lavorazione*): straight after milking, without skimming, without adding anything, just using whole fresh milk (*solamente con latte fresco integrale di mungitura*); d) the cycle of production and the aroma and taste it confers.[28]

To the 'integrity' of the milk and the optimal adaptation of the cheese-making cycle to its environment, the dossier adds a rich technical terminology, whose existence and current use in Bergamasco is used as evidence of the authenticity of the practices of locality it describes:

> One should and must add that the precise dialect lexicon of the dairy profession is a valid testimony to the traditional production of Formai de Mut, and in fact it is necessary to report here at least the essential lexicon in order to understand any argument about it.[29]

Particular attention is given to the justification of an apparently banal word *mut*, literally 'mountain', to explain that Formai de Mut does not mean *any* mountain cheese:

> There are three significant ways to refer to the word 'mut': *'ndà al mut* = to go to the mountain, namely to the high pasture (*alpeggio*); *cargà 'l mut* = literally to load the mountain, the high pasture (*alpeggio*) namely to take cattle to it, in numbers compatible with the size of the pasture; *descarga 'l mut* = to unload the *alpeggio*, namely to leave the pasture.[30]

When spelling out technical requirements and procedures, the overly descriptive protocol for Formai de Mut simply states that the milk comes from Brown breed cows locally fed on grass and hay, and integrated with silage maize or grains mix in the winter, *as needed*.[31] When this addendum was requested to convert the DOC into PDO, in 1992, integrating the cows' diet was obviously not perceived as a fault. This must have become a sensitive issue during the following fifteen years of debates on what constitutes 'heritage' cheese – as the *querelle* of the Bitto Storico gave ample grounds for debating, raising exceptions and rethinking the entire food chain, from grass to starter cultures. In fact, in 2009, the allowance of 3 kilos of 'dry substance' (specified as maize, barley, wheat, soy or molasses for no more than 3 per cent of the daily ration) to the diet of PDO Bitto-making cows was considered an outrage by the Bitto Rebels supported by Slow Food. The PDO Bitto protocol also spells out that hay (instead of grass) cannot be given unless in case of exceptional weather circumstances that impede outdoor grazing: hay is for emergency integration only, *di solo soccorso*.[32]

From a comparison of their production protocols, both Bitto and Formai de Mut clearly belong to the same family of upland, fat, cooked and matured wheels. Formai de Mut spells out that milk is not skimmed and no ferments are added in the curdling process. The curd is cut to grains the size of rice, at a temperature slightly lower than Bitto (45° to 47°C instead of Bitto's 48 to 52°C). Both techniques resemble those of Parmigiano Reggiano and Grana Padano, including finely cutting the curds and draining it in moulds under pressure (*fase di spurgo*), if not for the lower temperatures, which do not dry up the curd as much as in these harder cheeses. Dry salt is applied (in the case of Formai de Mut, bathing in a salty solution is also acceptable). While Formai de Mut does not prescribe a minimum ageing, in the case of Bitto the wheels can only be branded from the seventy-first day of maturation.[33]

The Formai de Mut DOC dossier spends more space exhibiting evidence of a direct tie to the transhumant tradition of the Bergamini than specifying how the cheese is actually made. What would otherwise look like a meandering linguistic-historical detour is deployed to establish precisely such link across space, time and geography, using the language of tradition and continuity. Instead of quoting published evidence in the local history scholarship (which is not thin, but can be repetitive), the Formai de Mut report opts for oral history and (without calling it such) ethnography. In other words, the report states what is under everyone's eyes, witnessing the obvious: these people make cheese, they use the dialect term *mut* for their higher pastures, and call their cheese 'mountain cheese'. The document articulates a further syllogism: these people make this cheese, *and* cheese-makers all around Lombardy are called 'Bergamo-people' (*Bergamini*)! Therefore Formai de Mut is a historically rooted practice of locality that has left a mark in language. As heritage, this cheese has to be preserved and it has to be made with this name *only* here.

This argument uses the poetics of dialect to establish an economic history, and to state a political claim. Which is why the dossier is wordy and reads almost as a literary contribution to local historical scholarship. By contrast, in cases where politics has *already* prevailed over poetics, as for Bitto, such long-windedness has been substituted by a meagre three-page list of technical specifications. Formai de Mut, the upland cheese of the Bergamasque valleys, received the mixed blessing of an early PDO, so small that it would support an authentically local production, combined with early bad management and late competition from a nobler neighbour, Bitto. Out-priced by Bitto PDO and out-famed by the Bitto Rebels, it remains the laughingstock of commentators who point at a PDO that never had a reason to exist, and apparently even picked the wrong name. One question remains to be asked: these Bergamasque cheese-makers, variously depicted in local rumours and the national press as scheming foxes *and* naive simpletons, as parochial *and* overambitious, stinking rich *but* conned and bankrupted by a cunning outsider . . . Why did they not call their cheese Bitto, if they could?

First, because in 1985 the PDO of Bitto with its current, enlarged production area was yet a decade to come. Second, because their alternative to a PDO 'of their own' was calling their cheese – like everyone else – after the name of a village just south of them, at the doorstep of the Upper Val Brembana: Branzi. This is the reconstruction that Corti (2011) offers of the district's history: while the area straddling the northern and southern versant of the Bergamasque alps was well known for producing a fat cheese of high nutritional quality during the summer *alpeggio*, unsurprisingly a number of variations and denominations came in use over time.

Mixing cow milk with varying proportions of goat milk and 'cooking' the milk directly on the pastures was the Bitto variation. The northern versant, known as Valtellina and currently under the province of Sondrio at the border with Switzerland, would trade this cheese in the fall, upon the herders' return, at the market of Morbegno, from whence it would be taken to localities around Lake Como for refining and maturing to be then sold in Milan (see map 1). The southern versant, namely the upper reaches of Val Brembana, also traded in Bitto cheese between the eighteenth and the nineteenth centuries. A summer high-pasture cheese *tipo Bitto* or 'like Bitto' would be traded southbound, in the village of Branzi in Val Brembana, to be refined and matured in the Bergamo area, often with added saffron, and be sold in Venice and Rome. South-bound 'Bitto-like' upland cheese, however, took the name of its market town, Branzi, where it was traded in September at the Fair of St. Matthew's.

In sum, it seems plausible to presume that Bitto, Branzi and Formai de Mut are different names for what was originally one general technique for making 'cooked' cheese in the summer pastures, with or without goat milk additions, which diversified in time.[34] But since 1985 the Upper Val Brembana could call its cheese Formai de Mut instead – a community-bound PDO that distinguished their own 'upland cheese' from any unspecified upland cheese 'like Bitto' or 'like Branzi'. Which one would you make?

The Unachieved PDO: Branzi

'Branzi is in the sorriest state of all' – a comment back in September 2006 by Lucia (a pseudonym), a business woman running the family cheese-maturing enterprise in Val Taleggio, after a dinner with an ex village mayor, a dairy farmer, and her husband and partner in business:

> Branzi producers are desperate. They do not have an acknowledged image, nor price, nor trademark. It's madness. They did not invest on their own territory. Our ecomuseum project instead is just the opposite: we need to attract people here to eat our cheese, *here* in this valley. It's like when you go wine tasting in the cellars. When you are in the cellar the wine tastes better. There are both environmental and psychological factors that make you think that that wine is good. (Lucia, 1 September 2006, dinner with entrepreneurs and administrators of the valley)

I will return to the ecomuseum project for Val Taleggio in Chapter 6. Here, the comparison was between Val Taleggio and Upper Val Brembana. Similarly to the case of Strachitunt, another producer filed a competitive PDO request for Branzi cheese at the same time as the producers of Branzi in Val Brembana. 'No, this is actually worse' – circumstantiate my cheese-making friends.

> 'This is more complicated because Branzi was actually made also by the guys in the other valley, lower down.'
>
> 'The family originally comes from upper Val Brembana you know? They took away the art with them.'
>
> 'They made a consortium without the people from Branzi, hoping to take them by surprise.'
>
> 'Yeah, they got some other mountain people in too.'
>
> 'But how can you get a denomination for Branzi if Branzi is not in the consortium? It's checkmate.' (conversations with Lucia, Evaristo and Anchise, 8 August 2006)

An article published in a culinary magazine described the situation in 2011 as that of a 'cold war'. The press reported that with 120,000 wheels produced per year, the business of Branzi, 'one of the most *tipici* and well-known cheeses of the Bergamo area', has a value of €15 million (Vitali 2011). Two separate consortia were established among competing but related family enterprises, all of which are well established in the local dairy industry. One consortium, based in the village of Branzi, gathers members of Val Brembana and Val Taleggio; the second one is based in the lower reaches of Val Cavallina but also includes Valle Imagna. Just to complicate matters there is a third sizeable producer, located in Upper Val Brembana near Branzi, related to one of the members of the latter consortium, who has joined neither of them. The upland consortium produces half of the lowland one (but would be on a par with the competitors if the independent dairy in the very same valley joined them). They claim *tipicità* and tradition over the others, and scorn those who have been making Branzi 'only for the latest twenty or thirty years'.[35]

Each of the two main competing Branzi creameries harnesses support from local institutions to claim continuity of Branzi production. The Val Cavallina producer counts fifty-five years of production, twenty-five of which continuously under one trademark. They claim to invest on locality, only sourcing cheese from the Bergamasque valleys; they are even prepared to acknowledge a distinction between their own 'lower lands', a hilly area at the border of Bergamo and Brescia, near Lake Garda, and the upland production of the Bergamasque mountains in and around the village of Branzi in Val Brembana. But their quantities (65,000 wheels as declared to the press)[36] would certainly outnumber those of the mountain 'cousins' (with 38,000 wheels a year according to the same press source, 26,000 wheels of about 10.5 kilos each in 2014 according to the producers themselves).[37] I gathered their story from a number of professional operators.

> the *Latteria Sociale di Branzi* [cooperative dairy of Branzi] has presented a PDO request at the same time and for the same denomination as a dairy of a neighbouring valley. Notice that the two leading families originate from Valle Brembana, in fact just a few kilometres apart, in Branzi and in a village shortly higher up. The cheese-makers of the upper valley have migrated to the neighbouring vale, lower and ampler and much better connected, and grown big. Now the regional experts look at the two homonymous requests and say *when you two come together, we'll underwrite your request – jointly*. It will never happen. (Antonio, a pseudonym, 20 August 2013)

'So the regional bureaucrats said, when you come together to file jointly we'll consider the case' – tells me another Slow Food member and cheese-connoisseur of the area, at the Sagra dello Strachitunt of October 2013, almost word for word. Battista (a pseudonym) confirmed what I had been told by another dairy expert seven years before, during my dinner in Val Taleggio, and again in the summer of 2014: no truce was in sight. 'You see the region has the duty to verify if the PDO proposals are functional, if they have a chance to survive'. This confirmed the casual comments gathered at the Fiera del Bitto in 2004 about the Bitto *querelle*: that the first duty of a consortium is to guarantee its own survival. This is a standard contention against small PDOs. But the demise of the Branzi PDO ambitions did not depend on a scarce production. Their quantities far exceed both productions of Bitto, for example: PDO Bitto was estimated at 27,000 wheels in 2006, while heritage Bitto branded 882 wheels in 2004 (out of the 4,500 produced on the high pastures, as most are not selected for ageing [*invecchiamento*]).[38] The Branzi impasse regarded the impossibility to determine an issue of boundaries without winning an argument of prestige. While the former can be conceded legally, the latter has to be won commercially. 'It's just as if I asked the minister to certify that heritage Bitto is better than PDO Bitto. It will always be open for discussion, it is not an objective matter.'[39]

In the case of Branzi, quantity matters – possibly to the detriment of prestige. The village of Branzi was the big attractor of the upland cheese market throughout the nineteenth century, while it entered a steep decline at the turn of the century and even more so between the World Wars. From the 191 tons of upland cheese sold at the Fair of 'the Branzi' in 1910 the market dropped to less than half the quantity in the 1930s, due, according to local historians, to the net decrease of cattle herds that would graze the high pastures (Corti 2011). Interviews with people born in the late 1920s and 1930s confirm that they already practiced 'transhumance' at a much more confined level – practically, transhumance had become a local business of the mountains in the form of *alpeggio* (Carminati and Locatelli 2004). This was the result of the progressive sedentarization of the Bergamini who were establishing large, intensive dairy concerns in the Lombard plains and were no more interested in driving productive herds uphill during the summers as originally described by Jacini (1882: 26).[40]

Transhumance reversed, as it increasingly became a way for lowland producers to save on grass by driving not yet productive heifers to the mountains, paying rent per capita (*paghe*) to mountain breeders (as they do to this day) for keeping them on the pastures to 'get strong', being tended by inexperienced youth or with scarce monitoring, as they do not require milking. *Alpeggio* increasingly became a local business, with only mountain herds moving to and from mountain village and upper pastures, often mixed with the 'renter herds' of calves and steers. Thus milk production dwindled, and upland cheese became a rarity. This was the situation I found at the end of the 1990s, when I began fieldwork in Val Taleggio.

The demise of the *alpeggio* convinced the dairy cooperative of Branzi to diversify production and to inaugurate a semi-fat cheese, obtained from skimmed milk from the day before. Previously, Branzi cheese was nothing other than 'mountain cheese' made in the upper Val Brembana . . . alias Bitto made south of the ridge of the Alpi Orobie, argues Corti (2011). To prove this theory, Branzi and Bitto still share the characteristic concave shape: instead of bulging out like squat barrels, both Bitto and Branzi look like slightly sucked-in cylinders. If Branzi was nothing other than Bitto, Formai de Mut was nothing other than Branzi. Formai de Mut does not have a concave shape, but that was allegedly dropped, as Formai de Mut was in search of a distinctive identity, and how could it gain and keep a DOC of its own, if it looked exactly like Bitto and Branzi? And how could Branzi producers be chastised for having opted for a skimmed cheese, or Formai de Mut for having reduced the size of their wheels?

The boundaries between the three upland cheeses showcased in this chapter (Bitto, Formai de Mut and Branzi) would then be more fluid and porous than actually marketed. This should hardly come as surprise. Upland communities historically straddle mountain ridges and consider lowland rivers as their external borders – not the other way around as it is today because of the predominance of lowland logistics and road infrastructure (Grasseni 2009). As a result, the entire area straddling the ridge of the Alpi Orobie, both north and south of them, was characterized by one basic way of making mountain cheese. Well into the Middle Ages, across the mountain pass of St. Mark's, the Strada Priula – not a road but a mountain trail – connected Bergamo and Sondrio and acted as a focal point of transit and rest for traders. The cheese they transported would now be called, according to procedural and commercial vicissitudes: Bitto, or Formai de Mut, or Branzi.

This theory is itself a deliberate repositioning of very real socioeconomic actors within a charged scenario, poised for distinction. It is in the name of their uniqueness, and not of their underlying sameness, that the producers of the Branzi Cooperative Dairy (Latteria Sociale di Branzi) have now established a commercial coalition, named I Principi delle Orobie (the Princes of the Orobie mountains) together with the other niche cheeses of the region: Formai de Mut of the Upper Val Brembana, Val Taleggio's Strachitunt, plus the three Slow Food Presidia: the Bitto Rebels of course, and two recent additions of Val Brembana: Agrì of Valtorta, and Stracchino all'antica delle Valli Orobiche ('Old-time Stracchino of the Bergamasque Mountains'). The commercial prowess and the resilience of this coalition still needs to be put to the test of time, as it was only launched in 2013, but the alliance achieved a high profile on the occasion of the Milan Expo, the universal exhibition held between May and October 2015, whose theme was Feeding the Planet. I will return to the strategy and tactics of this coalition of local cheeses in Chapter 6.

To conclude, community-PDO Formai de Mut, Slow-Food presidium Bitto Storico and partisan Branzi mark as many practices of locality which, when they succeed, produce named places in the same breath as their placed-named cheeses. Locality is consequently striven for, demarcated and defended with as many strategies, in order to establish name-sovereignty and thus ultimately prestige and a competitive edge on a discerning market.

Notes

1. http://www.ilsole24ore.com/art/notizie/2013–12–07/forbes-incorona-cucina-emilia-romagna-e-tesoro-paese-151345.shtml?uuid=ABU9Nbi.
2. Casarrigoni, personal communication, 1 June 2015.
3. As the name says, Presidia are commercial enclosures aimed at safeguarding niche productions (whether crops – such as certain types of salads or artichokes – or the end products of more complex food manufacturing processes, such as lard or cheese). See the world atlas of Slow Food Presidia retrieved 22 June 2015 from http://www.fondazioneslowfood.com/en/slow-food-presidia/?-id_pg=11.
4. State Archive documentation going over the border dispute between the Dukedom of Milan and the Republic of Venice reveals that, in the 1300s 'well matured' *stracchini* were requested to Val Taleggio to pay feudal dues to the Milanese Duke. In particular Sergio Salvetti (1989: 94) quotes a manuscript conserved in Bergamo's State Archive, written by Abbot Mazzoleni at the beginning of the eighteenth century (*Memorie relative al territorio bergamasco in ordine alfabetico relativamente ai singoli comuni*) according to which in the second half of the fourteenth century, under the Dukes of Milan Bernabò Visconti and his son Rodolfo, Val Taleggio owed an annual tribute made of 'two hundred measures of good, fine looking and well matured cheese' (*ducentum pensa casei boni pulchri ac bene axaxonati*). This author interprets '*ben axaxonati*' as 'well-laid' or 'well-sat' on wooden axes, hence well-matured. This source specifies that half of the two hundred 'good-tasting, good-looking, and well-stationed' forms of cheese should be submitted at Christmas and half at Easter. Many thanks to Arrigo Arrigoni for bringing this source to my attention.
5. First with a regional decree (DPR 10 September 1985) with which it gained the DOC national label (Denominazione di Origine Controllata, as per national law n. 125 of 1954). Subsequently, in 1996, as the national denominations of origin were subsumed in

European designations, it became a PDO (protected designation of origin) with the first cohort of Italian cheeses that were recognized at European level (including Parmesan, Taleggio, and Gorgonzola) with CE Regulation n. 1107 of 12 June 1996.

6. Piero Sardo used this expression in his speech on 25 April 2010, at a public conference held at the Humanitaria society of Milan. See Grasseni 2012.
7. News and documentation of the association, consortium and presidium are available online: http://www.formaggiobitto.com/.
8. By converse, the production protocol of PDO Bitto officially published on the website of the Ministry for Agriculture contemplates 'a nonmandatory addition of raw goat milk for *no more than* 10%' (*eventuale aggiunta di latte caprino crudo in misura non superiore al 10%*). Retrieved 6 August 2014 from http://www.politicheagricole.it/flex/cm/pages/ServeBLOB.php/L/IT/IDPagina/3340.
9. This was in sum the content of an informal conversation I had at the stand of the consortium at the Fiera del Bitto in Morbegno on 16 October 2004. Its content is confirmed by the interview to Fausto Gusmeroli, quoted in Corti (2006a: 33–34). Gusmeroli, secretary of the Bitto consortium in the 1980s, spells out that the idea of widening the designated area of production was meant to favour a return to high-pasture grazing (*alpeggio*), which was being progressively abandoned because of the self-evident hardship connected with living on top of a mountain for three months a year.
10. 'È consentito l'utilizzo di fermenti autoctoni che valorizzino la microflora casearia spontanea', *Disciplinare di produzione della Denominazione di Origine Protetta 'Bitto'*, no date, published online by the Ministry of Agriculture. Retrieved 3 April 2014 from http://www.politicheagricole.it/flex/cm/pages/ServeAttachment.php/L/IT/D/e%252F7%252Ff%252FD.2e6bbd4bed2d7c4f3a19/P/BLOB%3AID%3D3340.
11. The ministry inspection took place in the Fall of 2009 and resulted in heavy fines. Retrieved 6 August 2014 from http://www.ruralpini.it/Inforegioni02.11.09.htm.
12. Paolo Ciapparelli, interviewed by Luigina Giliberti, in 'Alpeggi e Affari, La Guerra del Bitto', *Corriere della Sera* 14 October 2005, 12. This attracted the harsh criticisms of journalist Giuseppe Cremonesi against the Bitto Rebels: 'Polemiche casearie. Sul Bitto è bagarre: 13 produttori (su 110) lasciano il consorzio'. Retrieved 5 August 2014 from http://www.asa-press.com/r-archivio-rubriche/filiera/filiera10.html.
13. 'Lettera alla redazione di ASA-PRESS dalla Redazione di Cheesetime', 27 June 2006, published 28 June 2006. Retrieved 5 August 2014 from http://www.asa-press.com/r-archivio-rubriche/filiera/filiera30.html.
14. Comunicato stampa n. 4 del 25/08/2004, *Un concorso unico per il Bitto e un premio speciale per i produttori delle valli storiche alla prossima fiera.*
15. L. Gilberti, 'Alpeggi e Affari, la guerra del Bitto', *Corriere della Sera* 14 October 2005, 12.
16. 'Tra Valtellina e Val Brembana l'annosa questione del Bitto orobico', *Italia a Tavola*, 21 June 2011. Retrieved 5 August 2014 from http://www.italiaatavola.net/articolo.aspx?id=21282. My translation from the Italian.
17. The website of the Italian Ministry for Agriculture lists the current production protocols for all forty-seven DOP cheeses that are EU approved. Retrieved 6 August 2014 from http://www.politicheagricole.it/flex/cm/pages/ServeBLOB.php/L/IT/IDPagina/3340.
18. 'Il Bitto è un formaggio orobico e non tanto valtellinese' (Corti 2011).
19. On http://www.ruralpini.it/Inforegioni08.06.11Bitto-formaggio.orobico.htm the animal husbandry scholar Michele Corti reports a map on which he annotates the areas of

production historically documented for Bitto and its variations, to show how its original production spans the ridge of the Bergamasque Alps instead of being located within the boundaries of the province of Sondrio.

20. Consorzio dei Produttori per la tutela e la valorizzazione del Formai de Mut dell'Alta Val Brembana, no date. *Formai de Mut dell'Alta Val Brembana*. Camera di Commercio di Bergamo. Picked up from the premises of the PDO dairy in Valtorta, in the winter of 1999.
21. Ibid.
22. 'Giovani. Disoccupazione record al 44,2%'. *Repubblica Economia e Finanza*, 30 September 2014. Retrieved 26 June 2015 from http://www.repubblica.it/economia/2014/09/30/news/istat_disoccupazione-96979435/. The 'northern question' is a play of words on the historical 'southern question', namely the persisting socio-cultural divide between a richer northern Italy and a poorer southern Italy (see Schneider 1998).
23. Battistini Francesco, 'Vivere a Piazza Brembana, nel paese più ricco d'Italia', *Corriere della Sera*, 15 February 1992, 41.
24. 8 June 2011. Retrieved 5 August 2014 from http://www.ruralpini.it/Inforegioni08.06.11Bitto-formaggio.orobico.htm.
25. Yet these data (of 2003) can help to contextualize this as the smallest PDO production in Lombardy at the time: Bitto PDO 270 tons; Valtellina Casera 1,426 tons; Taleggio 9,715 tons; Gorgonzola 22,529 tons; Grana Padano 98,557 tons (De Biasi and Stecchi 2004: 45). As confirmed by the producers, in 2014 5,638 wheels of Formai de Mut dell'Alta Valle Brembana DOP were produced, of which 1,963 during the summer from the high pastures and 3,675 from the winter village creameries. With an average weight of 10 kg (each wheel can weigh between 8 and 12 kilos) this is a production of about 56 tons. (Source: F. M., Latteria Valtorta, personal communication, 2 June 2015).
26. This problem was explicitly mentioned during my first visit to the Formai de Mut PDO dairy in Valtorta, in 1999.
27. Both Bitto and Formai de Mut PDO production protocols are official documents for public consultation. Retrieved 6 August 2014 from http://www.politicheagricole.it/flex/cm/pages/ServeBLOB.php/L/IT/IDPagina/3340.
28. Consorzio Formaggio 'De Mut' Alta Valle Brembana 1985: 5.
29. Ibid.
30. My translation from the original, in Italian: 'Si può e si deve dire che anche il preciso lessico dialettale del settore è una valida testimonianza della tradizionale produzione del formai de mut, ed anzi è necessario presentare almeno il lessico essenziale per la comprensione dì un discorso sull'argomento. Si è detto del vocabolo *mut* e si debbono riferire significativi modi di dire connessi: *'ndà al mut* = andare al monte, all'alpeggio; *cargà 'l mut* = letteralmente 'caricare il monte, l'alpeggio' ossia condurvi il bestiame, in numero compatibile con la dimensione dell'alpeggio stesso; *descarga 'l mut* = scaricare l'alpeggio, venir via' (Consorzio Formaggio 'De Mut' Alta Valle Brembana 1985: 6).
31. 'Oggi come anticamente l'alimentazione del bestiame vaccino deve essere costituita da foraggi verdi od affienati che derivano da prato, da pascolo, da prato-pascolo o da prato della zona di produzione oltre ad eventuali integrazioni con miscele di cereali e, nel periodo invernale, con insilati di mais o erba' (Consorzio Tutela 'Formai de Mut' dell'Alta Valle Brembana 1995: 3).

32. From the original PDO protocol for Bitto cheese, in Italian: 'a) l'alimentazione delle bovine lattifere deve essere costituita da erba di pascolo degli alpeggi dell'area delimitata all'art.2. Al fine di mantenere il corretto livello di benessere animale, è consentita per le lattifere una integrazione dell'alimentazione da pascolo, fissata nei limiti massimi di kg 3 di sostanza secca al giorno, con i seguenti alimenti: mais, orzo, frumento, soia, melasso nella quantità non superiore al 3%. È ammesso l'impiego di sale pastorizio. È ammessa inoltre un'alimentazione di solo soccorso a base di fieno di prato stabile, non superiore al 5%, nel caso in cui si verifichino eventi meteorici straordinari che non consentono il pascolamento (quali neve, grandine) e limitatamente al tempo necessario al ripristino delle normali condizioni.' Ministero delle Politiche Agricole Alimentari e Forestali, Provvedimento 3 dicembre 2009. Modifica del disciplinare di produzione della denominazione «Bitto», registrata in qualita' di denominazione di origine protetta (09A15041). Retrieved 27 August 2016 from http://217.56.218.163/testi/itaPROVMPAAF03122009p70.txt.
33. See article 3c of the Bitto DOP protocol (my translation from the Italian original): 'Coagulation is obtained through the use of calf rennet. The curd is cut at a temperature between 48 and 52°C. This operation lasts about 30 minutes, until the curd is cut into grains the size of rice. Once cast, the paste is laid in traditional moulds that give it a distinctive concave shape. Salt is added dry, or through immersion in salty water. Ageing begins in *casere d'alpe* and is completed in the lower valley, using the natural climatic adaptation of the production zone. Maturation lasts at least seventy days; from the seventieth day from the production date, the Consorzio di Tutela, after approval from its appointed board of control, brands the wheels as described under article 4.' (Disciplinare di Produzione della Denominazione di Origine Protetta 'Bitto', n.d., 1).

    Compare this description with the 'method of production' section of the Formai de Mut PDO protocol (my translation from the Italian original): 'The milk coagulates at a temperature between 35 and 37°C, adding rennet so that it curds in 30 minutes. The cheese must be produced with the traditional technology: first the curd is cut, then it is heated up to a temperature of 45–47°C, then it is stirred away from the fire. The paste must be pressed to purge the whey, then apt moulds are used, called *fasére*. Salt can be applied dry or in water solutions, every other day, for 8 to 12 days.' (Consorzio Tutela 'Formai de Mut' dell'Alta Valle Brembana 1995: 3.).
34. Michele Corti, a paladin of the cause of the Bitto Rebels, has researched extensively about the historical routes of the Bitto cheese. Comparing different authors, he concludes: 'Melazzini peremptorily distinguished Bitto from Branzi, while Serpieri is uncertain about the difference and calls 'Bitto' also the Bergamasque production coming from Val Brembana and destined to the market of Branzi. Such incoherence expresses the ambiguities of a process of construction of typicity [*le ambiguità di un processo di costruzione della tipicità*], which oscillates between a technique-driven definition and a geographical definition, between the quality requested by market demands and conditions of production, and which determines the actual offer (including the cheese-makers competences, the quality of the pastures, they types of management of the pastures and of the transformation of milk). Both the produce destined to the market of Morbegno and that destined to the market of Branzi can be legitimately considered as precursors of contemporary Bitto' (Corti 2011: 100).

35. Vitali (2011). Francesco Maroni, director of the Latteria Sociale di Branzi, and secretary of the Consorzio dei Produttori del formaggio Branzi, explains the reason for their qualms with the Consorzio Tutela Formaggio Branzi. Once again the claims of self-defined 'protectors' and self-evaluated effective 'producers' are at odds.
36. Claudio Paleni, president of the Consorzio Tutela Formaggio Branzi and owner of the homonymous dairy based in Casazza. Interview released to Roberto Vitali, 'Guerra Fredda tra Consorzi. Per il Branzi la DOP resta lontana' Primo Piano del 19 luglio 2011. Retrieved 3 April 2014 from http://www.italiaatavola.net/articolo.aspx?id=21875.
37. Casarrigoni, personal communication. 6 June 2015.
38. Associazione Produttori Valli del Bitto, *Comunicato Stampa del 10/11/2004*.
39. Evaristo, a pseudonym, agrofood technician, interviewed in Val Taleggio 8 August 2006.
40. Corti (2006b) describes and documents this historical process of sedentarization.

Conclusion of Part I

In the Bergamasque Alps – as anywhere else – we do not find a fixed landscape of singular cheeses, each with its own *tipicità* that can be held up as *patrimonio*. Not because the tradition of making mountain cheese could be deconstructed away. Not because it was altogether 'invented'. But because such tradition has taken shape over a *longue dureé* of relocations, kinship alliances and ruptures, shifting commercial supremacy and a cartography of continuous trade and rivalries that is evolving to this day.

This chapter singled out the stories of Bitto, Formai de Mut, and Branzi, contextualizing their serendipities within the contours of a uniquely rich and diverse area of production: the mountainous region straddling the provinces of Bergamo, Sondrio and Lecco, across the northern and southern slopes of the Alpi Orobie, a mountain ridge also known as Alpi Orobiche or pre-Alps. One of these three upland cheeses (Formai de Mut) had its protected denomination established as early as 1985 with a very small area of production, and kept it small, despite the financial misadventures of its founding consortium. A PDO was established in 1995 for Bitto cheese too. However, this area of production largely exceeded that of the original Bitto valleys, which engendered their 'rebellion' and subsequent exit from the consortium, with the result that they could no longer call their cheese 'Bitto'. Vocally supported by Slow Food, they effectively won the war in the commercial arena: in 2015 a single wheel of fifteen-year matured heritage Bitto scored the staggering price of €163 per kilo at auction,[1] and the standard price soared to €17 per 100g.[2] In the best tradition of diplomatic history, on 11 November 2014 a 'peace of the Bitto' (*La Pace del Bitto*) was announced. With a view to recompose the fractured Bitto landscape in preparation of the Universal Exhibition (EXPO 2015) soon to be held in Milan, under the auspices of Sondrio's chamber of commerce, the president of the Bitto Storico consortium and the president of the PDO consortium Valtellina Casera e Bitto signed a joined document, announcing that 'the two methods of Bitto production coexist and cooperate in the strategy of local and touristic promotion of Valtellina'.[3] In the case of Branzi, a PDO procedure was not even initiated, as two competing claims were submitted: one from a coalition of upland producers from Val Brembana and Val Taleggio, one from lowland producers together with the neighbouring Valle Imagna.

With marketing competition soaring, the cheese palette offered to customers is increasingly diversified and customized, testing the limits of local creativity: before obtaining the PDO for Strachitunt, the distributor of Strachitunt in Val Taleggio introduced an ample range of innovative products: beginning with an 'Imperial Red' and an 'Imperial Black', natural blue cheeses refined, respectively, in Sicilian dessert wine and in balsamic vinegar. Other radically 'invented' local products are named after local architectural and geographical landmarks such as Pizzino or Roccolo Divino (*roccolo* being the name of a traditional structure for bird-hunting in the woods), including new cheeses with added red hot chili pepper or black truffle. On the other hand, the war of the cheeses is fought over purity of tradition, boundaries of production areas and genealogies of practice.

Purity is regularly called into play but highly negotiable. Purity, in terms of what can be fed to the milking cows and what can be added or not to the curdling process, played a paramount role in the Bitto *querelle*: the director of the PDO consortium for Bitto and Casera was harshly criticized by the gastronomy magazine *Cheesetime* for having legitimated the use of fodder during the *alpeggio*.[4] As we shall see in Chapter 5, purity will also play an important role in the failed negotiations to establish a Slow Food presidium for Strachitunt in Val Taleggio.

The fiercest wars of the cheeses are fought over boundaries. At the Fiera del Bitto in Morbegno, in 2004, just before the 'rebellion' resulted in its final measure – secession – I conversed with a Bitto maker not residing in the Bitto valleys. He simply stated that he had recently moved from one side of Valtellina to the other, and that if the Bitto rebels where right, he could not continue to make Bitto. As Harry West (2012: 8) notices, in fact, the French regime of the Appellation d'Origine Controlée (AOC), equivalent to and indeed subsumed from1996 onwards under the European PDO/IGP/STG system of geographical designations together with its Italian counterpart DOC (Denominazione di Origine Controllata), does not contemplate distinguishing cheeses *by their makers* but rather *by a technique and area of production* – each of which are intimately enfolded, to the point that location designates technique and eventually taste.

Genealogy, on the other hand, deals with the transmission of knowledge. Branzi is a thorny issue because the competing consortium boasts continuity of production as a family enterprise, having moved out of their mountain village to establish themselves 'lower down'. Mobility – whether historically documented as transhumance or a recent resettlement of specific producers – is an inevitable crack in the veritable 'metaphysics of sedentarism' (Malkki 1992) of geographical indications, which imply that certain bodies of environmental and material knowledge are fixed in places. Cheese-making knowledge though, like herds, tends to travel and has done so for centuries. Embodied knowledge of course is much more difficult to pinpoint and fence off than boundaries, and this is the conundrum of the Bitto rebels, as my cheese-making friends commented: no officer of the Ministry for Agriculture could deliberate once and for all that their cheese is better because it is made closer to the river Bitto.

Each of these factors is skilfully harnessed and performed by the contenders. The obvious mismatch between geography and genealogy was used against the Bitto rebels by those who noticed that their coordinator was not even a cheese-maker by trade, but a tile-merchant! On the other hand, to support significantly higher prices for significantly lower quantities, the 'Bitto Rebels' introduced the practice of branding individual wheels from specific pastures for those who request them in advance – sometimes even with a personal dedication from the cheese-maker. There is also a 'Vault of the Just', where extra-long matured wheels are deposited for personalities and professionals who have defended the cause of the Bitto delle Valli del Bitto: journalists, historians and Slow Food organizers. This *Sancta Sanctorum*, half sacred half commercial, adds a new edge to the idea of 'customization'. Wheels of Bitto Storico are by now collectors' items, bearing the name of the exact pasture where they were made.

Furthermore, historical documentation and normative documents from competing authorities are used strategically. For example the Branzi-based cooperative creamery (*latteria sociale*) invoked the authority of the Bergamo Chamber of Commerce, since its trademark (*marchio camerale*) 'Bergamo Città dei Mille . . . Sapori', established in 1997, includes Branzi among its quality products and spells out in the protocol of production that the area for Branzi production is only Valle Brembana (including Val Taleggio), Valle Imagna and parts of Valle Seriana (not Val Cavallina where their largest competitor is located).[5] The Branzi competitor in lower Val Cavallina debunks the authority of the chamber of commerce by saying: 'the production zone was limited in this way upon direct intervention of the Branzi cooperative, *who got there before us*', implying that lobbying plays a heavy role in determining boundaries and terms of the trademark. He adds that 'that protocol is not binding'![6] As a higher authority, he cites the *Elenco dei Prodotti Agroalimentari Tradizionali della Regione Lombardia*, published by the Lombardy regional government in 2000, as the first regional list of 'traditional agro-food products' of the region. This list includes Branzi and mentions both Val Brembana and Val Cavallina as sites of production.[7]

As we shall see in the rest of the book, this shifting alliance with agencies and institutions will become strategic to the success of Strachitunt, which gained in notoriety and prestige with the help of Slow Food, not unlike Bitto, but in the end did not lend itself to the strictures of a presidium and preferred to pursue the longer-term strategy of an institutional recognition: a Europe-wide PDO, thus daring to repeat the risky move of establishing a very small, territorial geographical indications like that of the ill-fated Formai de Mut. As we shall see in Part 2, the Branzi stalemate also provides a useful comparison with the struggle of Val Taleggio to define its miniature PDO, Strachitunt, vis-à-vis competing producers in the lowlands of Bergamo. Like the Branzi competing consortium, the consortium for the protection of Strachitunt also ignored the authority of the chamber of commerce, as its trademark conceded Strachitunt production to the entire province of Bergamo, including the lowlands. The PDO was harnessed as a higher authority precisely against this.

The protagonists of these parallel struggles are aware of each other's plight and use them rhetorically to advance one's own cause: 'We don't want to end up like our colleagues from Valtellina, who have widened their production area for Bitto only to find that the heritage producers paddle against and withdraw from the rest of the consortium' – warns the president of the upland Branzi consortium.[8] 'This comparison is out of place' retorts the president of the lowland consortium – 'because in Valtellina the production area was expanded to *territories that did not have the tradition and the production*, which we have had for decades'.[9] Beyond the quandaries of this specific confrontation, the same keywords recur on both sides of the argument: a bounded locality claims the practice of a specific way of making cheese, without disruptions of the continuity of production. Such was the claim of Formai de Mut, so eloquently made in a sixteen-page protocol. Similarly, Branzi does not have a PDO production protocol, but the rhetoric of the upland consortium speaks volumes: 'If we believe in the words *tipico* and *tradizionale* we have to circumscribe the zone of production to the mountains and vales that have been producing this cheese for centuries.'[10] Strachitunt has a yearly production of less than one tenth of their Branzi neighbours, but both use the argument that upland cheese is radically different from lowland cheese. As we shall see in Part II, in the case of Strachitunt the mountain producers successfully restricted the PDO denomination to Val Taleggio only, and the lowland producers had to change the name of their cheese.

A dual geography of upland and lowland cheeses underscores each case, and its contentiousness is articulated through issues of denomination. On the one hand we have the high-ranking, aged upland cheeses: fatter, bigger, cooked, sometimes spiced with saffron, thus solidly fit for long routes of transportation and fit to yield high prices – or, earlier, high conversion rates with wines, salt and brocade. Mountain producers argue that this was, and should remain exclusively, their prerogative. On the other hand there is the lowland world of fresh, smaller, unpretentious, raw and skimmed cheeses, made for everyday consumption and family self-subsistence with a simple recipe, often not even requiring heating but rather acidification or curdling at the cows' body temperature immediately after milking. This is the family of *strachì* and its descendant, Taleggio. As we shall see next, Strachitunt is a post-transhumant hybrid, which straddles such geography of opposites.

At the outset of Part I, Anchise's plaidoyer carefully balanced the defence of authenticity with the pragmatism of a merchant. His argument is definitely distinct from that of the 'rebel' cheese-makers of the Bitto valleys, who consider 'heritage Bitto' only high-pasture seasonal production. By recalling how 'we do not have cows at 1,500 meters altitude all year round' he is making a rhetorical shortcut to realism, hinting at the fact that an *alpeggio*-only production would limit Strachitunt to a hyper-niche, and would thus be uneconomical. The strategy of the Strachitunt consortium privileged *tipicità* over purity, and used genealogy to support its claim to Strachitunt as *patrimonio* of the valley. Is Strachitunt really a patrimony of the people of Val Taleggio? Part II shows how, over a process that lasted more than eleven years, the founders of the Strachitunt consortium managed to convince not only each other but their own fellow-residents that yes, it is, and that not to bestow a PDO on *Strachitunt* would have been equivalent to stripping Val Taleggio of its own right to self-determination.

Notes

1. 'Battuto all'asta per 163 euro al kg. È un Bitto Storico della Val Brembana', *L'Eco di Bergamo* 18 May 2015. Retrieved 26 December 2015 from http://www.ecodibergamo.it/stories/Cronaca/battuto-allasta-per-163-euro-al-kge-un-bitto-storico-della-val-brembana_1121286_11/.
2. 'Bitto storico: prezzo alle stelle', *L'Eco di Bergamo* 5 October 2015. Retrieved 26 December 2015 from http://www.ecodibergamo.it/stories/Economia/bitto-storico-prezzo-alle-stellefino-a-17-euro-alletto-ma-va-a-ruba_1144377_11/.
3. 'La pace del Bitto', 11 November 2014. Retrieved 26 December 2015 from http://www.formaggiobitto.com/bitto-storico ('I due metodi di produzione di Bitto con l'accordo dell'11 novembre 2014 coesistono e collaborano nella strategia di promozione territoriale e turistica della Valtellina'). However, by July 2016 the peace was already over. The 'Bitto Rebels' announced that they would drop the name 'Bitto' altogether and would adopt the word 'Storico' in a new trademark. (*Comunicato Ufficiale,* 23 July 2016, retrieved 27 August 2016 from http://www.formaggiobitto.com/it/news/58-comunicato-ufficiale)
4. Stefano Mariotti, editor of *Cheesetime*: 'these people talk about tradition but look at quantity' (Anno 2, n. 5, p. 4), 2006.
5. Retrieved 5 May 2015 from http://www.bg.camcom.gov.it/millesapori/it/approfondimenti/regolamento/. The ellipsis is included in the official name of the trademark.
6. 'Quel disciplinare non ha comunque alcun valore vincolante', Claudio Paleni quoted in Vitali (2011).
7. 21 April 2000, Supplement n.5 to Bulletin n.16 (*Bollettino Ufficiale della Regione Lombardia*, retrieved 9 August 2014 from http://www.consultazioniburl.servizirl.it/pdf/2000/03165.pdf). The president of the lowland consortium is right to notice that this datum has changed: in its last update of March 2014, the production area for Branzi is 'Upper Val Brembana' *only* (Bollettino Ufficiale Regione Lombardia, Serie Ordinaria

n. 10, 7 March 2014. Retrieved 9 August 2014 from http://www.agricoltura.regione.lombardia.it/shared/ccurl/326/685/Estratto%20da%20SEO10_07-03-2014[1].pdf).

8. Francesco Maroni of the Latteria Sociale di Branzi quoted in Vitali (2011).
9. Claudio Paleni quoted in Vitali (2011).
10. Francesco Maroni of the Latteria Sociale di Branzi quoted in Vitali (2011).

PART

II

We, the People of Val Taleggio

CHAPTER 3

A Geography of Opposites

Having appreciated the intricacies of the cheese system of the Bergamasque Alps, Part II introduces a further triangulation of competing but intimately related cheeses: *stracchino* (in dialect: *strachì*), Taleggio PDO, and Strachitunt. While Bitto, Branzi and Formai de Mut are upland cheeses – at least originally made during the *alpeggio* – *strachì* and Taleggio are tied to the lowlands and to the transhumant tradition of the cattle herders and cheese-makers of Lombardy, known as Bergamini. Strachitunt, I will argue, is neither of the lowlands nor of the uplands. The belaboured birth of its PDO is due precisely to the struggle of demonstrating how it should not be considered as a cheese of the lowlands. But it is no upland cheese, either, as its production, by choice, is not exclusively tied to the *alpeggio* season in the high pastures (as Bitto Storico is). Strachitunt is a post-transhumant reinvention. In order to appreciate this, we focus first on the transhumant cheese-making tradition of the Bergamini.

Straddling Uplands and Lowlands

The Bergamini, an expression that betrays their Bergamasque origin, were seasonal herders who connected the 'opposite worlds' of upland and lowland: the *alpeggio* and the *marcita* (De Biasi and Stecchi 2004: 26). Itinerant dairy herders (and thus forcibly cheese-makers), they profited by the invention of the *marcite*, the irrigated pasture lands of the plains south of Milan, worked originally by monastic orders since the fourteenth century. The *marcite* (literally: mouldy lands) exploit the natural spring waters of Lombardy's foothills (known as *fontanili*), which permeate the grassland throughout the year, preventing frost as they flow at a constant 10°C. Constantly irrigated, the *marcite* thus yield enough grass for seven to nine cuts a year. The Cistercian monks developed canals, to harness a natural plenitude of water that allowed for rich crops and a local dairy tradition even in ancient times (but also caused widespread malaises: see De Biasi and

Stecchi 2004: 37). Transhumance was the most sustainable way of exploiting upland and lowland pastures in turn, at the peak of their seasonal availability. The Bergamini or *malghesi* would drive their herds uphill in spring and return to the lowlands in the fall to eat the hay made in the summer by lowland farmers, at an affordable price and in exchange for manuring their fields, thus feeding the herds through the winter. This would imply moving away from the mountain base-village several times a year, either to station in the high pastures, or to 'winter away' (*invernare*) in the lowlands after the fall (Jacini 1882: 26-27; cf. Carminati and Locatelli 2004).

Celebrated in Stefano Jacini's multivolume survey on the state of Italian agriculture in 1882, the Lombard *marcite* are the very reason for the existence of fresh and easy to transport whole milk cheese such as *stracchino.* It is by now a refrain of tourist brochures and culinary volumes that *stracchino* owns its name to the tired cows (*vacche stracche*) of the Bergamini's transhumance, as originally noted by Count Jacini. However, Jacini's comments about the pastoral economy of these herders revealed some discomfort with their liminal condition. In fact, he wished malghesi and transhumance away – as 'the last remnants of a prehistoric society in the middle of a modern world' (1882: 22) – to be replaced by a fully modernized dairy industry. As he explained with his *Report* to the newly formed government cadres of the Kingdom of Italy, Lombardy was then a meticulously managed, high-yield agricultural landscape with the highest population density in the continent and a vocation for industrial agriculture:

> The agrarian system of the irrigated Lombard lowlands is something quite unique in rural Europe, but the erudite ruling classes of Italy have no idea of it. The natural fertility of the soil is close to zero, but production has reached a yield threshold perhaps unsurpassed in Europe. However, productivity is entirely artificial and has been accrued with immense effort and capital, and immense capital is likewise needed every day to maintain it. Irrigation has a decisive influence on this type of agriculture, which cannot be fruitfully carried out if not in the form of vast and intensive cultivation. Land property is only meaningful in medium and large sizes; however, to conduct it as latifundia would be impossible. There are three main contracted roles: the owner, the manager and the worker. The big hirers have the intelligence and the capital, while material labour is a secondary factor. A farm in the irrigated lowlands is organized just like a manufacturing firm. In particular the area of the *marcite* has the highest grass production in the world. Then there are the rice lands and the rotating fallow fields. To the perfection obtained in the production of forage corresponds a backward dairy industry. (Jacini 1882: 99, my translation)

The *malghesi* or Bergamini were protagonists of cattle transhumance in Lombardy. Historical sources identify their operations as early as the fifteenth century, when systematic irrigation works in the Lombard lowlands made an unprecedented amount of forage available. The Bergamini were not poor as they owned their often numerous herds, but lived like 'nomads' (Jacini 1882: 25) and for this reason were scorned by the sedentary but cash-strapped sharecroppers of the lowlands, by waged agricultural workers and by the residents of the mountain villages alike (Corti 2006b). The latter alternated subsistence agriculture (notably animal husbandry, as crops were scarce) with skilled migrant labour as lumberjacks, carpenters, stonemasons and ironmongers – all of which are still average occupations for the Bergamasque mountain dwellers (Bertolotti et al. 1979; Viazzo 1989). Unlike these guild-like skilled labourers, the Bergamini were not organized in unions and associations: they were individuals or at most families, owning up to a hundred productive heifers according to Jacini (1882: 25) but reduced to herds as small as fifteen cows in living memory (Carminati and Locatelli 2004: 414).

Following the recent local historical research gathered about the Bergamini, their culture seems to have been conservative and patriarchal but freed from the bonds of the mountain villages from which they came. They could afford to live a 'masculine' life at the borders of acceptable societal arrangements: oral testimonies register comments about the fact that they might live away from their families for months or did not bother to go to church (Corti 2006b). However, they were the bearers of needed skills, both in cheese-making and in curing ham. In his report of 1882, Count Jacini criticizes the scarce capacities of the *casari* (cheese-makers) making *grana* cheese in the Lombard plains, as they would not be able to control or foretell the quality of the cheese they made. It is worth reading word for word his criticism, as it reminds us of how important the craft of cheese-making was, even at the dawn of industrial food manufacture:

> Dairy farmers who make cheese themselves exist, but are few. Generally they sell their milk to dairy industries. But both in the first and in the second case, apt personnel is always lacking, namely, people with that special instruction that is indispensable for good manufacturing. In the year 1881, with so much progress in basic and applied chemistry in the dairy industry, a cheese-maker will talk about the cheese he is making as if it was a gamble. 'Will it come out well?' he asks. And in fact some cheeses made in a certain period of the year are called 'the gambles'. (Jacini 1882: 122).[1]

These observations echo the comments I gathered among contemporary cheese-makers: their skilled practice is so personal that the production of an entire dairy is identified with the individual cheese-maker: 'I used to buy *crescenza* cheese from dairy XY, where Mr. B. used to make cheese. Since he left, it is not the same cheese. So I now buy it from where he moved to' (Cesare, a cheese merchant, Salone del Gusto Slow Food, Torino, October 2004).

Heather Paxson also reports on the 'knack' (or lack of it) of American cheese-makers: not all homesteaders had it, and part of the drive for an industrialization of cheese-making was caused by the unfavourable variability of home-made dairies (Paxson 2013: 136–37). Similarly, those who could master the unfathomable art of cheese-making would eventually establish the food industry of Lombardy, which still bears the name of the original founding families (Arrigoni, Invernizzi, Locatelli, Galbani etc.).[2] Most of these surnames originate in the valleys of Lecco and Bergamo – notably Valsassina, Val Taleggio and the neighbouring Valle Imagna – which together enjoyed access to the vast and rich pastures available at a relatively low altitude just north of Milan. One finds that different branches of the same family may have set up in time large businesses and even competing enterprises.

In this context, *strachì* (*stracchino*), means simply 'fresh cheese'. It was part of the breeder's diet, was not prestigious merchandise, and its name did not bring distinctive associations with particular places (as did instead Bitto and Branzi). However, *strachì* was made and especially aged and refined in Val Taleggio. The valley was rich in water and had easily reached high pastures for summer grazing. Unlike neighbouring valleys where cheese was aged in natural caves, the availability of streams and woods had allowed to develop a local architectural technique to provide aired and cool storage places for maturing cheese: the *caselli*. These were built directly upon spring waters or astride a stream, with raised entrances and a canal cutting across the shed. Shallow copper milk containers could be immersed in water allowing to cool the milk and wait for cream to surface without acidifying through heat. In other cases it is reported that fish could be kept alive, trapped in the stream water flowing through the *casello* and then sold fresh to vendors. North-facing windows allowed for ventilation and cheese slabs could be lined on wooden planks along the walls. In the summer, cheese could be made directly here. The dirt floor was treated with lime – charcoal and lime production being both specialties of this area rich in woods, requiring cooking limestone or wood at a constant heat in large piles over several days, in cone-shaped sites called respectively *calchère* (for limestone) and *poiàc* (for charcoal). According to testimonies gathered in the valley, the *caselli* were often built and owned in common by several users. This widespread technique was still in use up until the beginning of the 1900s, but then the buildings fell in disrepair or were converted for other uses.[3] Such uses are telling of a cheese-making technique that is seasonal and mobile, but not nomadic.

As we saw in the Introduction, transhumance proper is an all-year cyclical movement of herds (typically sheep, but in Lombardy this involved mixed sheep, goat and cattle herds) covering hundreds of miles in seasonal circuits from uplands to lowlands, often across regional and even national borders (Jones 2005). Long sheep routes kept flocks on the move the year round, straddling the Alps well into Switzerland or France (Albera and Lebaudy 2001). Instead of practicing a seminomadic pastoralism with roaming sheep, the *bergamì* stationed with cattle herds for longer periods in customary areas, taking them to manure the fields in the lowlands and buying winter hay in exchange. Cattle herds would then move to the original mountain pastures during the summer, eating the grass of the higher pastures and providing milk for cheese. Short-term *alpeggio* in stone abodes on the summer pastures allowed making cooked mountain cheese for high-end commerce. *Strachì* instead suited mobile adjustments as its cheese-making practice was considered easy and unencumbered by the need for heating and maturing. According to witnesses interviewed by local historians in Val Taleggio, *malghese* would be the commonly used word in Italian for *bergamì* (Carminati and Locatelli 2004), where *malga* or *bergamina* means its herd (Consorzio Formaggio 'De Mut' Alta Valle Brembana 1985: 3).

Even upland cheese is a seasonal production closely tied not to one *locality* but to the curdling and maturing *practices* that arose in tight conjunction with the mobility of several families across a series of upland 'stations', from summer ascension to the early fall descent. Establishing a specific 'area of production' for PDOs of transhumant traditions then, is particularly fraught. Even more than Bitto, Branzi and Formai de Mut, *stracchino* is characterized by the seasonal comings and goings of cattle herds. In order to understand how *strachì* came to be Stracchino di Taleggio and hence Taleggio cheese tout court will require switching back and forth between Italian and Bergamasco: the thesis of local historians and cheese experts is that *stracchino* just meant what Jacini describes: a soft, low-value, raw cheese made in haste from tired cows by cowboys on the move. However, one could refer to *strachì* made in specific places, such as *strachì de Taecc* (*stracchino* from Val Taleggio) or *strachì de Gorgonzola* (*stracchino* made in Gorgonzola), or made at a specific time of the year, such as *strachì quartirolo*: made from the milk of cows eating the 'fourth' (*quarto*) grass-cut in the *marcite*. From an earlier document of 1784 we can understand the rich diversity of such practices. Reviewing the Lombard agricultural production for the Austrian government, Ludwig Mitterpacher describes *stracchino* as a soft cheese domestically produced, fatty and easy to make and to preserve without faults. He also records a double-cream recipe, *stracchino di due panne*, that he gives as extinct:

> *Stracchini* are made with freshly drawn milk, consequently not skimmed. It quickly curdles thanks to the use of the same rennet employed for cheese [*formaggio*] and it is not as easily faulty as cheese is. However, rennet must be added in a warm and sheltered location, away from drafts. Once the curd is cast into round or square shapes, salt is added. Firstly on top, to allow it to melt, then on the bottom, thus flip-siding each slab. Since *stracchini* are better if made of rich substance, cream from other skimmed milks can be added. This diversifies the type of *stracchini*, and the latter are called *stracchini* of two creams [*di due panere*]. (Mitterpacher 1784: II, 361)[4]

Each of the surviving cheese-making techniques for *strachì* have become identified as a specific product: Gorgonzola, *stracchino*, Crescenza, Quartirolo Lombardo, and of course Taleggio. There is little doubt that Valle Taleggio gave its name to Taleggio cheese. But the significance of this fact is debated. Val Taleggio was a place of stationing and maturing for *strachì*. Its vocational industry consisted of ageing and refining cheese for commercialization. It makes perfect sense that the valley's able merchants sold 'their' *stracchini* with success, to the point of identifying the product with *their* place of origin. The '*stracchino* of Val Taleggio' earned prizes in international gourmet competitions at the beginning of the twentieth century, thanks to expat restaurant owners who maintained active networks with refiners in Val Taleggio. In particular, Strachini di Taleggio [*sic*] won the gold medal in the twenty-sixth Exposition Internationale de Cuisine, d'Alimentation et d'Hygiene in Paris, in 1909.[5] In 1918, 'Taleggio' is recorded in the Modern Dictionary of the Italian Language by Alfredo Panzini, denoting cheese (Stefanelli 1998: 50). Still to this day, people in Val Taleggio refer to Taleggio as *strachì*, using dialect. To them Taleggio cheese is nothing other than the PDO qualification of the *stracchino* that Jacini was talking about. However, not everyone agrees that it would still make sense to talk about Taleggio and *stracchino* interchangeably.

This is because since 1996 Taleggio is a PDO cheese with a specific protocol of production, while *stracchino* is not a protected denomination and denotes a generic soft, uncooked cheese, usually much fresher than Taleggio, only aged for ten to fifteen days. Taleggio is characterized by a standard square shape (precisely 18 to 20 cm wide, as the protocol prescribes) and mild, creamy taste. Whole, usually pasteurized milk is curdled with calf rennet at 32–35°C (roughly the milking temperature, but nothing prescribes that it should not be refrigerated and reheated, which is the norm in industrial production). The curd is cut down to grains the size of a hazelnut, letting it rest in between to favour the release of whey. In industrial production, this is done by mechanical arms of different sizes while it used to be done by hand with bowl-shaped copper cutters (in Bergamasco: *basla*) and finished with a finer cheese cutter (*spino*). Once cast in square shapes, salt can be added dry by hand, or more commonly by immersion in salty solutions. Taleggio needs maturing for thirty-five days in cellars at a temperature of 5°C and at about 80 per cent humidity to receive the consortium brand. Each slab weighs about 2 kilos (precisely between 1.7 and 2.2 kg as prescribed by the production protocol) and they are recursively brushed with salt and water to obtain the characteristic pink and thin washed rind (Stefanelli 1998: 46–51).[6]

When Taleggio gained a Denomination of Controlled Origin (DOC) in 1954, its recipe was widely known and widespread along the paths of transhumance connecting Alpine peaks and winter lowland pastures; the square *strachì* had become (and still is) a staple food for the Lombard plains. As a result, the consortium established in 1979 granted an area of production practically as wide as

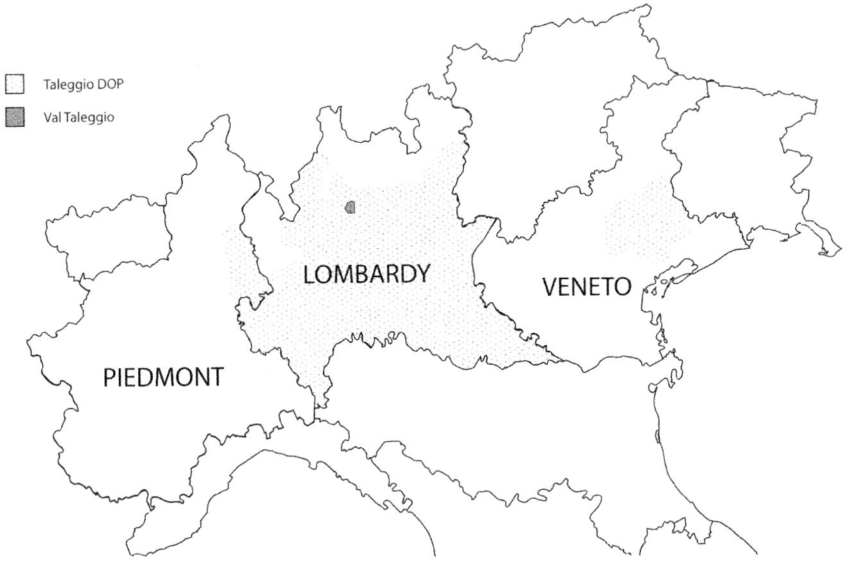

Map 2. Production area of Taleggio PDO vis-à-vis Val Taleggio. Map produced by Federico De Musso.

northern Italy.[7] Map 2 highlights the size of Val Taleggio compared to the area of production of 'Taleggio DOP'.

For *stracchino* there is no geographic designation at all: indicatively it is produced in the northern Italian regions of Piedmont, Lombardy and Veneto, but anyone can make a cheese and call it *stracchino*. Consequently, there is no consortium that can monitor and report on production quantities. Table 2 provides an overview of the starkly differing productions of the upland and lowland cheeses discussed so far (six, if we account for the separate productions of PDO Bitto and Slow Food Bitto Storico). By the time it obtained DOC denomination, Taleggio was so ubiquitously known, produced and eaten that one could argue that the geographical indication carried no added value beyond its sheer volume.

Strachitunt PDO	Bitto PDO	Bitto Storico Slow Food	Formai de Mut PDO	Branzi FTB (Latteria Sociale Branzi)	Taleggio PDO
23.89	240	15	56.38	273	860 (of which 21.6 produced in Val Taleggio)

Table 2. Production (in tons per year) of Strachitunt PDO, Bitto PDO, Consorzio Salvaguardia Bitto Storico/Presidio Slow Food, Formai de Mut dell'Alta Val Brembana PDO, Branzi FTB (Formaggio Tipico Branzi/Latteria Sociale di Branzi), Taleggio PDO.[8]

The bulk of Taleggio and *stracchino* production is industrial, largely located in the lowlands south of Milan. Milk comes from the intensive dairy farms of the surrounding plains. For this mass production, the connection between a singular product and a distinctive 'sense of place' had not been *lost* – it just never was there, as *strachì* was the unassuming by-product of transhumant milking, whereby the breeder had to quickly transform the milk of 'tired' cows, without the aid of fire – and move on. This is not the interpretation of the Val Taleggio entrepreneurs. To them, the behest of DOC certification to such a wide area of production (then converted into PDO in 1996) meant a catastrophic loss. They missed the chance to market 'their own' Taleggio – a cheese that after all carries the name of their valley!

In the next chapter we will see how, faced by this stalemate, the cheese-makers of Val Taleggio adaptively and creatively fought what appeared as a lost war for a long time. Crushed as they were between an undistinctive (because too big) PDO area of production for Taleggio, and an unrewarding local production of near-domestic *stracchini*, they reinvented Strachitunt. Initially, they attempted to get recognition for their own 'naming' interventions on Taleggio cheese itself, based on arguments about the history and specificity of Taleggio from Val Taleggio. Then, banned from naming their valley's cheese in a distinctive way, they resuscitated *another strachì* from Val Taleggio, namely the round *strachì* or *strachì tund*, now Strachitunt PDO.

How Taleggio Cheese Failed the Taleggio Valley

On 29 July 2014 I was in a Slow Cooking restaurant in Bergamo, recently opened but carefully provisioned. Slow Cooking is a network of fourteen Lombard restaurants whose mission is to offer locally sourced wines and foods.[9] Its menu featured 'porked veal' (*vitello porchettato*), namely marinated veal wrapped in bacon and slow-roasted, *violino di pecora* (sheep ham), fish from the Lombard lakes and of course Strachitunt. I overheard the owner casually explaining that 'Taleggio cheese is obviously named after the Taleggio valley, but *there* they don't call it Taleggio of course. They call it *strachì*.' A poignant remark that sums up in twenty words the pride and plight of Val Taleggio over ownership of Taleggio cheese. In a signed preface to a volume of twenty-one interviews with surviving *Bergamini* of Val Taleggio, the owner of the dairy who sponsored the publication writes:

> How is it possible that we cannot even use the name of our *strachì quader*? How come it is now owned by a consortium that, without the consent of our valley, of its administrations and of its population, has taken away the name 'Taleggio'? How is it that Strachitunt, born on our *alpeggi*, thus belonging to

> the history of these villages, is continuously faked by lowland producers, when it would be an important resource for our valley?[10]

This tirade requires contextualizing. Vigilance and supervision on the production and commerce of Taleggio cheese is the task of the Consorzio Tutela Taleggio (CTT) . This is a not-for-profit association of producers, whose mission is to preserve Taleggio cheese from fraud, monitor its quality and promote it commercially. Its main activities consist in providing technical assistance to milk producers and creameries, and monitoring the employment of the denomination 'Taleggio' in the public domain. It was on the basis of this privilege that CTT intervened with a legal admonition against the dairy cooperative of Val Taleggio and its main merchant and refiner in 2006, as they had attempted to commercialize the Taleggio cheese made in Val Taleggio with the name Stracchino di Taleggio. The consortium's claim was that the word 'Taleggio' appeared in the name Stracchino di Taleggio in a different way than the one prescribed by its PDO. The protected designation of origin for Taleggio cheese is simply *Taleggio*, and any further specification would be misleading for the consumer. Thus adjectives, appellatives or restrictive specifications are banned from Taleggio's PDO. 'Stracchino di Taleggio' implies that Taleggio is indeed a place before it is a cheese, and further that Taleggio cheese of Val Taleggio is better, or more authentic, more *tipico*, than the rest of the Taleggio cheese produced within the PDO production area.

But what is *stracchino*, other than Taleggio by another name? As we saw, originally they were the very same thing (the latter took its name from the former, for being matured in the Taleggio valley). Taleggio, *taècc* in the local dialect, did not even mean 'cheese' but probably 'beech', a common tree in the woods of the valley (Da Lezze 1988). Taleggio cheese would be nothing else but a *strachì* made in the valley of the beech trees. Commercially though, the former is now a PDO with a specific protocol and area of production, while the latter is not. Barred from characterizing their Taleggio as local, and stuck in the procedure for the recognition of Strachitunt as a PDO cheese,[11] the dairy cooperative of Val Taleggio opted to produce its own cheese under the name of Stracchino di Vedeseta, after the name of the village that hosts the valley's creamery. But they could not specify their cheese with a designation bearing the name of the valley of origin: Taleggio. In other words, they could not differentiate autochthonous Taleggio production from PDO Taleggio cheese, despite the fact that Taleggio is the very name of one of the two municipalities of which Val Taleggio consists (see Figure 1).

The local cheese-makers believed that the only development perspective for Val Taleggio lay in its capacity to both differentiate itself from an industrial mass production and to calibrate itself to the demand for niche cheeses. Hence their investment on Strachitunt Valtaleggio and on the Stracchino di Vedeseta, both

Figure 1. Road sign for the municipality of Taleggio in Val Taleggio. Photograph by Angelo Hankins.

made with locally sourced raw milk. At this point Strachitunt did not have a PDO and the specification Strachitunt Valtaleggio was essential to distinguish it from what the valley's producers considered imitations. Both Strachitunt Valtaleggio and Stracchino di Vedeseta were then produced at the cooperative dairy of Val Taleggio and commercialized by Arrigoni Valtaleggio.

Until October 2010 in fact the main Taleggio cheese producer in Italy was Arrigoni Valtaleggio, a business including a large creamery and dairy-farming enterprise in the Bergamasque lowlands as well as maturing cellars and a commercial distribution network based in Val Taleggio. This firm distributed Taleggio cheese in northern Italy for its main part but also exported to the United States, Canada, Japan and Europe, especially Germany and Austria, both as its own produce and through supply contracts under major distribution brands such as Carrefour, Metro and Iper. According to data provided by the producer itself, the annual production of Taleggio in 2006 was 9,195,854 forms in 2005, of which 24.4 per cent were sold by the Arrigoni group. Vertically integrated, they made cheese with milk produced in their own sheds: 15 tons of milk a day produced by about 1,000 cows, 800 of which were in production around the year, and prospects to raise them to 2,000. At that point Arrigoni Valtaleggio could boast that

> we produce more than Cademartori, more than Mauri. We have an organic supply chain, GM free, plus a mountain cheese supply. *But* we cannot sell

Figure 2. Strachitunt Valtaleggio and Stracchino di Vedeseta. Publicity postcard of 'Arrigoni Valtaleggio', 2007. Reproduced with permission from Casarrigoni.

> our mountain cheese, which is produced at 1,000 meters altitude, *as organic* because it is not certified. We could not even meet the demand for organic cheese with our mountain production. Demand for genuine and good cheese is huge, upland production is tiny and the number of producers is decreasing. (Arrigoni Val Taleggio manager, audio-recorded conversation, 1 September 2006)

The scenario that should be avoided would be to end up like neighbouring Valsassina, another historic seat of transhumance and dairy farming: 'There is no one left making cheese in Valsassina. They still make eight tons of milk, and sell it in the lowlands to make mozzarella with it!' (Lucia, cheese entrepreneur, 1 September 2006). The disdainful reference to mozzarella, a Southern tradition and a completely different type of cheese-making technique than the autochthonous ones, spoke volumes of the fear of assimilation to a nondescript 'other', a loss of memory and identity.

Despite operating in a sound economic environment, as partners of a much larger industrial group in the lowlands, the cheese-makers of Val Taleggio also believed that Taleggio cheese had failed them, and on the basis of this they advanced a number of requests to the CTT, the Taleggio PDO consortium, as mentioned above: to receive a 'royalty' on Taleggio sales for the development of the valley, to have the administrative seat of the consortium moved to the valley, to have at least symbolically the brand number 1 to mark the valley's production, finally, to create a subdenomination as there is for Camembert, for a Taleggio *tipico* of Val Taleggio. All were turned down. According to the valley's point of view, it was myopic not to let diversity thrive. Mass production is identical across the spectrum, and price cannot be helped by that: 'Asiago is all the same, because it is produced in four main dairies only' (Lucia, cheese entrepreneur, 1 September 2006).

Furthermore, some of the bigger industries seem to hold the designation of Taleggio in such low esteem that they began to reverse-brand it, using just their family name (as in the case of Cademartori). In honesty, the main refiner of the valley explained that it would be difficult to obtain concessions for the valley when still working under the umbrella of an industrial group: 'But despite the fact that my lowland partners do not agree, I am convinced that they owe us something' (Arrigoni Val Taleggio manager, 1 September 2006).

After six years of partnering with the main national Taleggio producer, as of 2010 this Val Taleggio refiner went solo as an independent business entirely based in the valley. It was a bold move. At this point the prospects for the valley's growth hinged on its dwindling dairy farming. Promoting a unique local product was the only viable project to resuscitate the valley, encouraging the use of local pastures and hay so as to have a locally sourced, branded, possibly organic production that can sell at twice the price as nonorganic:

> For our organic supply chain we buy fifteen tons of organic milk a week from the lowlands of Pavia, in the middle of rice fields! Here, our mountain cooperative makes seventeen tons a week alone![12] If it was all organic, we would not even have to buy it. And we could sell it at elitist price because GM free milk is sought after and paid for 30 per cent more than average milk, which is already much pricier than elsewhere in Europe. This is *good* mountain milk, not *watery* milk! Instead, we sell our organic Gorgonzola to Austrian and German organic chains. Instead of buying 400 tons of silage a year, our farmers should make 100 tons of hay more a year. (Arrigoni Val Taleggio manager, 1 September 2006).

Still not organic, to this day there are only two milk producers and cheese-makers of a notable size in the valley: the farming family who salvaged the recipe for Strachitunt and the valley cooperative dairy. The family farm is in any case a prominent member of the cooperative, and both entered the consortium for Strachitunt. Many others knew how to make both Strachitunt and *strachì* (and some made it) but could not sell it. Some may be ageing farmers with no interest in growth, some lacked the resources – financial or entrepreneurial – to upgrade their facilities to comply with ever-increasing regulations (refurbishing their buildings, getting professional help to write their HACCP protocol, or applying for a commercial license). A rumour regarded one farmer who invested in building works on his cowshed and creamery, only to have the license denied because of a technical mistake in how to line up entrances and exits from the dairy room. On the other hand, the progress made toward obtaining the PDO for Strachitunt, however slow, convinced local dairy farmers to produce it. By the end of May 2009, the regional administration approved the dossier and gave the go-ahead for a ministerial hearing at the national level. By then, eleven producers altogether in the valley made about 4,000 wheels a year out of 200 tons of locally produced raw milk.[13] Hence the pride of the consortium's president, who could state 'our Consorzio per la tutela dello Strachitunt (Consortium for the Protection of Strachitunt) should rather be called Consortium for the Protection and Salvage of the Traditions, Culture, and History of Our Valley'.[14]

Milk for Strachitunt is all worked *a munta calda*, meaning curdled at body temperature straight after milking as requested by the PDO protocol. This is as an essential character of the Val Taleggio operations because it demands a very short distance from the milk collection point and the point of transformation (otherwise the milk would go cold and would need reheating to be 'started' for coagulation). This of course requires some coordination and logistics: the cooperative cheese-maker must be ready to transform the milk as soon as it reaches the creamery. It also guarantees that the geographical boundaries of the consortium stay small, *operationalizing* so to speak the policing of local boundaries. The Strachitunt production area could not be any larger than Val Taleggio because there would be no time to transport the milk to the creamery.

Furthermore the partnership between the valley's only creamery and the valley's main refiner established at once a regime of monopoly, according to some, and a safety valve for a local production of uneven quality and quantity, in the opinion of others. The valley's main merchant would guarantee maturing facilities, packaging and logistics all year round – whichever the product, its quantity or its attractiveness. Within this agreement, the valley's producers cooperative grew – but only slightly: its production capacity is reported as increased of about 15 per cent in fifteen years.[15] However, there were recurrent complaints about the quality of the produce and its lack of diversification. Initially, the cooperative only produced Taleggio PDO alongside undistinguished *formagella*: a common name for any fresh, round, fat, cooked cheese, also usually described as *tipo Branzi* ('like Branzi').

Criticisms of the cooperative management and of the cheese-making procedure varied from scepticism about pooling milk from different dairy farms to specific complaints about managing the curdling process in the cooperative building, including accusations of reheating the milk and airing the rooms at the wrong time, thus interfering with the delicate phase during which the milk curdles and the curd settles. Such level of detailed criticisms of the cheese-making skills – or lack thereof – of the master cheese maker were often openly discussed in front of me by the refiner, the customers and the producers – often all of whom were local residents. The *casaro*, also a valley's resident, was in effect replaced in the following years by a new master and apprentice, again local youth (actually relatives of the initial *casaro*).

Despite the intense degree of interconnection between individuals, family enterprises and kin relations, producers' cooperation in the valley was scarce to say the least, and could easily lead to long-drawn discrepancies even within the same household. This notwithstanding the fact that the Alpine region boasts a historically documented tradition of collective management of herds and pasture-land, often with associated cheese-making tasks. According to local historians, collective agreements to manage herds and make cheese on the high pastures (*Società di Alpeggio*) were running still into the 1940s, pooling and transforming milk during the *alpeggio* season in many localities of the Bergamasque Alps.[16] As for Val Taleggio, in 1934, notary public Antonio Leidi in Bergamo certified the existence of a cooperative of producers with twenty members conferring milk.

However the recent history of dairy cooperatives in the Bergamasque mountains is dotted with difficulties and hurdles. Val Taleggio's own cooperative site was built by the Mountain Community Administration with development funds in 1980 but remained abandoned for a decade, so that in 1991 it had to be restored even before the only two milk-conferring members of the valley's cooperative were ready to move their herds in the stable. The site offered a cow shed with inbuilt milk conduits to the dairy locales, plus a family apartment for the cheese-maker and a shop for selling the dairy products. The herds are not held collectively but rather each farmer pays rent to the cooperative for using the shed as a private site. No one would delegate the care of their animals to a cooperative employee for lack of trust. Not far from Val Taleggio, in Sambucco of Dossena, an analogous structure built for cooperative management was never adopted for collective production and was left to ruin. When I visited it in 1999, it stood just next to an overcrowded family-owned dairy farm.

Since then, I had many occasions to learn that scepticism of collective management is engrained in the local entrepreneurial culture. In February 1999 I took part in an excursion to a cooperative dairy and cowshed in Parma with a party of Bergamasque family farmers. The visit was organized by the trade union Coldiretti to exhibit the 'best practices' of Parmigiano Reggiano – a cooperative. Their scepticism about the collective management style was palpable.

Some commented that if the cows belong to the cooperative then they are everyone's and no one's, and that the cheese-makers of parmesan cooperatives are nothing but cooperative employees so how can they be passionate about it? Yet we were visiting a state-of-the-art shed hosting two hundred Friesian cows, freely perambulating and accessing individually rationed meals thanks to a microchip on their collars. This was (and still is) dream technology for the Lombard mountains just a couple of hours drive away, mainly because of their cost vis-à-vis the minute size of mountain operations. When my hosts introduced the first free range shed in the valley, people flocked to come and see 'the mess' of unchained cows free to move around, being rounded up for milking. The first days were hard. Then both cows and farmers learnt what to do when it was milking time, and now visiting the milking shed of my host family is a fixture for passers-by. The president of the Strachitunt consortium was dismissive of the lack of entrepreneurial initiative of some cooperative members: he commented that with the exception of one family, they want to have their milk paid for but would not invest their private money in it.

Since the end of the 1990s, also thanks to development funds from EU Objective 5B for marginal rural areas, the Val Taleggio cooperative consistently invested on modernizing the creamery, buying a refrigerated truck to transport milk from conferring members, and their own maturing fridge. A cooperative usually offers better prices for milk to conferring members than industrial dairies, which would not pay a premium on quality. However, once accessing a perceivably high-quality milk, producers also have the interest to make cheese themselves in order to sell it privately. The final decision inevitably depends on a pragmatic calculus of resources and capacities. Sometimes the cheese produced at the cooperative site was not perceived to be as excellent as the craft cheese made by individual families, and these internal competitions in a very small place could feed fault lines between or even across families. For example, the family previously mentioned for developing a state-of-the-art free-range stable was also criticized for maintaining their own cheese-making line instead of investing fully in the cooperative enterprise. Their cheese was considered better than the cooperative's, and thus sought after by private consumers and cheese merchants. The risk was that only low-quality or too small producers would find it attractive to confer milk to the cooperative. On the other hand, precisely because of the fragility of mountain dairy farming, a cooperative must be able to buy out all the milk in all seasons and to transform it accordingly.

The extreme divergence among cultures of collaboration between farming entrepreneurs across northern Italy could also be explained in terms of the diverse political subcultures, ranging from an individualist ('white') entrepreneurial style associated with conservative party politics and a collectivist ('red') cooperative management style. The latter are associated with regions that have a history of communist and socialist public administrations, the former with Christian

Democracy strongholds (Messina 2006).[17] One could also imagine that the collective management of pastureland at a time of intensive seasonal migration, up until the last century, was not necessarily a cultural preference of mountain farmers as much as a viable solution to a common problem. Charismatic leaders such as parish priests or local notables could tip the balance and drive collective entrepreneurship, corralling a sufficient number of local smallholders.

Consistently with this tradition of personal leadership and in order to stop divisive local dynamics, Strachitunt was salvaged by an individual cheese-maker much celebrated in the press, but developed by the cooperative enterprise with milk from the entire valley. This was hoped to become the developmental device to jump-start the valley. Strachitunt PDO seemed to answer Val Taleggio's plight to defend a distinctive local production from a widespread but generic designation of origin for Taleggio PDO, which detracted from its price and impeded a singular product identity, to the detriment of its mountain producers. In order to achieve the PDO though, something more than a bureaucratic procedure was needed. Strachitunt producers and their leader had to convince themselves and the rest of the world that their cheese was indeed unique.

Notes

1. My translation from the Italian original, here transcribed: 'I conduttori che fabbricano il formaggio per proprio conto esistono ma sono pochi. Generalmente invece essi vendono il latte ad appositi industriali che esercitano il caseificio. Ma tanto nel primo caso quanto nel secondo, manca sempre il personale adatto all'uopo, fornito cioè di quella istruzione speciale che è indispensabile per il buon andamento dell'industria. In pieno 1881, con tanti progressi della chimica generale e della chimica applicata al caseificio, un casaro vi parla di un formaggio che sta fabbricando come di una giuocata al lotto. "Chi sa se riuscirà?" dice egli. Ed è perciò che determinate quantità di formaggi prodotti in un dato periodo si sogliono chiamare *le sorti*' (Jacini 1882: 122).
2. We find a similar dynamic not only in dairy but also in its related cured meat industry, as pig-rearing was the porcine counterpart of cheese-making in the animal husbandry practice of using whey from curdling as a nutrient for domestic pig-breeding. While ageing salami in one's own cellar is very much felt as a family tradition, especially in the lowlands of Bergamo, Milan and Lodi, a profitable intensive agribusiness has evolved out of the customary domestic pig-rearing as accompaniment to small-scale dairy farming.
3. Barbara Pesenti Bolò and Erika Arrigoni, as volunteers of Val Taleggio's Ecomuseum, have authored the reports on 'high pastures' (*alpeggi*), 'high pastures abodes' (*malghe*) and '*caselli*' for the community map of Val Taleggio. Retrieved 7 May 2015 from http://www.osservatoriovaltaleggio.it/index.php?option=com_content&view=article&id=45&Itemid=54. The Community Maps reports on limestone and charcoal production were authored by Roberta Gabbatore.
4. Many thanks to Prof. Gaetano Forni for allowing me to consult his personal copy in 2001. The volume is currently digitized on Google Books from a copy held at Harvard Widener Library.

5. The recipient of the prize was the grandfather of the retired school teacher of Vedeseta in Val Taleggio, who reportedly traded internationally and opened a restaurant in London. The teacher keeps the prize certificate in a frame, and showed it on a national Sunday television program devoted to culinary and rural practices: *Linea Verde*, RAI, 7 December 1997 (see also local press coverage on *L'Eco di Bergamo*, 12 August 1998). Another medal was won in 1911 in S. Pellegrino, then a fashionable international thermal resort at the heart of Val Brembana.
6. The official website of the Taleggio PDO consortium spells out the production protocol and specifies the geographical area of production, straddling Piedmont, Lombardy and Veneto. Retrieved 7 May 2015 from http://www.taleggio.it.
7. The production area of Taleggio PDO are the provinces of Bergamo, Brescia, Como, Cremona, Lecco, Lodi, Milano and Pavia in Lombardy; Novara in Piedmont; and Treviso in Veneto – an area straddling the entire Pianura Padana of northern Italy from west to east.
8. Data regard 2014 and were gathered in June 2014 from: Latteria Sociale di Branzi/ Formaggio Tipico Branzi; Consorzio Tutela Valtellina Casera e Bitto; Consorzio Salvaguardia Bitto Storico; Latteria Valtorta/ Consorzio Formai de Mut dell'Alta Valle Brembana; Consorzio Strachitunt/ Cooperativa Agricola Sant'Antonio di Vedeseta; Casarrigoni srl.
9. See www.slowcooking.org.
10. Carminati and Locatelli (2004: 16). Signed Preface, December 2004.
11. Even though already in 2006 the procedure for a PDO for Strachitunt was considered 'at an advanced stage' and the local press reported it as almost a *fait accompli*. See Sergio Tiraboschi, 'Zootecnia, ultimo trittico in Valle Brembana', *L'Eco di Bergamo*, 5 October 2006, 30.
12. Data from 2014 confirm slightly lower production rates: the Val Taleggio producers cooperative transforms 685 tons of milk per year, or 1.9 tons a day (Casarrigoni, 1 June 2015).
13. 'L'unico Cru "a due paste". 11 produttori, 4mila forme', *L'Eco di Bergamo* 28 May 2009, 44.
14. President of the Consortium for the Protection of Strachitunt (interview of 15 August 2006).
15. The data of the Mountain Community administration (*Comunità Montana Valle Brembana*) of 1998 recorded the cooperative's capacity at 580 tons of milk a year (GAL Valle Brembana, *Piano di Azione Locale*, 1998: 149). Data from 2014 confirm a slightly increased production of 685 tons of milk per year (Casarrigoni, personal communication, 1 June 2015).
16. Società di Alpeggio are registered in the villages of Castione, Bratto and Dorga in Val Seriana; Ornica and Valtorta in Val Brembana; and Schilpario in Val di Scalve (Gherardi and Oldrati 1997: 19 and 141; Corti 2004: 125 and 84).
17. See Messina (2006) on Veneto (cf. Stacul 2003 on Friuli); Mocarelli (2013) on the history of the Chianti consortium, or Ulin (1996) on Southwest France wine cooperatives for a transnational comparison.

CHAPTER 4

The Best Cheese in Italy

At the turn of the millennium, the *strachì* of Val Taleggio began to be well known again. My host, farmer Guglielmo, had appeared on national television as early as 1997, on the Sunday program *Linea Verde* (the Green Line), about food and agriculture. He showed his raw milk *strachì*, but Strachitunt was not mentioned. The popular TV presenter Fazzuoli stressed that Guglielmo was making Taleggio with raw milk, something of interest for the debates of the day. At the time, Strachitunt was considered a dwindling family production of no particular interest. A cheese merchant associated with Slow Food had idiosyncratically rekindled its production, by ordering a few wheels from Guglielmo's *alpeggio* to sell it at his Bergamo shop. This operation remained low-key for quite a few years. In time, through the network of connoisseurs of Slow Food, Strachitunt began to be known to chefs, refiners and gourmands. The site of the consortium acknowledges chef Gianfranco Vissani, who in 2002 declared that Strachitunt 'is the best cheese in Italy'.[1] After Vissani's visit, it began customary to quote that the valley of Taleggio cultivated two lines of production: *strachì-quader* (the square *strachì* then evolved into Taleggio cheese) and *strachì-tunt* (round *strachì*).

Chefs and food journalists wield significant power when they evaluate local foods. Letizia Bindi has commented on the paramount role of haute cuisine movers and shakers (elite restaurant owners, culinary journalists, media personalities) in shaping discourses and destinies of specific items of 'heritage foods' (2012). In Val Taleggio, gastronomy journalist Elio Ghisalberti, after reprimanding the restaurant owners of Val Taleggio for failing to promote the valley's cheeses, became a prominent supporter, first of a project to create a Slow Food presidium for Strachitunt (dicussed in Chapter 5), then of its PDO consortium. On the other hand the culinary critic Edoardo Raspelli, prominent on the national scene and featured in gastronomic television programmes, dispensed a succinct analysis of the Bergamasque food scene on the local newspaper[2] celebrating Taleggio, Formai de Mut and Branzi but criticizing Strachitunt as 'too niche'. He praised both the lowland producers of Strachitunt and the Val Taleggio producers, thus implicitly avoiding supporting the endeavour of obtaining a PDO for the mountains only. At the same time, he celebrated the culinary 'excellence' of the entire province, giving a specific mentioning to certain producers and restaurants in a full newspaper page.

Why so much ado about Strachitunt? Its difference does not lie in shape only. This round *strachì* is made with raw, unpasteurized milk with a rather sophisticated technique of mixing layers of curds from two different days (typically the curd of the night before with that of the morning) so that natural moulds develop during the maturing phase. This is aided by puncturing the cheese during maturation with copper needles, so that it is exposed to the 'air' and the environmental bacteria of the maturing station. This procedure is similar to Gorgonzola, which is typically striated with bluish lines along the furrows left by the needles. But in the case of Gorgonzola, the bacterial cultures (*Penicillium glaucum* or *Penicillium roqueforti*) are inoculated. Strachitunt instead develops its moulds naturally. This allegedly requires more dexterity and a carefully managed 'stationing' environment. Natural blue moulds develop inside the wheel weighing 6 kilos, about 25 centimetres wide and up to 18 centimetres high, making Strachitunt look like a harder Gorgonzola and endowing it with a sharp taste – not for the uninitiated. Unlike the creamy *strachì quader*, Strachitunt can only be appreciated in small quantities, and defies standardization: not only each wheel, but each *slice* potentially contains devilish sharp mouthfuls of natural 'blue', co-existing with the smouldering proteins that give it the habitual sweet and creamy taste of Taleggio.[3] As the microbiology of each maturing environment is unique, so is the end product, it is claimed. In fact one cannot even predict *if* – let alone how much – a wheel of Strachitunt will actually look blue inside, and hence how (if at all) piquant its slices will be to the mouth.

This natural blue cheese with its complex and unpredictable texture was salvaged from oblivion thanks to a carefully orchestrated and persistent campaign, shared by Slow Food, local refiners and merchants, and nationally profiled chefs and food journalists. As a result, Farmer Guglielmo and his family became prominent in the valley and beyond, cast as 'saviours' of authentic traditional mountain cheese. Guglielmo appeared on local, then national media – including on national television. In the meantime, his four daughters-in-law were staffing the cooperative cheese-shop and the stands at the valley's fairs. I was witnessing the emergence of a local elite, winning all the prizes at the valley's cattle fair, obtaining the presidency of the dairy co-operative, and eventually taking over the abandoned pastures of the neighbours whose heirs had gone to work elsewhere. Kings of a ghost valley, this family, which had once hosted me as a visual anthropology student, and with whom I had lived under the same roof for two consecutive summers in the high pastures as a Ph.D. student in 1997 and 1998, now give testimonials on national television. They are regularly invited to the Slow Food Salone del Gusto in Turin, to the international Cheese fair in Bra, as well as to the global happening Terra Madre – ideated by Carlo Petrini to facilitate peasant networking under the auspices of the Slow Food Foundation for Biodiversity. They also became a testimonial of traditional cheese-making in the recently established Ecomuseum of Valtaleggio. Well beyond starring in my humble student film *Those Who Don't Work, Don't Make Love* (1998), they had been capable of 'seeing bifocally' (Peters 1997): while casting their public peasant persona in a global heritage scenario, they upgraded their herd and scaled up their business, investing in innovative opportunities (including hosting inexperienced apprentices like me and others I met on their premises, some of whom have grown to professional distinction and political engagement, eventually enriching their network.

Despite the key role played by these individual protagonists, Strachitunt was chorally performed. In the following section I describe the public coming of age of Strachitunt as a PDO cheese: the public hearing of the case for Strachitunt, moderated by an officer of the Ministry for Agriculture, at Vedeseta in Val Taleggio. On a cool and sombre day of the fall of 2010, Val Taleggio finally came under the spotlight, called to prove itself as the cohesive community that it never was,[4] to publicly testify to the sheer existence of a cheese of its own. After having failed to profit from Taleggio PDO with much collective chagrin, the entire community of Val Taleggio actually showed up at the public reading of the proposed production protocol for Strachitunt. An act that could have been simply bureaucratic was turned into a collective ritual, almost a public declaration that 'we, the people of Val Taleggio', own Strachitunt and demand public recognition of (at least) that name.

The Public Trial of Strachitunt

On Friday, 29 October 2010, all of Vedeseta's 216 residents and three municipal employees seemed to have rallied for a show of presence. The president of the consortium, who is also the main cheese merchant of the valley and – at the time – also served as president of the valley's Ecomuseum, played the host in the crowded municipal hall. A public hearing had been called according to official procedure – to give anyone the opportunity of claiming a stake to the issue, whether to concede Strachitunt a protected designation of origin. From the start, thanks to the unprecedented participation to the community hearing, the meeting accrued a higher political significance. As it was spelled out by the consortium's president from the outset:

> This is an event that we are sharing today for normative and bureaucratic reasons, but we have engaged in this project in collaboration with four munici-

palities [Taleggio, Vedeseta, Blello and Gerosa] and thanks to the political representatives that have supported this project at local and national level. This is not a project of a single cooperative, or a single producer, or a single consortium, or a single person, but of a locality, of a population, of a history, of a culture. (29 October 2010, Vedeseta Municipal Hall, public meeting, audio-recorded)

In his opening speech, the president of the Strachitunt consortium made reference to the long procedure that began with the establishment of the consortium in October 2002. Some embarrassment was caused by the casual opening remark of the mayor, who, being the official host of the event, spoke first but immediately gave the microphone to the president of the consortium as 'the person directly interested in this matter'. While thanking the local administrations ('some more, some less') for their support, the latter reminded the audience that this was not meant to be a one-man project but a strategic and participated plan for the valley: 'We are very well prepared and have done our homework, we know how to manage a consortium. Our produce is not improvised. We can provide all answers and guarantees. We know how to make it.' He then added, as if to anticipate the critique that PDOs are ill-suited for small productions (on which we return in the following section): 'This product exists, its history exists. Someone makes it, someone will continue to make it. Our milk exists. Volume is not an issue, and was never requested as such.'[5] He continued: 'We want to make good produce according to our capacities. Obviously, this project entails an ambition to develop and to grow, also in terms of the local animal husbandry economy as well as tourism and restaurants.'[6]

After this preamble, he landed a veritable *coup de théâtre* on the audience: 'I have to read out a communication that has just arrived at 9:39 am at the fax of the municipality of Vedeseta, which as you know is the seat of our consortium. It comes from the Comunità Montana Lario Orientale/Valle San Martino.' This mountain community acted as the legal representative of the interests of the dairy cooperatives and milk producers of the neighbouring valleys, lying immediately to the east in the province of Lecco. The upper pastures of these upland communities border with those of Val Taleggio, specifically the Piani di Artavaggio directly across from Mount Resegone and at walking distance from Piani di Bobbio, a well-visited sky-resort particularly popular in the Milanese area. On the basis of this adjacency of producers and pastures, the fax read:

Your product is part of a tradition that belongs also to our mountains. We kindly ask that you expand the area of production as per your protocol to this area, without altering the technical and procedural component of your protocol. We will follow up with a formal request signed by our cooperatives and producers. Signed: The officer responsible for Agriculture of the Mountain

> Community Administration. (Fax read out at the public meeting by the President of the Strachitunt consortium, 29 October 2010, Vedeseta Municipal Hall, audio-recorded).

The Strachitunt consortium president was visibly annoyed and became more so as he read on, shaking the fax in his hands as if the untimely claim was in need of an immediate rebuttal:

> We will verify the historicity of this claim. But I wish to state my surprise! We have studied the history of this cheese, and we know where it was produced. Are we a group of terrorists, having secret meetings to define the history of a cheese? We have sent out invitations and calls for seven years to the neighbouring administrations . . . how can we complain about the future of agriculture if this is the timeliness of their responses?

There followed a very long round of applause from the crammed auditorium. Beyond the apparent untimeliness of this request, the consortium members knew well that a number of exceptions had already been raised by lowland producers wishing to brand their cheese as Strachitunt. More claims from neighbouring upland communities would add to the procedural obstacles, and would slow down even further the achievement of the designation.

By then all the seventy seats were taken and more people kept arriving, adding themselves to the ones already standing at the back – an extraordinary audience indeed for a valley of scarcely 800 residents altogether, between the two municipalities of Taleggio and Vedeseta. This dramatic preamble happened under the eyes of the male functionary of the Ministry for Agriculture that had been appositely sent from Rome, and of two female officers of the Lombardy regional administration who had followed the Strachitunt dossier. Finally given the right to speak, he introduced himself in a Roman accent that those present did not fail to notice, introduced his two colleagues from the Lombardy administration, and asked to take the signatures of all those present. There followed a long pause because photocopies of the production protocol (*disciplinare di produzione*) needed to be provided for all the convened, and this had to be arranged in the municipal offices next door, as the available copies were far outnumbered by the signatories. He then announced that 'today is only a step in the process for the recognition of a Protected Designation of Origin for Strachitunt cheese'. He proceeded to explain very clearly that 'today's public hearing comes as a response to the consortium to have their name registered, firstly by the Lombardy regional government, then, after regional approval was conceded, by the national Ministry'. After the positive evaluation by the regional administration, published in June 2009,[7] the national Ministry of Agriculture had set this date (a year and a half later).

> Hence the open hearing. The protocol is for now a *norma volontaria*, namely the consortium members voluntarily abide to a self-imposed protocol. Today this discipline will be publicly verified and hence published on the *Gazzetta Ufficiale* [the national bulletin that publishes all official ordinances and laws in Italy]. After thirty days, should there be no oppositions or written requests for changes to the protocol, the minister sends the request to the European Commission, *which has its own long and complex procedure*. Once registered by the European Commission, this voluntary discipline becomes binding. That means that in order to brand one's produce as Strachitunt, at that point all producers *must* abide by the protocol – and this will be controlled by a supervisory committee. (Representative of the Ministry of Agriculture, 29 October 2010, Vedeseta Municipal Hall, public meeting, audio-recorded).

Then began the public reading of the production protocol for Strachitunt, as proposed by the consortium. The protocol establishes that Strachitunt is 'produced with the ancient technique of the two curds' (*prodotto con l'antica tecnica delle due paste*) and subsequently matured for at least two and a half months, having as sole area of production the four mountain municipalities of Taleggio, Vedeseta, Gerosa and Blello.

There followed several interventions and interjections, including from the very competitors that had already engaged in a number of regional appeals against the restriction of the Strachitunt area of production to the sole Val Taleggio. 'We humbly ask to continue to produce what we already make' – was the very reasonable stance presented. But the retired primary school teacher of the village, sitting next to me, immediately hissed, 'We already have so little, and these ones from the lowland want to take away even our name, our own identity!' A cow breeder of the neighbouring valleys mentioned in the fax simply stated

> We used to produce Strachitunt too, in our high pastures in Valsassina. We humbly want this production to remain within our circle of small producers, not of merchants and traders who have cut our legs . . . we only heard of this presentation yesterday. Our administrators, as you can see, are not even here . . . (M.vL., 29 October 2010, Vedeseta Municipal Hall, public meeting, audio-recorded)

To these exceedingly humble interventions, there was the immediate retort of the regional administration representative: 'We have given the outmost visibility to this event, it was published in the news of our website' (Dr. Parma, 29 October 2010, Vedeseta Municipal Hall, public meeting, audio-recorded). There were a number of circumstantial supportive interventions from notable speakers, such as a senator of the Republic, the Mountain Community Officer of Agriculture for Val Brembana, and the vice-mayors of both Vedeseta and Blello, two of the municipalities involved in the consortium. Most of them expressed the plight of mountain agriculture *in general*, and listed a number of obstacles to local development, such as bureaucratic permits and audits, as underlined by the president of the regional conservation park of the Orobie Bergamasche. A number of practitioners wished to have their testimony recorded: farmer Placido from Pizzino in Val Taleggio stated that Strachitunt was commonly made up until forty years before, and called *gorgonzola*. The naming issue was brought up again and again . . . why was Strachitunt not so well known? Because it was made under various names, from *gorgonzola* to *strachì-tund*, argued some. But now it must be clear that Strachitunt it is and no other name must be used, not even *Strachitund* with a 'd', which would create consumers' confusion, authoritatively stated a culinary journalist.[8] The same journalist stated that he personally wrote about the Strachitunt production of Val Taleggio in 1985 and that should be enough to testify continuity of production in this locality.

But the main controversy regarded the distinction from competing producers outside Val Taleggio, an issue raised in person by the president of a dairy cooperative in the Bergamasque lowlands. This Latteria Sociale boasts a history of collaboration with the local farmers cooperative and cooperative credit union, and represented three creameries producing Strachitunt. The cooperative's president mentioned literature that testified how already at the end of the nineteenth century, in connection with the transhumance of dairy herds, the winter milk production would be used to make cheese in the lowlands. Thus Strachitunt would have been made by itinerant *Bergamini*, not only in the Bergamasque lowlands but also in the Milanese plains. Moreover, he contended that the Bergamo Chamber of Commerce had already approved a production protocol (*disciplinare di produzione*) for an identically named cheese (Strachitunt) under its trademark *Bergamo Città dei Mille . . . Sapori*, established in 1997 – this protocol allegedly being 'practically identical' to that of Val Taleggio.[9] This trademark did not make any distinction between specific areas of production within the province of Bergamo. Thus it should only be fair to include in the PDO all the producers within the province of Bergamo – he claimed.

In the crowded municipal hall of Vedeseta, the defenders of Val Taleggio's Strachitunt retorted that the chamber of commerce's protocol was not as binding as the PDO. 'The *Città dei Mille . . . Sapori* guidelines are simply a privately agreed code of conduct among members of a collective trademark', spelled out the journalist. He underlined the important distinction between a commercial trademark and a producers' trademark, the latter being more stringent because it also specifies a board that implements controls on protocol abidance. Val Taleggio producers should not be blamed for seeking to establish a more stringent quality certification: the proliferation of commercial trademarks such as those supported by the chamber of commerce, i.e. *Bergamo Città dei Mille . . . Sapori*, confuse the consumers, who are confronted with a plethora of logos and certifications without knowing exactly what is being certified – he claimed. Is it the abidance to the production protocol? Is it the political support from the chamber of commerce? Is it just an agreement between distributors, to pool together under one visual identity? Instead, PDO and PGI are the lawful ways to certify abidance by protocols that the producers have agreed to respect, checked by a control committee.

Historically then, the defenders of the mountain Strachitunt maintained that transhumant herders did not make cheese but simply sold their milk to the big creameries of the lowland such as Invernizzi or Galbani. While some Strachitunt might have been occasionally produced, the law established that a continuous production and commercialization of the product within a certain area for at least twenty-five years had to be documented. Finally, came the decisive argument, namely, the taste of place: 'We privilege a product that is intimately connected to one territory, because of its sensorial characteristics [*caratteristiche organolettiche*]' spelled out the president of the Strachitunt consortium. 'Behind a name there must be a territory: Strachitunt made here is not like Strachitunt made anywhere else' (president of the Strachitunt consortium, 29 October 2010, Vedeseta Municipal Hall, public meeting, audio-recorded).[10]

The conclusive rationale for limiting the area of production was thus spelled out on the consistency of one locality with the taste of the foodstuff manufactured there. This argument was further supported by the municipality of another neighbouring village, Brembilla, notably outside the production protocol area. The councillor for agriculture of Brembilla, himself an agronomy consultant, argued that he was opposed to an enlargement of the production area *even though his municipality would benefit from it*, because as an agronomist he was in favour of conserving *un sistema di allevamento tipico* (a *tipico* breeding system), that of the Brown breed, which is losing out to stronger dairy producers (notably Friesian cows) in the lowlands.[11] One of the notable differences between the two protocols, strengthening the argument of the taste of place, was that Val Taleggio's Strachitunt can only be made from local milk of Brown cows. The very first of the 'characteristics regulated and guaranteed by the Strachitunt Valtaleggio Consortium' in fact is the 'area of production', spelled out as 'the municipalities of Taleggio, Vedeseta, Gerosa and Blello (from 700 to 2000 metres above sea level)'. The same localities are also the 'area of origin of the milk', specifying that the type of cows producing that milk must be 'only Brown Alpine breed'. Furthermore, their diet must be 'mainly grass and hay from the area of production'. These quotes are taken verbatim, in English, from the postcards produced by the Strachitunt consortium as soon as they obtained the PDO 'transitory protection' (*protezione transitoria*: Figure 3). This is a temporary designation that applies the PDO regime nation-wide, while the protocol is being approved at European level.

Milk for the cheese made under the chamber of commerce trademark could come from anywhere within the province of Bergamo; it was not specified which breed should produce the milk; and 'up to 50%' of the hay for the cows' feeding should be from grass growing within the province. While the province of Bergamo is an administrative area of over 2,700 square kilometres inhabited by more than 1 million residents, the four mountain municipalities of the Strachitunt protocol cover about 80 square kilometres with no more than 1,000 inhabitants altogether. By making this distinction, we can understand what seems to be at first sight a hair-splitting controversy, and appreciate the Strachitunt strategy for sovereignty over local economies and environments, which consistently underscored the discourse of this niche PDO.

Finally the main competitor of the concept of a Strachitunt of Val Taleggio spoke. As a winner of several prizes for the excellent quality of his dairy, *his* Strachitunt was acknowledged best cheese in Lombardy already in 2002.[12] He resented that an agreement had not been found between the Val Taleggio consortium and the Chamber of Commerce. This was allegedly a political choice, and the mayor of Taleggio – then president of the Mountain Community of Val Brembana – was named as the main political actor against such agreement. The competitor criticized such politics of territorial exceptionalism, as neither useful to support small producers nor successful commercially. He argued that as vice-president of the consortium for the protection of Taleggio PDO, he could claim that Taleggio cheese is renowned and sold globally thanks to a politics of high volumes and large production areas ('Taleggio cheese is in America because *we* sell it'). He added that his strategic choice is to buy and transform quality milk from smallholders, thus supporting local economies, whether they breed cows in the mountains or in the lowlands. This goes to the benefit of *quality* milk producers, he claimed, while there is no direct connection between keeping the production area small and real economic benefit to smallholders. None of these critiques are easy to rebut, and in fact to these day it is not proven that the PDO strategy will result in a renaissance of the valley, besides benefitting those competitive entrepreneurs who were already emergent protagonists of an otherwise stagnant valley.

After hours of denunciations, lamentations and reciprocal accusations, the laconic comment of the ministry officer was that since the regional administration had already expressed a motivated positive opinion on conceding the PDO, it was not the ministry's responsibility to interrupt the procedure because of lack of local agreement. Exceptions could be filed within thirty days of the publication of the ministry's report on the *Gazzetta Ufficiale*, the law's national bulletin.

In the meantime though, the public hearing of Strachitunt had been successfully turned into the public trial of all those who did *not* want a PDO for the valley. The aseptic procedure of reading out and discussing the production protocol, article by article, gave way to the pleas of the consortium's president, of the dairy farmers, of the local administrators and even of notables appearing for the occasion such as the local representative at the Senate of the Republic. The grievances and passions raised were of another, more encompassing nature than the production protocol of an obscure type of double-paste, natural blue mountain cheese. In effect, the Strachitunt supporters stole the stage from the public officiators, and in turn this reinforced the role of the consortium's president. Had this event been less attended, or the community performance less in tune with his own, his position could have been difficult, owing to the overlapping of many roles in one person, and perhaps it would have backfired with open accusations of conflict of interest. Instead, the event had a concerted and dramatic nature, a choral performance of a community protecting something as intrinsic as their own name.

PDO Italian Style?

Following the public hearing of 29 October 2010, the national decree of the Ministry for Agriculture was published on 21 January 2011 thus giving thirty days for filing exceptions and complaints to the competing dairies of Valsassina in the neighbouring province of Lecco and of the Bergamasque lowlands. Punctually in February 2011, three large dairies filed their official recourse, requesting that the area of production be extended to the entire province of Bergamo as per the previously existing chamber of commerce protocol. This required an evaluation of the counterproposal, a negotiating meeting in Rome (which took place in February 2012), a conclusive evaluation of the request (in May 2012) and a final deliberation, protocolled by the Ministry of Agriculture in September 2012. Only at that point could the request for PDO registration be transmitted to Brussels. The exceptions of the lowland producers, arguing that the transhumant cheese-making tradition itself is the historical source of the dissemination of the Strachitunt recipe straddling mountains and lowlands, were turned down. Strachitunt had finally been decried as *a post-transhumant cheese* of Val Taleggio only.

On 7 March 2014 Strachitunt was officially entered in the European 'Register of protected designations of origin and protected geographical indications' with Commission Regulation (EU) Number 244/2014, published in twenty-three languages.[13] In fact, this was largely a bureaucratic implementation. The decisive step had been made on 19 January 2011 with the announcement on the Italian *Gazzetta Ufficiale* (the national registry of laws) that the Italian Ministry of Agriculture had granted Strachitunt the transitory status of a protected designation of origin (PDO), preliminarily valid within the national borders.[14] This is the standard procedure to grant PDO denominations, as they are examined and approved first at regional level, then at national level, and finally acquired at European level if no competing claims are raised. That more than two years elapsed even to complete the last stage is a symptom of how fraught this acquisition was, including a one-and-a-half-year-long appeal from a competing producer that was left out of the production area.

Figure 3. Front and back of a postcard produced by the Strachitunt consortium (Sagra dello Strachitunt, October 2013). 'Protezione transitoria' is visible in small letters under 'DOP'.

The final granting of PDO status was celebrated in the local press, notably the province-wide *L'Eco di Bergamo* that had covered the vicissitudes of the consortium since the alleged claim that Strachitunt was the best cheese in Italy. Strachitunt is variously described as *il gioiello della Val Taleggio* (Val Taleggio's jewel), *vaccino erborinato a latte crudo* (raw, cow-milk blue cheese), or *il papà del gorgonzola* (Gorgonzola's Dad). 'Now we have to aim to produce up to 8,000 wheels a year', one reads in the accompanying interviews,[15] and this gives a sense of how local is the significance of this economy.[16] However, the political significance of obtaining a protected designation for a tiny production is signalled by the fact that it was the newly nominated Minister for Agriculture, a man from Bergamo, to announce the news.[17] After the PDO was conferred to Val Taleggio only, the lowland homonymous production had to change its name. The designation Strachitunt is, as the acronym says, protected against producers outside the authorized production zone who might want to call their produce with the same name. Thus the chamber of commerce changed its production protocol to '*erborinato bergamasco*' while the lowland competitor established its own trademark, *Blutunt.* 'Erborinato' means 'with moulds' or simply 'blue cheese', a category under which Gorgonzola or Stilton would fall.

What makes Strachitunt unique? Its protocol is characterized by the *lack* of certain ingredients (notably lactic cultures) and standard procedures (notably pasteurization): it must be made with 'full-fat raw (unpasteurized) milk, worked at the temperature of the animal (not cooled or heated) of a single milking (*a munta calda*), with rennet and salt. Lactic cultures are not used'. The only margin left to discretion is the diet of the cows: milk must be from cows of 'only Brown Alpine breed', whose diet must be '*mainly* grass and hay from the area of production'. Considering the local tendency to abandon local pastures for imported alfalfa grass and hay, this clause leaves the local breeders time to reverse-engineer their logistics of production. With the prospect of increasing the cattle units in the valley, the farmers left in the valley could reasonably invest more on local grasslands and thus reclaim pasture land from encroaching woods and shrubs.

However, as I will show in Chapter 5, on this very clause local negotiations to obtain a Slow Food Presidium for Strachitunt had ground to a halt a decade before. Strachitunt had been showcased at the Slow Food Salone del Gusto in October 2004 in Turin, and at the Cheese fair at Bra in 2003. But the Slow Food expectation that the cows' diet would not include any fodder, at least during the *alpeggio*, was considered taxing by local producers, who had invested on high-yield cows which in turn 'simply cannot live on grass alone'. Glossing over the issue of fodder in the protocol, and not even prescribing that *all* the grass comes from Val Taleggio, had been a necessary compromise to establish the Strachitunt coalition. The result is a stress on the dairy technique rather than on the production's ecology. Strachitunt is referred to as 'blue cheese obtained from combining curds from two stages twelve hours apart [*due paste*]', namely a 'natural blue cheese' or 'the father of Gorgonzola'. This cheese *could* be beneficial to local development, but would not *per se* engender it. While the consortium hopes to set in motion a virtuous circle leading to the renaissance of Val Taleggio, it can for now only insist on the uniqueness of the dairy technique and of its clear boundaries, while it does not *prescribe* a more sustainable use of the local territory. The postcard in Figure 4 defines Strachitunt as 'a precious gem of the cheese-making tradition of Val Taleggio, more than 1,000 years old'. The antiquity claim ennobles the recipe and technique of curdling, maturing and refining, but distracts from the issue of the raw material.

Size and weight was always a matter of distinction for the Val Taleggio producers, who scorned their lowland competitors for 'making Strachitunt the size of a *formagella*' (Lucia, cheese entrepreneur, 1 September 2006). Size is not a capricious decision. It has important impact on transportation, logistics and marketability: smaller sizes always sell better in today's customized market. The round wheel is much heavier and bigger than a 'square' *strachì*, more difficult to transport and longer to mature. The option of Strachitunt was to keep the prestigious size and weight of an upland cheese. However, only over a year after

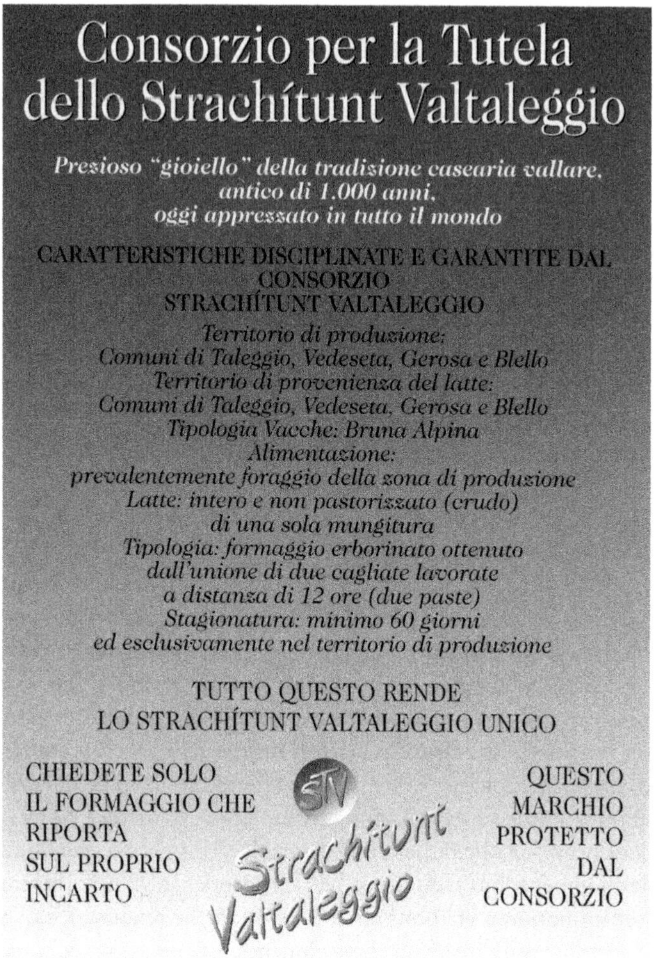

Figure 4. Promotional postcard for Strachitunt, Slow Food Salone del Gusto, 21 October 2004.

the PDO was bestowed, the consortium had to rather sheepishly file for a modification of the production protocol 'for commercial reasons', to decrease the height of the wheels, as it appeared that they had shrunk in actual practice, as reported in the local paper.[18] The maturation time of Strachitunt also adapted itself to PDO strategy. The PDO protocol sets it to seventy-five days (as it is for Blutunt), but it was 'minimum 60 days' in 2004 when it was presented at the Slow Food Salone del Gusto in Turin (see Figure 4).[19] Strachitunt lowered the ageing period as much as possible to keep up with the competition while maintaining the length of a respectable upland cheese, with recommended three months and up to five as I noted down in interviews in 2006, and of which we find trace in the guided gustatory 'suasion' of a tasting session held in Turin in 2004 (described in Chapter 5).

These strategic recalibrations are not the only reason for which 'PDOs Italian style' came under critical spotlight. Strachitunt obtained a Europe-wide protected designation of origin for a consortium of eleven members, including three refiners, six dairy farmers, two cheese-makers – one a cooperative and one family enterprise that is also the valley's major milk producer. Certainly this comes to the rescue of artisan local production. In the local press, the fact that the province of Bergamo hosts nine PDO cheeses is often mentioned as proof of a 'dairy leadership' over the competing mountainous areas of Cuneo in Piedmont and Brescia in Lombardy, with 'only' seven and five PDO cheeses each. But there are vocal critics of this 'protected denomination Italian style', as Strachitunt brings the number of Italian PDO products to 261.

In a press article entitled 'Quando la Dop all'Italiana rischia il flop' (PDO Italian-style risks a flop), representatives of Nomisma, a socio-economic research group founded in the 1980s under the auspices of the Banca Nazionale del Lavoro, underlined how this kind of niche-PDO are trademarks for conservation rather than for product development ('marchi di tutela, non di lancio dei prodotti', Di Mambro 2009). In other words, it would be unthinkable to imagine that a substantial growth in Strachitunt production would follow the bestowing of the PDO, considering how small the production area actually is. However, the consortium members hoped that the forthcoming universal Exposition (Expo 2015) held in 2015 in Milan on the topic of 'Feeding the Planet' would be a significant boost for Strachitunt sales, and already boasted orders from the United States, Canada, Japan and – in Europe – the Netherlands and Germany. For example, it was anticipated that the long-standing interest for Strachitunt cheese on the part of Slow Food, even though it did not develop into a presidium, would grant it a placement among the permanent Slow Food exhibition of Italian 'food excellence' in the Italian pavilion.[20]

The accusation of being a PDO 'Italian style' deserves contextualizing. In 2003, there were 153 Italian protected designations altogether (this is inclusive of three typologies of protected designations, namely 'protected designations of origin' or PDO, 'protected geographical indications' or IGT, and 'guaranteed traditional specialties' or STG). Gambera and Surra, in a Slow Food–sponsored handbook for cheese connoisseurs, list the thirty Italian PDO cheeses that were originally registered in 1996 – eight of which are produced in Lombardy.[21] These original repertoires featured both broad commercial productions such as Taleggio (but also Gorgonzola, Grana Padano or Parmigiano Reggiano), and niche productions of upland communities such as Formai de Mut of the Upper Val Brembana and Bitto. From this point of view, Strachitunt seems to be perfectly legitimated to feature alongside other minuscule mountain dairy products such as Formai de Mut. But the fact that ten years later there are 264 Italian PDO foods provides the proverbial food for thought.

Specifically regarding cheese, the debate turned once more on what makes a cheese *tipico*. If any cheese can be *tipico*, then what is an non-*tipico* cheese? In 2007 there were thirty-one Italian PDO cheeses altogether (with the only addition of Ricotta Romana, Roman cottage cheese). An update at the end of 2012 counted forty-six (still excluding Strachitunt, which obtained its PDO in 2014): the number of PDOs had increased by 50 per cent in five years. It was largely understood in the circle of professional operators that being registered in the lists of national and regional traditional products would be important, not so much in terms of obtaining a quality certification, as much as to qualify for national exceptions to the many forms of auditing, which many felt were more apt for large industrial concerns than for family entrepreneurs or village cooperatives.

As we have seen, since the 1990s,[22] EU regulations began to introduce stringent safety criteria for food production, introducing self-auditing practices such as HACCP (Hazard Analysis Critical Control Points) at every level of production. Certifying traditional products seemed an efficacious means to keep draconian applications of EU hygiene laws at bay to preserve niche productions. By certifying exceptional conditions and contexts, national and regional authorities could claim that traditional products should be exempted from an immediate implementation. This argument won over time, and exemptions were made.[23]

However, after ten years, critics noticed that there seemed to be more 'certified traditional cheeses' than actually known cheeses! A national list of traditional food products of Italy, published in 2000, identified about five hundred cheeses as 'traditional products': municipalities, province administrations and regional councils, as well as Mountain Communities and Chambers of Commerce, were concurring to map and identify as many traditional products as possible.[24] *Caseus*, the professional magazine of the National Organization of Cheese Tasters (ONAF), denounced in 2006 that only about four hundred cheeses altogether had been previously catalogued by independent associations, quoting the Slow Food cheese atlas as a more representative picture than the national list of the traditional food products of the Ministry for Agriculture.[25] ONAF experts warned against the commercial implications of this largely political strategy. They felt that the proliferation of certifications of traditional status, bestowed by a number of agencies, could only disorient the customer if it was not substantiated by clear categories and a well-grounded fame for their products. This debate resurfaced at the public hearing described in the previous section, when it was argued that the chamber of commerce protocol alone did not provide the quality assurance of a PDO.

One category that is evoked with mixed feelings by professional operators is that of the *nostrano*: anyone can claim that their products are *nostrani*, as the word literally means 'our own'. Once a common-sense word for local products, implying a genuine provenance and skilled craft, the same word is now looked down on by more refined cultures of food quality. Discerning marketers want to avoid the category of the *nostrano*, which evokes simplistic operations of ambiguous quality such as the kind of 'local foods' one finds at the proliferating *sagre*, popular feasts that include selling and consuming food or beverages on special occasions or calendar events. Seasonal foods usually feature: as in *sagra della castagna*, the chestnut fair, or *sagra del fungo*, the mushroom fair. The occasion may mark a traditional milestone in the agrarian cycle, such as St. Martin's Day, or local religious celebrations (such as the many patron saint feasts that are organized at municipal or village level), but can also be newly set up (the Strachitunt *sagra* began to be officiated every October in 2006). Superseding parish-church communal meals on festive days, the business of *sagre* has taken off at a national level, reaching its seasonal peak in the summers. An exposé in the national press denounced in 2013 'the business of 30,000 *sagre*. Restaurant owners appeal to the antitrust authority: it is untaxed, unfair competition and typical meals [*il piatto tipico*] are by now a chimera'.[26]

For small producers such as mountain cheese-makers, however, savvier marketing than '*sagra*-business' requires all-year-round logistics and investments. Assuring consistent and recognizable imagery (both of the product and of its packaging and associated visual identity) mean sizable expenses for professional photography, publicity, translations, packaging paper and brochures. Logos carry a political as well as graphic importance and the protagonists in the trade, as we shall see in Part III, are highly aware of it. However, traditional producers should also have enough human resources to be able to be visible at a number of events, from local festivals to commercial fairs, with stands and tasting sessions, giving out literature, nibbles or gadgets.

A number of local administrations support these efforts with territorial trademarks. For example, the certification 'produce of Val Brembana' was launched as early as 1998 by the Mountain Community of Val Brembana (of which Val Taleggio is a branch). In December 2004, according to conversations with local operators of the mountain bureau, the trademark did not seem to have quite taken off commercially. As participating in the consortium is a service, producers had to pay a fee and were not so keen to do so without a return in increased sales. Successively, the trademark became increasingly prominent at the province-wide yearly Agricultural fair of Bergamo (Fiera di Sant'Alessandro) as well as in local tourist events such as Festinvalle. Trademarked products of Valle Brembana are especially its mountain cheeses, but also organic fruit and vegetables and other local goods such as honeybee-based beauty products and wood furniture. At the time of writing, the list of trademarked produce has risen from the initial dozen to 45, including 11 goat cheese producers and 18 cow cheese producers respectively, of course enlisting the Strachitunt consortium too.[27]

The logic of local trademarks is not free of political considerations and participates in the many controversies over territorial exceptionalism. So for instance the Bergamo Chamber of Commerce trademark *Bergamo Città dei Mille . . . Sapori* was mentioned both in the Branzi and in the Strachitunt controversy: competing consortia called upon the authority of the chamber or vice versa dismissed it as a matter of 'getting there first'.[28] As explained in the previous section, the lowland competitors of Strachitunt upheld this trademark to argue that the PDO production area should have been consistent with it. The competitors proved valiant, reaping prizes for their Strachitunt and profiling themselves as potential 'heirs' of the cheese-making skills of Val Taleggio. Not coincidentally, their website boasts that their cheese is 'son of Taleggio and father of Gorgonzola'.[29] Both cheeses count on the distinctive recipe of combining curd from the night before with curd from the morning milking (as dairy farming usually prescribes milking twice a day). This family enterprise also boasts continuous cheese-making tradition over four generations, its own European quality certification, as well as a newly restructured site of production (entirely rebuilt in 1994). Its 'dairy excellence' was acknowledged on the pages of the local newspaper by nationally esteemed culinary expert Edoardo Raspelli. The producer's website boasts that their Blutunt, when it was still legally called Strachitunt, reaped prizes from 2002 to 2014, from Milan's Expo of Taste (Expo dei sapori) to Slow Food's own blue cheese excellence diploma (Diploma di Eccellenza Slow Food Infiniti Blu). To bestow a PDO to Val Taleggio only was in their words 'a great lost chance for our territory':

> I have always maintained it and I am not the only one, since Bergamo's Chamber of Commerce has time ago listed our Bergamasque Strachitunt in its trademark *Città dei Mille . . . Sapori*, without posing any internal boundaries to its geographical area of pertinence: the entire province of Bergamo. We could have just all got along, working on the production protocol, and avoid this diaspora. What is the need for a PDO? What did this cheese need protecting against? We are talking about niche products, minimal quantities that is absurd to aggravate with unnecessary costs. (M. T., published interview in Ghezzi 2013: 7).

This argument rehearses the logic used in many similar conflicts between niche producers on the one side, and a wider pool of production capacities and commercial potential on the other, as in the case of the Bitto *querelle*. In 2014, with 47 PDO cheeses and a total of 264 protected foodstuffs (among PDOs, PGIs and TSGs) plus 523 protected wines (among DOCG, DOC, and IGT), Italy is the European country with the highest number of food products recognized by the European Union with a designation of origin or a geographical indication. This is underlined with pride on the relevant website of the Ministry for Agriculture 'as a demonstration of the high quality of our products and especially of the strong tie between Italian agro-food excellence to its territory of origin'.[30] The web page spells out further that 'the EU system of geographical indications favours the productive system and the economy of the territory, it safeguards the environment because this indissoluble link with the territory of origin demands the conservation of biodiversity and local ecosystems; it supports the social cohesion of the entire community. At the same time, thanks to the EU certification, consumers have a higher guarantee of traceability and food safety'.[31]

What is then Strachitunt? Is it the best cheese in Italy, the noble heir of a lost transhumant tradition, or is it 'a PDO Italian style'? PDO seems to be one of the tools that marginalized producers, disgruntled administrators, visionary merchants, celebrity chefs, activist scholars and paladin journalists may use to achieve possibly divergent objectives: economic survival, demographic salvage, a growth in business, more celebrity, the defence of a just cause and a good long saga to report on. Crucially, as shown in the previous section, such conflicting views and interests can synergize during key turning points, whether public events or private negotiations. These political dynamics can and do determine the fate of the cheese makers.

Notes

1. The consortium's website maintains a collection of press releases ranging from the local newspaper *L'Eco di Bergamo* to the professional magazine *Affari di Gola*, where it is reported that even before a consortium was created in Val Taleggio, chef Vissani claimed during his visit to the valley that the best cheeses in Italy come from the Bergamasque mountains and that *Strachì Tunt* [*sic*] is the best. Retrieved 15 August 2014 from http://strachitunt.it/.
2. *L'Eco di Bergamo* 25 August 2013, 11.
3. Two theses were written on Strachitunt by two students of Food Science at Milan University, about its historical origins and its microbiology. Both graduates became dairy consultants (at different times) for the Strachitunt consortium. See Belotti (2000) and Pesenti (2002).
4. This may sound like a sarcastic remark, but historically Val Taleggio was divided by no less than a national border for four centuries. The state border between the Dukedom of Milan and the Republic of Venice literally divided the valley in two halves, roughly corresponding to the current two municipalities of Taleggio (Venetian and Guelph) and Vedeseta (Milanese and Ghibellin). Popularly felt distinctions and animosity between the two communities are still celebrated, while border-stones (affectionately called *termenù*) are still visible in the pastures.
5. 'Il prodotto c'è, la storia c'è, c'è chi lo fa, c'è chi lo farà in futuro. Il latte esiste, i volumi non sono una questione, non ci sono mai stati richiesti.' 29 October 2010, Vedeseta Municipal Hall, president of the Strachitunt consortium, audio-recorded public speech.
6. 29 October 2010, Vedeseta Municipal Hall, public hearing.

7. Decreto della Direzione Generale Agricoltura n. 5101 del 22/05/2009, BURL n. 23 – Serie Ordinaria – 8/06/2009.
8. E. G., 29 October 2010, Vedeseta Municipal Hall, public hearing, audio-recorded. To be sure, the two theses devoted to Strachitunt production in Val Taleggio, defended in 2000 and 2002, both spell '*strachìtund*' with a d (Belotti 2000; Pesenti 2002), while the press reported the double name '*Strachì Tunt*' a number of times. At least initially it seemed more important to stress that Strachitunt was a kind of round-shaped *stracchino*, hence in line with the valley's historical production of 'Stracchino di Taleggio', and this is much clearer if the word *strachì* clearly appears as part of the name.
9. This is the date indicated by the Bergamo Chamber of Commerce. Retrieved 8 May 2015 from http://www.bg.camcom.gov.it/macroaree/promozione-e-ambiente/marchi-di-qualita/prodotti-dei-mille-sapori/.
10. 'Come viene qui lo Strachitunt non viene in nessun altro posto', president of the Strachitunt consortium, 29 October 2010, Vedeseta Municipal Hall public hearing, audio-recorded.
11. P. M., E. G., 29 October 2010, Vedeseta Municipal Hall, public hearing, audio-recorded.
12. Retrieved 8 May 2015 from http://www.caseificiotaddei.it/prodotti/blutunt.html This website lists more recent prizes including a silver medal at the UK World Cheese Award.
13. The implementing regulation is viewable at: http://eur-lex.europa.eu/legal-content/EN/TXT/;jsessionid=WhqQTD0Rqst1TKkhNdRgndZyY4vwJ4dMPJ02gCg1djWnm9FtM6q8!-451414052?uri=uriserv:OJ.L_.2014.074.01.0031.01.ENG, retrieved 26 May 2014.
14. Ministero delle Politiche Agricole, Alimentari e Forestali. Comunicato: 'Proposta di riconoscimento della denominazione di origine protetta "Strachitunt" (11A00491)', *Gazzetta Ufficiale Serie Generale* n.14 del 19–1-2011.
15. Maurizio Ferrari, 'Strachitunt, c'è l'OK di Bruxelles. Ora la Dop vale in tutta Europa', *L'Eco di Bergamo*, 15 March 2014.
16. Maurizio Ferrari, 'E' Dop: Strachitunt nella storia', *L'Eco di Bergamo*, 21 January 2011.
17. 'La Val Taleggio esulta: Strachitunt è Dop a livello europeo', Bergamonews, 14 March 2014. Retrieved 26 May 2014 from www.bergamonews.it.
18. *L'Eco di Bergamo*, 7 August 2015: from the original height of 15 to 18 centimetres, the production had to stop to request a lower height of 10 to 18 centimetres (keeping the diameter of 25 to 28 centimetres and consequently diminishing its weight to between 4 and 6 kilograms).
19. A list of prizes won, and a technical description of the production protocol for Blutunt are online on the website of the dairy that produces it: http://www.caseificiotaddei.it/prodotti/blutunt.html, retrieved 21 August 2014.
20. 'Expo 2015 con i Formaggi Orobici, degustazioni al via della rassegna', http://forum.valbrembanaweb.com/novita-valle-brembana-f52/news-cronaca-dalla-valle-brembana-t5406–405.html, retrieved 26 May 2014.
21. Gambera and Surra (2003: 224–25). This happened in two instalments, namely on 12 June 1996 and 1 July 1996 respectively with European Community (CE) Regulation 1107 and 1263.
22. See directive 93/43/CEE of the Council of Europe, 14 June 1993, on food products hygiene.
23. The European Community regulation CE N. 852 of 2004, while regarding HACCP as a universal method for producer's self-regulation (identifying critical control points in the

production of foodstuffs for commercial sales), concedes exceptions to small productions and gives the nation-states margins to legislate on exceptions, specifically to allow the continuation of 'traditional methods' and to keep into consideration the added hurdles of 'food enterprises located in regions with particular geographical aggravations' (art. 13.4, retrieved 31 July 2014 from http://www.agroqualita.it/doc/reg_ce_852_2004.pdf).

24. The list of traditional food products of Lombardy was established in 2000 following national legislation, namely Minister's Decree (DM) n. 350 of 8 September 1999. This called on regional authorities to establish a national list of traditional food products, which were not protected by European designations such as PDO, PGI or TSG. This list, *Elenco dei Prodotti Agroalimentari Tradizionali della Regione Lombardia*, was published by the Lombardy regional government on 21 April 2000 in Supplement n.5 to Bulletin n.16. It was then included in the national list of traditional food products by Minister's Decree on 18 July 2000. Regional decree number 241 of 8 June 2004 (Supplement to the *Bollettino Ufficiale della Regione Lombardia*) regulated how this list should be updated over time. A first revised list was published with Minister's Decree n. 174 of 2005. The ninth update for Lombardy, published in March 2014, includes 264 traditional food products. Retrieved 20 June 2014 from http://www.agricoltura.regione.lombardia.it/cs/Satellite?c=Redazionale_P&childpagename=DG_Agricoltura%2FDetail&cid=1213305628183&pagename=DG_AGRWrapper.
25. R. Rubino, *Caseus*, n. 4, 2006, 1.
26. Corrado Zunino, 'Il business delle trentamila sagre. Esposto dei ristoratori all'Antitrust. 'Concorrenza sleale e niente tasse'. Confcommercio: ormai il piatto tipico è un'illusione', *La Repubblica*, 15 August 2013, 25.
27. A full list is made available on the website of the Mountain Community administration. Retrieved 21 June 2014 from http://www.vallebrembana.com/export/sites/default/agricoltura/documenti/Brochure-Prodotti_2010L.pdf.
28. 'City of a Thousand Flavours' refers to the historical motto of Bergamo, 'City of the Thousand' (*Città dei Mille*), Bergamo having contributed a consistent number of volunteers to the thousand-strong brigade that Giuseppe Garibaldi led to Sicily in 1860, as part of a successful military campaign that ultimately resulted in the unification of Italy under the Savoy.
29. http://www.mangiartipico.it/prodotti/formaggi/strachitunt.html#tabs-1.
30. http://www.politicheagricole.it/flex/cm/pages/ServeBLOB.php/L/IT/IDPagina/309, retrieved 1 August 2014.
31. http://www.politicheagricole.it/flex/cm/pages/ServeBLOB.php/L/IT/IDPagina/309, retrieved 1 August 2014.

Conclusion of Part II

Obtaining a status of territorial exception for Strachitunt was a strategic and political choice whose significance is not exhausted in a marketing strategy. Unsurprisingly, the market reveals itself as an arena where much more than money is exchanged or is at stake – as the furious schoolteacher of Val Taleggio reminded me when she accused 'those lowland merchants' of trying to steal Val Taleggio's own name from their inhabitants.

This strategy was complicated by the fact that Val Taleggio is not so much known as a cheese-*making* valley as much as a cheese-*maturing* location, where to this day the five to six family enterprises that package and distribute various types of cheese certainly *mature* it in the valley, but don't necessarily *make* it there. While there is nothing dishonourable about it, the territorial exception of defending the borders of Val Taleggio as a specific area of production was complicated by an established practice of mobility and labour division, by which the most established cheese-refiners and merchants in Val Taleggio were not necessarily local cheese-makers too. Both in the case of the upland cheeses discussed in Part I (Bitto, Formai de Mut and Branzi) and in the case of the lowland cheeses introduced in Part II (Taleggio, *stracchino*) we appreciated how transhumant herding mobilized techniques and genealogies of cheese-making, both in the uplands and in the lowlands of Lombardy. Reinventing Strachitunt thus meant responding to the need of territorial branding by at once differentiating it from the ubiquitous Taleggio *and* also establishing a novel, sedentary tradition: cheese made within Val Taleggio, matured in Val Taleggio, with milk from cows fed in Val Taleggio.

Comparisons are instructive. When the 'Bitto Rebels' were heralded by Slow Food activists as 'resisting cheese-makers', the cheese-makers of Val Taleggio were still striving for visibility. Their timid attempts to revamp a 'Taleggio cheese truly from Val Taleggio' was censored by the Taleggio PDO consortium, but did not grant them per se the external support that would cast them as heroes in an epic David-versus-Goliath battle against a large PDO consortium.

In fact, as we shall see in Part III, right from the beginning Slow Food was part of the local deliberations on how to best strategize to reappropriate a cheese that would bear the valley's own name. However, uncertain between accepting Slow Food's uncompromising agenda or fighting through their wars with lowland competitors to obtain a Strachitunt PDO on their own terms, the Val Taleggio cheese-makers muddled through claims for exceptions and premature announcements. An alliance between milk producers, cheese-makers and refiners proved laborious despite, or probably *because of* the very local nature of this coalition. Not only the complexity of the regulatory context, but also the fraught relations between some of the cheese merchants and the exceptions of some of the producers made many doubt the success of the PDO project. In the meantime, the population of Val Taleggio continued to shrink, and the bush continued to encroach the pastureland.

As we shall see next, these contested choices, as well as what were perceived as 'elitist' and 'primitivistic' understandings of how to salvage mountain farming, came to the surface at key ethnographic moments during the eleven-year-long process of obtaining the Strachitunt PDO. In order to fully appreciate *how* and *why* serendipitous convergences over name-sovereignty alternate with long-drawn enmities and legal exceptions, we must take a further ethnographic step. The language of *tipicità* and *patrimonio* would not by themselves do the cultural work of heritage distinction, without a corresponding discourse and practice of sensorial discernment. Far from spontaneous, this is also appropriated and performed to substantiate claims to territorial exceptionalism and dairy excellence. The heritage arena is then shaped by the ways in which the actors involved position themselves and make food heritage visible, felt and tasted.

PART

III

Dulcamara's Senses

CHAPTER 5

Marketing the Sensorium

Gaetano Donizetti is Bergamo's musical heritage: a cosmopolitan author of several melodramas, after whom the town's municipal theatre is named. In Donizetti's opera *L'Elisir d'Amore*, Dulcamara is the charlatan who sells love potions: the *elisir*. Dulcamara is also the name of a poison; in Italian, this sounds as an odd combination of sweet (*dolce*) and bitter (*amaro*).[1] Bittersweet is the aftertaste of the cheese wars I was witness to – the toxic collaborations and exasperated competition that sealed fates and made fortunes, in the name of *patrimonio* and *tipicità*.

Since my initial fieldwork in the Lombard Alps in 1997, I observed a momentous transformation in Val Taleggio, as my hosts were confronted with more and more stringent 'audit cultures' (Strathern 2000): visits by the breeders association to update the herd book; quality checks on the milk; loans for a bigger shed to accommodate the bigger, 'improved' cows and a milking parlour; then liaising with local politicians and farmers' trade unions to apply for European agricultural aid to service such loans. For *pater familias* Guglielmo and for the rest of the family, becoming the saviours of Strachitunt was just a tussle in a complex winning strategy that saw them excel as intensive milk producers (by mountain standards) while in the same breath being heralded as testimonials of a revered tradition.

An important part of this competitive performance was the need to market a complex sensorium to convey Strachitunt's uniqueness. The 2015 catalogue entry for Casarrigoni describes Strachitunt as a 'Traditional, naturally marbled 'double-paste' cheese', insisting that 'until a few decades ago, local dairy production was mainly focused on *stracchino* cheeses – called *Tunt* or *Quader* (round or square) depending on their shape. Strachitunt or "round stracchino" takes its name from this tradition.' Alongside such continuity, the entry insists on the 'naturally irregular marbling' granted by the dairy technique and by the raw milk. 'The aroma is characteristic of marbled cheeses, beginning with slightly milky hints followed by metallic tones. The flavour is aromatic and intense, ranging from mild to sharp depending on the degree of aging, fragrant and melt-in-your-mouth with a pleasant vegetal aftertaste.'[2] Consistent with the long-term strategy of reappropriating the stolen tradition of the *stracchini di Taleggio*, at a cheese-tasting session of the Slow Food Salone del Gusto of October 2004 the valley's dairy tradition was presented as producing two types of *strachì*: the round (*tund*) and the square (*quader*). The following section analyses that very cheese-tasting session (*Laboratorio del Gusto*), in which I took part.

Part III complicates the story of Strachitunt, as we learn that the Val Taleggio producers turned down speedier ways to obtain a commercial premium on their cheese – notably through a Slow Food presidium. Negotiations to set one up failed, because local farmers wanted to preserve their production routines, including substantial choices in favour of intensive milk production and progeny breed selection – according to a lowland model of productivity that farmers have been inculcated with since the 1960s. Paradoxically, it is precisely by these industrial standards that mountain agriculture is still by and large judged as unproductive and uneconomical – in one word, marginal. The strategic choice of Val Taleggio was not to profile themselves as 'upland cheese-makers' only. They decided to trademark *all* of the valley's Strachitunt production, not just the *alpeggio* season. Their reinvention of Strachitunt was thoroughly post-transhumant: it extolled the virtues and historicity of their mountain tradition, but did not establish a distinction between high-pasture production and winter production. It established a distinction between their area of production and the lowland producers based on 'a metaphysics of sedentarism' (Malkki 1992) rather than a recognition of the many borrowings and fluidities of a transhumant circulation of people, knowledge and cattle.

Slow Food and the Geometry of Val Taleggio

'. . . And tell me, by the way, do you think that Slow Food is acting wisely here?' Ugo pressed.[3] By 2006, cheese diatribes emerged as a fixture in the field of forces slowly redetermining the fates and fortunes of Val Taleggio. People who knew me well felt free to have an honest conversation, eliciting my own views on thorny and divisive subjects, such as why Slow Food had promoted the cause of Bitto Storico but failed to set up a presidium for Strachitunt in Valtaleggio, after supporting the 'reinvention' of this cheese as early as 2003.

> What happened with the plan for a Strachitunt presidium, you ask? There was a plan for presiding only the Strachitunt made *in alpeggio* . . . Preservation is ok, but there can be excess in protection [*tutela*]. They are a bit Taliban, they just wanted to make a presidium for the upland cheese. Cheese made in a certain way, only in the summer, only in the high pastures, with cows only eating grass . . . it was too restrictive. (Aronne, 11 August 2006)

Since this negotiation failed, the valley's main merchant had deserted the Cheese fair in Bra of 2005 and the Slow Food Salone del Gusto of 2006 in Turin. The Cheese fair only hosted the artisanal production of the one farming family in Val Taleggio making Strachitunt in *alpeggio*, and the diminished significance of this vis-à-vis the fate of the valley and its dairy economy was apparent to everyone, especially if contrasted with the veritable public debut of Strachitunt that Slow Food had choreographed in the framework of their Salone del Gusto just a couple of years before. What could have happened in less than two years, to justify such a fallout? Why was the president of the valley's dairy cooperative calling 'Taliban' the very Slow Food activists who had invested time, energy and resources in making the plight of Val Taleggio public?

On 21 October 2004, the Val Taleggio cooperative, the valley's main merchant and my host family had profiled together at Turin's Salone del Gusto – the renowned biennial Slow Food fair. Together, they had presented a session of guided tasting (*degustazione guidata*) of Stracchino di Vedeseta (notably, not Taleggio) from the valley's cooperative and Strachitunt made by farmer Guglielmo. The cheeses of Val Taleggio were featured in one of eighteen *Laboratori del Gusto* (Taste Labs), as part of Slow Food's initiatives to disseminate knowledge about 'the excellence of national artisanal food production' (*l'eccellenza della produzione artigiana nazionale*), offering wine and food coupled in guided tasting sessions presented by experts, producers, farmers, wine-makers and refiners. It was an important acknowledgement to the existence and relevance of Strachitunt. The session, which I filmed and recorded, was entitled 'The Geometry of Val Taleggio: *Strachì tunt* and *strachì quader*'. It was introduced by a high-ranking representative of Bergamo's Slow Food convivium, together with representatives of the Strachitunt consortium and of the valley's dairy cooperative, as well as the cheese merchant in person who was publicly credited for the 'commercial renaissance of Strachitunt'.

As stated right from the start of the *Laboratorio del Gusto* by the chair of the session, 'the heart of the issue here is the protection of these products', 'a fundamental economy for this area' that is 'representative of the Bergamasque territory'. A Strachitunt producer, Aronne (a pseudonym) was introduced as a *malgaro*, a transhumant cheese-maker, and thanked for the sacrifices of taking the family herd to the *alpeggio*. With well-rehearsed simplicity he stated:

> We have always made these cheeses, *strachì tunt* and *strachì quader* or *stracchino*. My father has made them all his life and my son goes with him to the *alpeggio*. Keep in mind that when we are at our winter station, we say *fondovalle*, bottom of the valley, but that means 1,000 meters above sea level. When we are in the high pastures we are at 2,000 meters. So life is pretty hard all year round. There you go, I am not a born Cicero.[4] (Aronne, a pseudonym. Salone del Gusto Slow Food, 21 October 2004, video-recorded)

He reaped a hearty applause. About fifty preregistered workshop participants sat in orderly rows as if in school desks, each supplied with a palette of six slices and three degustation glasses, paper documentation and headphones for both amplification and translation (at least two of them spoke no Italian – they told me they came from Australia). The audience was reminded by a gastronomy journalist, introduced as 'the culinary expert who has most worked and long striven for the cause of Strachitunt', that Slow Food's Salone del Gusto acquires novel and militant meaning in conjunction with the peasants assembly of Terra Madre:

> Those who still live this life merit every encouragement and our friendship. These are niche products and precisely because of this we must support them. His family makes sacrifices, not gains. These people have defended their territory with passion, they have defended these products, and deserve to be thanked. (E. G., Salone del Gusto Slow Food, 21 October 2004, video-recorded)

He then framed product identity as an issue of territorial defence and environmental conservation:

> The only way we can safeguard a territory is to safeguard the human presence on that territory. That means paying those who work on that land for what it costs them to produce their cheese. This is why we need to demand information, we need to know what we eat and *how* what we pay for is produced. That is how we can preserve the transhumant ecosystem [*l'ecosistema delle malghe*]. (E. G., Salone del Gusto Slow Food, 21 October 2004, video-recorded)

Commercial promotion through the protection of specific enclaves, combined with fair pricing, is believed to be the main alley to sustain an entire cultural economy and its environmental knowledge about locality, seasonality and sustainability. In fact, the presidia system is named after such notion, of a stronghold that can be presided over. On another occasion, a Slow Food activist spelled out their conservation mission in these terms: 'We do not forgo quality, but then we can reason about price' (Iva, a pseudonym, 20 August 2013). Demanding and paying for quality is thus a precondition for sustainable conservation, and the entire performance at the Slow Food Salone del Gusto was oriented toward educating the public about the qualities of Val Taleggio's cheeses. It was a very diverse public, potentially made of international buyers but also cosmopolitan gourmands, with superior expertise and motivation to appreciate the nuances of food identity.

First, we encountered Strachitunt visually: the title of the tasting workshop attuned us to its 'geometry'. Then came a good deal of listening. After the speeches mentioned above, the dairy technician of the Strachitunt consortium underlined that Strachitunt is not standardized as its natural mould develops without inoculating the paste with cultures. Therefore, the wheels of this 'blue' cheese can be whitish or greenish inside, more typically green if made in *alpeggio*, and white if the cows are fed on hay with a dry diet. In a raw milk artisanal product, 'every wheel tells its own story, actually every quarter in the case of *strachì quader*: sometimes only a whiff of air makes the difference' (Evaristo, Salone del Gusto Slow Food, 21 October 2004, video-recorded). Finally a professional cheese taster, introduced as an experienced instructor of the Slow Food's Master of Cheese, guided the gustatory session literally telling us what we were supposed to smell and taste. First he reminded us of using our hands, as tasting is also a tactile matter, and to keep in mind what happened under our teeth – whether we could spur clicking grains or 'marble' veins. We were all holding the customary palettes of cheese, beginning to taste with the slice 'at midday' in an imaginary clock of six slices.

As in the evaluation of cattle, any classification is based upon comparison. We began with the square *stracchini*. *Strachì quader* made in *alpeggio* was firstly contrasted with *strachì quader* of the *fondovalle* (namely a winter production). Each was consumed fresh, at fifteen days of ageing, with increasing maturation in a succession of more and more matured tastes. This crescendo led us from butter-like sensations, fresh, creamy, and slightly acidic, to detect 'woody' fragrances. At forty days, we could visually register the destructuring of the proteolytic undercrust, which looked like melting cheese, and the underwood aroma took over. We were alerted to the sandy texture of the tongue under the palate. At sixty days, the *strachì quader di alpeggio* gave 'a superior olfactory complexity', smelling no longer of milk but of grass and flowers. 'It is the floral scent of the morning dew on the upper pastures', we were told, and reminded to eat the crust as an integral part of the cheese: 'Not only is the crust edible but it gives the strongest sensation of intense underwood, almost of wet leaves.'

We were ready to approach the real protagonist, the 'round' *strachì*. The sliced Strachitunt wheel was exhibited for all to observe the different colouring of the two curds. Aromas of hay and dry grass, and a delicate taste of *Penicillum* combined, we were taught, into a 'suasion' (*suadenza*), that delicate and sweet pleasure of placing cheese in your mouth and keeping it there to melt. After ninety days, the olfactory sensation included floral grass including 'white flowers', while a bite at the bluish veins would deliver a precise underwood and fungal aroma of white *muffetta* – 'the mushrooms you can smell sometimes when hiking in the woods'. An apotheosis of delicacy would confirm the gustatory 'suasion' of Strachitunt in the mouth, this time defined as 'balance' between the fat creaminess and the blue tones of this champion of diversity. We were left with the promise of a sure (but delayed) acme: 'In thirty, forty days this cheese will deliver even ampler sensations. It is at 120–130 days that Strachitunt gets to the top.' With that in mind, we dived into the surprise dessert: a lime pudding with persimmon and melted Strachitunt. Revelling in the details of the recipe and preparation, the chef made a detectable faux-pas: 'This is an optimal Taleggio . . . oops I meant *stracchino*!' (Guided tasting workshop '*La geometria della Valtaleggio*', Salone del Gusto Slow Food, 21 October 2004, video-recorded).

The most detectable absence from the presentation in fact was the word *Taleggio*, notably mentioned at the outset to give a geographical coordinate (as in Val Taleggio) and henceforth substituted by *stracchino*, apart from a couple of lapses, accompanied by winks and nervous smiles that only added to the significance of this name boycott. What could have otherwise been presented as Taleggio was introduced as '*stracchino* di Vedeseta, a very ancient cheese produced exclusively in Val Taleggio, aged sixty days, square shaped and weighing about 2 kilos' (Evaristo). It was important to the local diatribe to underline the continuity of tradition and the intimate connection between Val Taleggio and its two '*stracchini*'. Moreover, substituting Taleggio by the dialect *strachì quader* (meaning nothing more than 'a square-shaped *stracchino*') would avoid accusations of abusing of a PDO-protected denomination, namely Taleggio.

This was not a paranoid speculation, as incidents had happened before. As recounted in Part II, in their constant quest for a named cheese that would distinguish the valley from the mass-produced, low-priced but PDO Taleggio cheese, the valley producers had tried introducing creative denominations and products such as 'Taleggio della Val Taleggio' and 'Stracchino di Taleggio' but had been chastised by the consortium for the protection of the Taleggio PDO denomination. When stating that already in 1966 the protocol for Taleggio extended the area of production to the entire Lombardy and beyond, the food journalist explained this state of things as a 'burglary, an identity theft'. Val Taleggio had been shoplifted of its culinary identity, and the issue at stake in this workshop was not tasting two cheeses from Lombardy but to side with 'those few who strive for a sanctimonious right of their own' (E. G., Salone del Gusto Slow Food, 21 October 2004, video-recorded).

The historical rooting of such right resided in the narrative account provided by Cesare (a pseudonym), the cheese-monger who salvaged Strachitunt by purposely ordering a consistent stream of wheels from farmer Guglielmo beginning at the end of the 1990s, to sell in his own shop in Bergamo. In his own words Cesare was 'one of Slow Food's oldest friends in Bergamo':

> I tasted my first Strachitunt nearly twenty years ago. I have the same job as my grandfather. He used to get cheese from Val Taleggio by horse-cart; he would meet the cheese-makers at S. Giovanni Bianco in Val Brembana – because there was no road back then. They would walk down and carry the wheels on their back. I have always sampled my *stracchino* – I am not calling it Taleggio, eh! – from Val Taleggio! There, I just noticed, they used to make another *strac-*

> *chino*, round, a kind of Gorgonzola. I asked to make some for me . . . 'No, no, it's too much work!' They just made it for self-consumption . . . I did not even dare calling it *Strachì tunt* in the shop, I did not want the dialect to diminish it . . . so I called it 'natural *erborinato*'. Then came all these chefs, and they fell in love with it, and I have been eating it for twenty years . . .! But it did need *refining*. We have *developed* this product. (Cesare, a pseudonym. Slow Food Salone del Gusto, 21 October 2004)

While confirming the script of a continuous tradition of generations after generations stepping into the same revered trade, the cheese-monger also claimed precedence in having *developed* and *refined* this cheese, once unpresentable both for its dialect name and for its noncommercial vocation. As a Slow Food early-day member and supporter, Cesare was doing with Strachitunt what in heritage studies has been identified as the work of 'cultural legitimization', both a 'performance of meaning making' and the creation of 'new meanings and values' (Smith and Akagawa 2009: 4–6). As part of this process, at the Salone del Gusto, subtle distinctions and name disobedience were being carried out in virtuoso manner in front of a public that was not local to Val Taleggio and not privy to the internal feuds and *coups-de-theatre* that had already several times changed the fortune – and name – of Val Taleggio's square and round cheeses.

Little did they know that an arm-wrestling was being carried out right in front of their very eyes – a performance behind the performance. In fact, the professional cheese taster invited for the purpose of guiding the tasting workshop went as far as announcing, at the end of a thoroughly successful session of both gustatory and moral suasion, that the production protocol for a Slow Food presidium of Strachitunt was in its final stages of definition and would entail that milk for Strachitunt made in *alpeggio* would come from cows exclusively fed on local grass and hay. While I watch again the footage I took of the session back in 2004, I cannot help but noticing that Aronne, sitting next to him, turns to the journalist at his other side and whispers while shaking his head. 'It will be difficult . . .' [*serà dificil*] I can read in Bergamasco dialect on his lips.

The presidium for Strachitunt would have crowned a special relationship to the valley that had been mediated through the very persons sitting at the panel in 2004. Already in 1997, while I was living with them, I had personally taken phone calls to my host family inviting them to the Lingotto district in Turin. 'You take it, this woman speaks too fast' – had been Lavinia's reaction – 'What does she want?' Slow Food was then an emerging phenomenon, building on a network of personal connections and professional reputation. The 2004 Turin session marked a high point in tactical convergence. But two years later, in 2006, talking to the entrepreneurs who somehow interpreted and represented the economy of the valley, I was sternly reminded that Slow Food is sponsored by very powerful food industries (Ugo, 8 August 2006),[5] and that the mission of the Strachitunt consortium was to obtain a PDO – *not* a presidium (Evaristo, 7 August 2006).

Aronne's calling Slow Food negotiators 'Taliban' in 2006 was a conscious linguistic marker for the state of things: with an obvious reference to the Afghanistan campaign, but calibrating the metaphor of radical militancy to his own context, he implied that Slow Food had an excessive and even damaging concern for purity; he blamed a zealot's concern with detail, while making the overall point that his business was in and of itself worthy. As one of the notables in his community of practice, he was experiencing precisely how 'the contemporary practices of "intangible" heritage make the immediacy of the consequences of heritage practices for local communities' political and cultural aspirations more obvious and apparent' (Smith and Akagawa 2009: 5).

The cultural work of distinction – which pertains to regimes of heritage – was colliding with the logic of territorial exception – which pertains to the regimes of geographical indications. In sum, once the public recognition of Strachitunt made it a sought-after cheese, a competition process had been triggered, as a result of which one would find several different productions going by that name on the market. To buffer this dangerous outcome, as a leading member of the dairy cooperative and of the cheese makers of Val Taleggio, Aronne needed that Strachitunt could exclusively designate a product made *within* the valley – nothing more binding than that. As we see in the following section, this was important to the dairy farmers of Val Taleggio, who are socialized into the aesthetics, the ethics, and the logics of breed 'improvement' through progeny selection.

Taliban and Improvers

I first talked to a local Slow Food coordinator, or *responsabile di Condotta*, Emanuele (a pseudonym), in the fall of 2006. We discussed the state of things with Val Taleggio's cheese, especially the fate of Strachitunt. At the time, even the denomination for the valley's soon-to-become flagship cheese had not settled. I initially picked up the name *Strachìtund* in my own publications, following Slow Food's own communication. This extolled the round-shaped (*tund*) natural blue cheese of Val Taleggio, contrasting it with the valleys' square-shaped *strachì*.

In September 2006, Emanuele (a pseudonym) had graciously agreed to meet for a coffee (an espresso, of course) at a newly opened café in the main square of downtown Bergamo, Piazza Pontida. The moment we were served he criticized the waiter for the poor service and the bad match of the home-toasted and instantly brewed coffee with dry biscuits that were served freely with our gourmet cup. They did not live up to the distinction of the brew, and he was upset that the newly established business was unable to set standards for itself. This first impression stuck with me. In the following years, throughout the 'engagement turn' that Slow Food had boldly taken, speaking out and standing up for the rights of marginalized peasants and brainwashed consumers, I could not relinquish the first impression of a consumer culture based on distinction as much as discernment, cherishing quality and service above all else, and requiring the social cultivation of the gourmand – a critique articulated early on by other scholars (Chrzan 2004). While the purpose of this ethnography was not that of observing Slow Food activists, the theme of the reinvention of cheese brought me to converse in depth with several of them. These repeated, often casual encounters over a long period of time helped me to nuance and facet this initial impression of elitism, and to appreciate the political commitment of their discerning sensorium.

Emanuele and four friends (all of whom I later met) had just established in 2005 a Slow Food *condotta* outside Bergamo. Their convivium stood out as something created in the peripheries, for the peripheries. In the city-centric idiom of Italian culture (Silverman 1975), where the town is a natural reference point for its 'civilization' embodied in the many bell towers to be found both in secular buildings and in churches, this sounded somewhat of an affront, perhaps a manifesto. Two teachers, two architects and one librarian, they were personally engaged at the time with the resurrection of an obscure cheese from Val Taleggio: Strachitunt. In May 2004 they had invited one of the charismatic leaders of Slow Food, Piero Sardo (currently president of the Slow Food Foundation for biodiversity) to present their project for a Slow Food presidium for this cheese.

The sourcing of the milk for Strachitunt was the crux of the matter. As already seen in Part II, this was 'accurately selected' but with no limits as to the area of provenance, in the chamber of commerce trademark for Strachitunt. With Strachitunt PDO, milk can only be produced in the municipalities of Taleggio, Sottochiesa, Gerosa and Blello. Crucially, neither the mountain producers nor the lowland competitors opted for a specific *quality* of the milk, or of the cow's diet – this is what put the Val Taleggio producers in contrast with their Slow Food supporters. The mountain farmers pledged only to use cows of the Brown breed, claiming that the latter is more specific to the mountain landscape and its cheese-making tradition. *But what do the cows eat?* Mountain grass? Or imported hay? Or multigrain, possibly GM fodder? Why do they need to eat grains to supplement a grass-and-hay diet? *What kind of Brown cows are these?* These were the issues that impeded a successful establishment of a Slow Food presidium for Strachitunt in Val Taleggio.

Progeny selection was firmly in place in Val Taleggio at the end of the 1990s, even in my host family's then forty-odd herd, and embryo-transfer techniques were beginning to be introduced. As a result of a pervasive politics of agricultural advice, each farm that dealt with the farmer's trade union was encouraged to register in the association for the promotion of breeding (APA) and to join one or another breed improvement herd register – in Lombardy this practically meant choosing the lowland, high-yield Friesians, or, in the mountains, Brown cows yielding high-protein milk ideal for cheese-making. Consultants of APA would often collaborate with trade union technicians to support chosen family farms with applying for development funds and agricultural aid, so that the option for progeny breeding is not simply a technical one. It amounts to entering a community of practice that will in turn inform, support and orient further developments. Farmers are judged by peers and advisors on the basis of their more or less 'modern' mentality about breed improvement, and low-yield herds are not considered worthy of survival.

Visually explicit benchmarks populate the 'socio-technical imaginary' (Jasanoff and Kim 2009) of cow breeders. Breed inspectors and breed experts follow the 'Linear Module for Morpho-Functional Evaluation' that was introduced in the 1980s in Wisconsin, identifying nineteen morpho-functional traits that should be handed down in progeny bulls and heifers. This international circulation of standards corresponds of course to an ideological narrative, conveyed in the bilingual adverts for progeny bull semen that populate professional magazines such as *Razza Bruna* – of which every farmer registered with the association for the advancement of the Italian Brown breed receives a copy.

The inculcation of acceptable productive standards translates into a tacit appreciation of 'functional beauty': animal shapes must be standardized, *calibrated* in fact, to the expectation of high yields (Grasseni 2005a, 2007c). Breed experts, performing as judges at all echelons of cattle fairs – from international arenas to mountain vales – refer to morpho-functional standards to evaluate the specimens they see. In other words, the aesthetics of intensive production percolates to very local levels: in Val Taleggio too, breeders receive professional recognition according to these standards. This is not just a matter of distinction but of *reputation*: in very close-knit circles of consultants, technicians and advisors it may mean receiving (or not) timely information, favourable evaluations, or viable advice on how to apply for funding, being eligible for incentives and receiving credit on investments.

Not coincidentally, two of the four sons in my host family have developed a career as breed experts of the Brown Breed and a third one practices as a licensed cattle inseminator. This means that often they act as judges in similar contexts as the one they operate in (and are judged by peers who may have well heard of their enterprise or have dealt with them professionally). The logic of the peer-review creates an inner circle of respected professionals, all of whom recognize a number of standards of propriety in what they do as animal breeders – standards that are in turn directly derived from the global industry striving for the intensification of milk production – which in Italy exceeds 9 tons of milk per year on average for a Friesian cow and 7 tons for a Brown cow. Only fifteen years ago, the average production for a Friesian in Italy was less than 8 tons a year and 5.4 tons for a Brown cow.[6]

Only nine men altogether in Italy have *breed inspector* rank – and my host family would entertain conversations with one of them regularly. This should be no surprise, as a cattle inspector of the Italian Brown breed association is routinely asked to evaluate the cattle stock of a number of areas of operation, as well as publicly performing the same evaluation skills in cattle fairs. Both at fairs and through visiting hundreds of cattle sheds a year, *his* judgement sets a standard for professional farmers (as of January 2015, all breed inspectors were men).[7] Every cattle fair judge delivers not only a final score, determining which specimens win, but also the equivalent of a Distinguished Lecture in the standardization of animal shape: explaining why one specimen is superior to the one filing next to her – whether by capacity of the udder, height of the ligament, height of the hoof or line of the spine. It is an ideological lecture, praising the superiority of selected cattle for the 'functional' objective of intensive dairy production. As I have elaborated elsewhere, the cattle fair trophies themselves – usually scale models of the Ideal Italian Brown cow – will be paraded in the farmers' living rooms and will mimic the standard figure of a hornless cow with a mighty udder and symmetrically placed teats – all of which is convenient for machine milking. Even plastic-cast toys implicitly follow this aesthetics (Grasseni 2005b).

Issues of environmental *and social* sustainability are tacitly implicated here. The bigger, voracious and sedentary 'Super Brown' cows produce a higher amount of milk but also of liquid and solid manure, which the steep and rocky mountain pastures cannot absorb. Their bones are brittle, and their joints are not supple enough to move at ease over uneven terrain as required by transhumant breeding, which implies travelling with cattle to the upper pastures. Multifunctional breeds have a lower environmental impact, and are being rediscovered as heritage landraces, but yield less milk. They are smaller, sturdier, plumper than selected high-yield cows, which some of the detractors of progeny selection equate to anorexic pin-ups, shaped by a logic of consumption into a form that is detrimental to their own survival.

Either way, these are strategic choices with long-lasting impact on the individual enterprise as well as the community, an impact that cannot be easily rethought and undone. A single farming family is unlikely to have the resources to reinvest on low-yielding and multifunctional breeds, without shield from crushing milk prices or the vagaries of niche markets for heritage cheese. Moreover, farmers are not only dependent on the market, but on local systems of patronage: trade unions, the regional government (which assigns European funds) and professional associations. This system markets a completely different animal aesthetics and functionality than the one that food activists and associations like Slow Food upholds.

I used the term 'skilled vision' to explain how the community of practitioners rallying around progeny cattle share a fundamental worldview that is not only functional to the ever-growing global food market but also populates the mind's eye. A dairy farmer learns to recognize a beautiful cow by manipulating plastic toys, revering trophies on the grandparents' mantelpieces, then becomes socialized in peer talk about genetic indexes and progeny lineages. One's friends, colleagues and professional reputation are enmeshed in economic calculations about milk price, milk quotas and agricultural aid opportunities. It should be no surprise, then, that the Slow Food request for cheese made with milk from cows that would 'only' eat grass was met with scepticism and was taken almost as an affront by the most 'modern' of the valley's farmers. The producers found themselves in the impossible situation of the double bind: meeting both the productive standards of breed 'improvement' and the purity criteria of Slow Food. As Aronne succinctly put it:

> If I tell my father that we should feed the cows on grass only, he'll tell me to f*** off! He says that in the old days the cows were starving and that now they fare much better, so the milk is better and the cheese must be better too, it's fatter and contains more protein. What is the point of looking into whether I give my cows a kilo of silage when there is the trade union that lobbies to make Strachitunt in the entire province like they did with Bitto for Sondrio . . . It's a question of finding reasonable compromises. I understand that it is no good to take the cows to the upper pastures just to then feed them silage, but if I give them some fodder as integration, it's different. And to those who say that we should convert to organic, I want to see what they do when a cow catches mastitis. Don't you give her antibiotics? At what price should I sell this Strachitunt then, to recoup my losses, if I produce half the milk and even lose some cows? (Aronne, a pseudonym, 11 August 2006)

In his eyes, the 'Taliban' food activists were not only zealots, they were anachronistic in their quest for authenticity. The public presentation of Strachitunt at the Turin Salone del Gusto in 2004 was part of a negotiation process to establish a Slow Food presidium in Val Taleggio. Unfortunately, this process was not successful, mainly because the producers would not bear the costs of reconverting their animal husbandry practices to the standards that Slow Food expected (namely avoiding grain-based fodder and the import of hay for their voracious cattle). Such a radical shift in the local models of animal 'improvement' – models that had been socially inculcated by generations of agricultural consultants and trade unions – was too momentous to be digested.

Elsewhere I have dwelt on how the aesthetic of productivity is a matter of subtle perceptions, of moral codes and well as production standards (Grasseni 2004). Slow Food's challenge to breed 'improvement' was perceived as luddite, purist to the point of backwardness: even 'Taliban'. In fact, Slow Food was further articulating the producers' argument of *tipicità* by adding the question of where the milk comes from *originally*. The animal body lives in intimate relationship with the ecology of the pasture and the shed, which implicates not only the *location* where herds are raised but whether actual pastureland is used, the proportion of grazed grass vis-à-vis imported hay or silage fodder, and even what kind of body is ingesting and transforming the milk: a sturdy mountain landrace, capable of climbing steep pastures, or a high-yield 'improved' Brown, larger, more voracious and more awkward in her movements, less resilient to the changes in diet and weather that the *alpeggio* imposes?

These arguments resurfaced during the public hearing for Strachitunt in 2009 described in Part II. When the Brembilla agronomist made reference to a 'typical' breeding system (*un sistema di allevamento tipico*), he was backed up by Aronne – who in the meantime had become the president of the valley's dairy cooperative. He explained that in response to the need to enhance the *tipicità* of their milk, the cooperative had decreased the use of imported maize silage in the cows' diet, adding that this meant a lot more work in terms of hay-making and storing hay in situ. This announcement shows how, as controversies evolved, local producers learnt to appreciate Slow Food's original argument, which now seemed 'systemic' but three years earlier was simply deemed 'radical' and primitivistic. The actors in the heritage arena – who never ceased to talk to each other in the best diplomatic tradition – had gradually repositioned themselves over time, to the effect that modern improvers now appreciated the necessity of some 'Taliban' stance.

Notes

1. *Amaro* is also the name, in Italian, for digestive liquors (commercial bitters). See the work of Thomas Hausschild for thought-provoking considerations on 'magic potions, bitter herbs and bitter liqueurs' and their humoral relation with 'our favourite modern and postmodern drink, produced from herbal extracts and secret recipes: Coca-Cola' (2005: 22). Hausschild positions love potions within a historical complex of 'archaic psychosomatic medicine' (2005: 23) very much alive in the uses and beliefs surrounding contemporary herbal remedies – both in Europe's 'West' and in Italy's 'South'.
2. Casarrigoni srl., export catalogue, personal communication 8 May 2015.
3. Conversation annotated in field notes. 8 August 2006, at Arrigoni Valtaleggio, Peghera, Val Taleggio. Interlocutors were Evaristo, Ugo and Tito (all pseudonyms).
4. Italians use the name of Cicero, the Roman philosopher and consul, to define generally the skill and practice of an orator. It is also used in everyday language to refer to a tour guide.
5. To this criticism, Antonio, a high-ranking Slow Food representative, retorted that 'this is really misunderstood in the light of ideologies that have no purchase in the current time . . . we run a publishing house, a university and a foundation. This grants us unsurpassed autonomy: we are free to write and say what we want. But every time we host a Market of the Earth [*mercato della terra*] or we launch a Master of Food, we have financial engagements. So if the sponsorship of Grana Padano allows me to take farmer Guglielmo to Mother Earth [*Terra Madre*] or the unknown Fiurì di Valtorta to Cheese in Bra, I am fine with that' (Antonio, a pseudonym, 20 August 2013).

6. The *Bollettino dei Controlli della produttività del latte* published by the Associazione Italiana Allevatori measures the increase of milk productivity since the first systematic data gathering in 1962. According to Governmental Decrees 24–5-1967 and 18–4-2000 and Law 15–1-1991 n.30, the Italian Breeders' Association (A.I.A.) carries out the activity of recording dairy cattle productivity. According to the data gathered in 2012–2013, 'The Italian Friesian breed has an average milk yield of kg. 9,140 ± 2,099 with fat percentage of 3.70 ± 0.51 and protein percentage of 3.30 ± 0.26. The Italian Brown Swiss breed presents an average milk yield of kg. 7,058 ± 1,898 with fat percentage of 4.00 ± 0.45 and protein percentage of 3.55 ± 0.29.' In Northern Italy 1,152,352 cows were recorded, representing 84.8 per cent of the entire population. They are located in 14,844 farms averaging 77.63 units per farm. In Central Italy, 61,171 cows were controlled in 933 farms, representing 4.5 per cent of the entire population averaging 65.56 units per farm. In Southern Italy and Islands 145,917 cows are located in 2,867 farms with an average of 50.89 units per farm.' Retrieved 21 August 2014 from http://bollettino.aia.it/bollettino/bollettino.htm.
7. The Associazione Nazionale Allevatori Razza Bruna Italiana (ANARB) updates its lists of breed experts and inspectors yearly. Retrieved 5 December 2015 from http://www.anarb.it/pagina.asp?ID=281&lang=it.

CHAPTER 6

Reinventing *Stracchino*

Fading away the plans for a Slow Food presidium for Strachitunt, and with the PDO only slowly materializing, another Slow Food presidium was established in 2010: that of the *stracchino* 'made in the old-way' (Stracchino all'Antica delle Valli Orobiche). This drew on a network of small-size, traditional cheese producers, but did not promote Val Taleggio specifically. The presidium of thirteen producers in the Bergamasque valleys includes only one in Val Taleggio. The idea is to pool together marginal but high-quality producers from Val Taleggio and the neighbouring Valle Imagna and upper Val Brembana. After the high hopes of 2004, the Strachitunt course diverged from that of Slow Food – only symbolically though, as at least one cheese-maker produces both Strachitunt for the PDO consortium and Stracchino all'antica for Slow Food. This is perfectly legitimate, but how is it relationally achieved, in a world where the next-door neighbour can be today's ally and tomorrow's fiercest competitor? This question requires introducing the mediator, the diplomat, the ambassador.

Over the years, I saw Antonio (a pseudonym) ascending from the role of local leader of a peripheral Slow Food convivium to a high-ranking officer in the regional, then national committees. Since 2006, we had several exchanges about alternative food networks, their relationship with Slow Food, and the mission and ambition of his organization. Our conversations had begun as a result of my research and had continued in reciprocally respectful distance, marked by awareness of our distinct roles. When I met him last time in August 2013, he gave me a number of promotional postcards. 'Plastic or taste-less cheese?! KEEP KALM and EAT STRACCHINO – the real one . . . taste the difference! F [for Facebook] Slow Food Lombardia.' I wondered if the consistent choice for 'Kalm' rather than 'calm' was a conscious pun on the ubiquitous postcards inspired by World War II British patriotic propaganda ('Keep calm and carry on').

The postcard compares and contrasts Strachitunt with the photograph of a plastic-wrapped *sottiletta* – the Italian word for sliced cheddar-type cheese of the kind produced industrially. Since the 1960s, a pervasive advertising campaign

Figure 5. Slow Food postcard, August 2013. Sottiletta vs. Strachitunt. Courtesy of Slow Food Italia.

publicized the handiness and freshness of these ubiquitous slices vis-à-vis bulky, smelly and quickly drying artisanal cheese. *Sottilette* are now used daily by Italians, for instance for quick toasties in bars or in cafés serving inexpensive lunch breaks. Opposed to the ideal-type of a *sottiletta*, the postcard shows three wheels of Strachitunt, lying on a straw bed, and displaying the consortium trademark. This sits in relief on the cylinder's face, exhibiting the uneven and well-dried greyish crust, while the slicing unveils the marbled paste and the blue streaks in the middle, uneven with moulds and cracks. It is a matter of *conviction* – which takes quite a lot of cultural work and aesthetic assumptions – that this second photograph should look more enticing or reassuring.

Some of this cultural work transpires from the accompanying caption, in English – at least potentially directed to an international buyer. The industrial cheese is described as 'plastic' altogether, and the fact that it is displayed half-wrapped in plastic film hammers the message home. The culprit is the very protective film that would keep *sottilette* hygienic and individually preserved, hence conveniently 'fresh'. They would never dehydrate – unlike the sliced surface of a cheese wheel, which easily gets dry, absorbs other aromas, or vice versa contaminates the rest of the fridge with a foul smell. Furthermore, *sottilette* in

Italy are universally considered 'taste-less', especially by comparison with 'real' cheeses such as Strachitunt.

Several other postcards were produced as part of the same series: this Slow Food campaign built on shared cultural discourse, using visualization to evoke a complex sensorium, rendered through shape, colour and wording. Designed to credit regional artisanal foodways against industrially produced and distributed foodstuffs, the 'keep kalm' postcards voice a bold call to establish no less than a new sensory order, as well as to revise everyday practice: shall we then use Strachitunt for our toasties during the office lunch?

'Keep kalm and make *caprino*' (goat cheese): in Figure 6 the postcard contrasts a plastic vat of spreadable cream cheese whose blue, white, silver and red corporate brand name has been Photoshopped out, with a basketful of craft goat cheeses of several shapes and dimensions: cone, square and round, with moulds coloured from yellowish to white-grey. It is the diversity of the latter that the iconography plays up as a way of conjuring 'taste', while the bleached-white cream cheese in the plastic vat is captioned as 'no-taste cheese'. Antonio gifted to me several other postcards of the same ilk, while we sipped red wine and ate exquisite charcuterie on a sweltering August afternoon, sitting at wooden tables on a shadowy terrace in Bergamo's upper town. While we watched the sweaty

Figure 6. Slow Food postcard, gathered August 2013. 'Make caprino' (goat cheese). Courtesy of Slow Food Italia.

tourists filing down Via Colleoni, I thumbed through the postcards: sliced white bread versus kneaded rolls and loaves ('No-taste or smelly bread?! Keep Kalm and become baker'); long-chain sea fish as opposed to local lake fish ('Stinking Fish? Keep Kalm and become fisherman'), industrial wine, iconically identified by tetra pack packages and one-size-fits-all definitions of 'white' and 'red', vis-à-vis a splashy toast in a stylish glass ('Bad wine?! Keep Kalm and become wine maker'); pre-cut salads and greens in plastic bags as opposed to a cornucopia of whole and colourful vegetables, artfully heaped on a wooden table ('Plastic vegetables?! Keep Kalm and become farmer'); 'Industrial or egg-taste beer? Keep Kalm and brew your beer'; '*Wurstel* or *salame*?' Keep Kalm and become butcher'.[1]

Antonio was handing me a call to resistance. 'Keeping calm' was just a precondition to action, a positive mind frame as opposed to despair, rage or listlessness, to then engage in a proactive stance against 'taste-less', 'plastic', 'smelly', 'stinking', 'industrial' or simply 'bad' food and drink. However, what was suggested (to become a baker, a fisherman, a butcher, a wine-maker, a farmer, or to brew one's beer as well as making one's goat cheese) takes skill, time, determination, resources and training. Usually one acquires them through apprenticeship and socialization in a network of peer-producers: not an easy task. Ironically the simplest action proposed, if I were to single it out of this experimental series of postcards, was that of 'eating *stracchino*. The real one'. The real one? Is there a fake one? What is *real stracchino*? Antonio's answer was different from the one of the cheese-makers of Val Taleggio and in order to appreciate it, one needs to be encultured to the language of taste.

A Language for Taste

As many of the other relationships that I cultivated over time, my correspondence with Antonio was partly made of one-to-one conversations, partly of commensality and participation in events such as the dinners organized by ONAF, the Organizzazione Nazionale Assaggiatori Formaggio. Analogously to the wine-tasting association ONAV (Associazione Nazionale Assaggiatori Vini) the national association of cheese-tasters runs intensive courses on the art of tasting cheese. It trains and examines certified cheese-tasters. I took part in the course offered by the Chamber of Commerce in the fall and winter of 2006, and received my diploma of cheese taster (*diploma di assaggiatore*) in December 2006. Here, I learnt to taste *stracchino*, Strachitunt, Bitto, Formai de Mut, Branzi, Taleggio, Gorgonzola, Grana Padano, Parmigiano Reggiano and other Italian cheeses. Above all, I learnt a language to describe the cheese sensorium. I particularly liked the teaching of the first day: 'A good professional taster should be able to grade a cheese 'good' even if she does not like it.' That was my case. I did not like them, though I discovered a partiality to Formai de Mut.

The course was offered free of charge to registered farmers and cheese-makers. It was aimed at the very producers that I had been doing fieldwork with, or interviewed, during the previous years. I met them all there: Aronne, Mario, Letizia (pseudonyms), each a representative of a distinctive lineage, of well-known families of cheese-makers and dairy-breeders of different parts of the province: Val Taleggio, Lower Val Brembana, Upper Val Brembana and the lower lands. The evening course was strategically located, not in the town of Bergamo, but in Zogno at the mouth of Val Brembana, easily reachable by all of them after a long day of work. The course consisted of theory and practice: we received sizable printouts about cheese microbiology, a book on cheese-tasting and several tasting report sheets to fill in and practice with – one for each cheese, mostly regional but also national: Emmentaler, Gorgonzola, Asiago, Fontina, Robiola di Roccaverano, Pecorino sardo, Scimudìn, Stracchino, Crescenza, Salva, Mozzarella di bufala, Caciocavallo silano, Caciocavallo ragusano, etc.

We were advised to taste in silence and with concentration, to abstain and withdraw from the everyday 'sensorial stress' of overcrowded plates and overlapping tastes. 'Taste alone is a little thing, it does not *move* us' – we were cautioned. But olfactory information is the matter of emotion: memory, alarm, pleasure. It is the smell that in some cases can trigger salivation! We would use our nose first, as *fragrance* and *aroma* are the proper domains of a first exposure to cheese. 'You smell with your nostrils, but you detect aroma with the back mucosae of the inside of your nose. So don't gulp. Bite, chew, use your tongue and press the rich air from your oral cavity into the nasal cavity *behind* your nose. That's *aroma*.' So instructed us Beppe Casolo, an esteemed ONAF instructor with a degree in agronomy, on our first lesson on 25 September 2006. This veritable synaesthetic initiation (Sutton 2006) consisted of seven distinct steps: to look, to touch, to smell, to bite, to spread the cheese in the mouth, to chew, to ingest – and wait for further sensation.

What could we sense? Some acidity remaining on the tongue? An aftertaste? Had the colour of crust and paste impressed itself on us? Did we eat both crust and paste? Were we capable of describing them distinctively? Was the cheese 'eye-spotted' (did it have an *occhiatura*, an eye-shaped series of minute holes that air creates in the paste)? and was this 'eye' as in a partridge, or was it rather the size of a rice seed, or a maize grain, or a pin-point? 'It melts in the mouth', 'the paste is adhesive to the palate', 'persistent taste', 'elasticity', 'acidulous', 'crystals' were all words we learnt as part of our shared vocabulary. In our exercises, we had to recognize unidentified smells from sources that would then be disclosed to us, to understand how much of our olfactory experience is instructed by expectations conveyed by visual information and memory. To prove that, my samples of lemon, honey and nougat became in my own perception jasmine, sweat and liquorice! . . . Moving on to taste proper, we would learn to articulate beyond the obvious. Sweet, salty, acid and bitter (and umami) were *not* sufficient descriptors.

'Hot', 'peppery', 'astringent', 'metallic', 'refreshing' vis-à-vis 'warming' were more eloquent terms.

Our expertise should consist of the capacity to observe, describe, compare and articulate a motivated evaluation of two or more cheeses. But, explained Dr Casolo, the mission of ONAF went beyond the mere instruction of cheese tasters. The goal of such instruction is the dissemination of a 'dairy culture': to educate to the diversity of cheese and its tastes (for example, explicitly mentioned was an appreciation of raw milk cheese). Furthermore, to offer such instruction directly to cheese-makers meant 'to give the producers the right weapons to sell their produce'. Another call to arms – we all knew, after all, that we operate in a regime of 'war of the cheeses' – and some of the people sitting on school benches next to me were the very protagonists of those wars.

In our tasting exercises, we used the *Scheda descrittiva ONAF per l'assaggio dei formaggi* (descriptive form for cheese-tasting). On each sheet we learnt to take note of category and denomination of the cheese (such as Pecorino Toscano di Pienza), and to articulate the results of our visual, olfactory, taste and tactile examinations: shape, crust, colour of the crust, as well as colour, structure, eye-spotting or blue streaks of the paste. Texture, aroma, taste and smell had to be described as exhaustively as possible. For example: 'lactic fragrance, good solubility, not persistent, scarcely elastic, modestly adhesive, fruity aroma, mild intensity with vegetal notes, compact, creamy paste with ivory reflexes, brick-coloured and wrinkly crust but intact, has an undesirable bitter aftertaste', was my description for the above mentioned Tuscan sheep cheese from Pienza.

To my surprise, I scored top grades, and graduated *assaggiatore* (taster) with higher marks than my cheese-making friends. That someone who had practically never eaten cheese would score higher than a professional cheese-maker confirmed the theoretical bias of the course, which was geared not to evaluate our knowledge of cheese, but rather our capacity to articulate it. My friends' knowledge and experience was undoubtedly infinitely superior to mine, but their training did not include a language to convey it. The chamber of commerce was right to encourage them to take the course and to equip them with adequate analytic and rhetorical weaponry, so that they could compete on a market that sold not cheese alone, but the sensorium around it.

The graduation dinner took place at the castle of Clanezzo, a medieval mansion now turned into a restaurant, and featured local wines and cheeses. One year later, in 2007, a similar ONAF event hosted the presentation of my book (in Italian) *La reinvenzione del Cibo*, where I described the plight of Val Taleggio, which could not name its cheese 'heritage Taleggio', nor 'Stracchino di Taleggio' nor 'Taleggio of Val Taleggio'. Antonio was discussant. Since then, our scattered conversations have ranged from the European GM regulation framework – too much of a compromise to be satisfactory for the Slow Food agenda – to the future of 'zero-mile' food systems. We shared scepticism for high-tech online platforms for product traceability, such as the ones just being invented at MIT Media Lab to be showcased at Milan's EXPO in 2015 as 'the supermarket of the future' (Oriani 2014). Design-oriented, they would digitally augment the experience of shoppers, measuring distances from farm to table by harnessing labelled data. The underlying agenda seemed to be one of making carbon foot-printing more conspicuous. But where is the engagement? – we asked – Where is the market square? Where are the peasants? And where is the community? We went back again and again to the idea of a new pedagogy of consumption – unsurprisingly, considering that we are both teachers.

Over the years, Antonio acted as a pivotal node in a painstakingly woven network, creating convergence between several social, economic and institutional actors who concern themselves with grassroots social innovation, environmental sustainability and resilience. Taking sustainability both in social and in environmental terms, sometimes too different to actually develop a common project, these actors were nevertheless all present in a series of seminars that Antonio authoritatively hosted in the framework of Terra Madre. Throughout the first half of 2012 the Lombard *condotte* (known abroad as *convivia*) focussed on sustainable agriculture: producing, consuming and supporting local foodstuffs – including new developments such as permaculture, but also a 'return to the future' through a renewed investment on mountain agriculture. Another innovative theme was 'the cultures of cultivation', specifically in connection with biodiversity and seed-saving. 'Dairy excellence' (*eccellenza casearia*) would position the Lombard mountains as the most viable local resource for significant short dairy chains. Solidarity economy was also explicitly championed as a form of ethical exchange by the anti-corporate economist Andrea di Stefano – practically a star amongst alternative consumers – and Vandana Shiva as guest of honour, in her role of vice president of Slow Food International.

As a result of this cultural and political investment, Slow Food maintained a high profile in debates about food sovereignty and, locally, it played an important role in the planning and organization of Milan's Expo 2015 – whose theme 'Feeding the Planet' attracted many industrial interests as well as criticisms from more radical alternative consumers. The declared ambition of Slow Food, explains Antonio, was to achieve a political directorship of all these intertwined themes:

> We have the vision, the capacity to keep all of these threads woven together, while other societal and institutional actors focus on specific aspects, such as environmental protection, heritage or solidarity economy. Our mission is to navigate these by keeping a clear steering towards environment-territory-soil consumption and on historicity-memory-quality of food-health. This is how we got to 40,000 members in Italy and 150,000 members worldwide, of which 4,500 are in Lombardy, our first region in Italy. We are the fourth largest Slow

> Food region in the world, more than California, more than Tuscany. (Antonio, a pseudonym, 20th August 2013).

It slowly dawned on me that alongside the conferences, Antonio was actually working to implement his own solution: in the name of Lombard 'dairy excellence', he would reinvent not a PDO for Val Taleggio, as my friends had done with Strachitunt, but rather *stracchino* itself: the very protagonist of the lost history of Lombard transhumance, the lowly cheese that Count Jacini described in 1882 as 'quickly' made (*all'infretta*, not a commendable descriptor) by the dairy breeders of the Bergamasque Alps, the *Bergamini*, in their resting stations, en route and hence with milk of tired cows (*strach, stracche*). Slow Food was reinventing a *fast* cheese!

Five years before, Antonio sat next to me at the momentous Slow Food National Assembly at Abano Terme in May 2010, where I was a delegate of his convivium (a *delegato di condotta*). He quietly broke down while Carlo Petrini spoke passionately about the fate of the world's peasants, their indigenous knowledge, their languages and dialects, their marginalization by the very food economies that they feed with their labour and skill. In a previous convivium's assembly, in preparation for the annual meeting, he had taken to heart Petrini's political turn, explaining to his own *Condotta* that Slow Food had a political mission and was a social movement, not a congregation of '*gastrosofi gaudenti*' (a highly creative hybrid neologism for 'gluttons' and 'philosophers' combined). This assembly was important and Antonio had invited me as an external auditor. It was graced by a personal visit of a close collaborator of Carlo Petrini – practically a personal envoy. Antonio stepped in his role the year after, subsequent to the national assembly of May 2010. His brain children, the two new Slow Food presidia of Valle Brembana and Imagna (namely, the cheeses Agrì and Stracchino all'Antica delle Valli Orobiche) were inaugurated that year, just in time to debut at the October Salone del Gusto in Turin.

Since then, Stracchino all'antica delle Valli Orobiche has been a Slow Food presidium gathering together eleven producers from the Bergamasque valleys (the Valli Orobiche) including Val Taleggio, the Upper Val Brembana and neighbouring Valle Imagna. *All'antica* literally means 'as in the old days'. This *stracchino* is made with raw milk *a munta calda* (like Strachitunt, it is curdled at the cow's milking temperature). As with Strachitunt, this drastically reduces the size of possible operations, as no refrigeration and re-heating of the milk is admitted, and requires greater cheese-making skills, because no starter cultures are added, as well as high-quality milk, which is worked unpasteurized. When I visited the Slow Food University of Gastronomy at Pollenzo and the wine 'ark' that Slow Food samples to publish their Wine Guide, in 2010, even Carlo Petrini himself, the founder of Slow Food, mentioned Celina of Valle Imagna, one of the cheese-makers of the Stracchino all'antica.[2]

In Valle Imagna, the presidium was given added meaning by the partially synergic initiative of the municipal administration of Corna Imagna, which encouraged the *stracchino* producers to form a cooperative and make cheese collectively. The 2010 initiative of the municipal administration, which invited all the locally active dairy farmers to renovate a municipal building and occupy it with a cooperative creamery, solved the marginalization of all those who can make cheese and do, but are not formally authorized to do it and thus to sell it. The cooperative building, renamed House of the Stracchino (*Casa dello Stracchino*), produced thirty *stracchini* a day in 2014, selling at €8 per kilo, from the milk of fifty cows owned by six producers. The House also serves as a social aggregation for youth associations and as selling point for other even smaller local productions such as chestnuts and fruit preserves.

The Valle Imagna initiative was positively reviewed by the Lombardy region's Institute for Research as an example of 'promotion of local agro-food systems of relevant socio-cultural interest'[3] and a model for the 'development of high-quality local traditional farming foodstuffs'. However, this is not per se the kind of economy that can create jobs. A more powerful tourist framework would be needed, including farmers markets, school trips, accommodation, cultural productions and events, etc. The interpretations of just *how* to achieve that are multiple and potentially conflicting: the expectations of the presidium and of the municipal initiatives seemed distinct. The latter would pool milk to make cheese collectively – even though the common criticism about pooling production is that quality will decrease – and establish a cooperative involving all the local breeders, rather than the three best cheese-makers only. Then, why make *only* stracchino rather than many other dairy products that sell more easily at farmers markets, such as yoghurt? Further, local institutional actors envisaged frameworks such as ecomuseums to attract tourism. Slow Food on the other hand would invest on dairy 'excellence' above everything else, while the municipality would rather keep everyone involved in the cooperative.

Not only the cheese-makers of Val Taleggio can reinvent their *strachì*. And so it was that while Val Taleggio placed all their stakes on a PDO for Strachitunt, neighbouring Valle Imagna opted for a softer path – a presidium Slow Food for a *stracchino* made 'as in the old days'. If Taleggio PDO failed its valley of origin, Stracchino all'antica also favours the neighbours without giving Val Taleggio a competitive edge, especially considering that the *Stracchino* presidium partially overlaps with the Strachitunt PDO (see Map 3).

Antonio's comment on these potential conflict of intents, in the summer of 2013, was:

> They have not yet understood the genuineness, the commercial potential, of this product! It bypasses the nozzle of the Taleggio denomination and in the same breath it acknowledges the cheese-making capacities *all around* Val

> Taleggio, because inside it, there is only one family that makes *stracchino* with raw milk *a munta calda*. (Antonio, a pseudonym, 20 August 2013)

Antonio was politely pointing to the fact that, with the demise of active farming in the last twenty years, quality cheese-making in Val Taleggio *in marketable quantity* is practically only possible either for the dairy cooperative or for one single family enterprise, that of the celebrated 'saviour' of Strachitunt. While the resurgence of *stracchino* in and around Val Taleggio certainly adds to the defence of its *tipicità*, Val Taleggio itself hosts no more than twenty breeding farms, of which the largest and most successful boasts around two hundred milking cows. This adds to present and past competitions a survivalist edge, and animosities

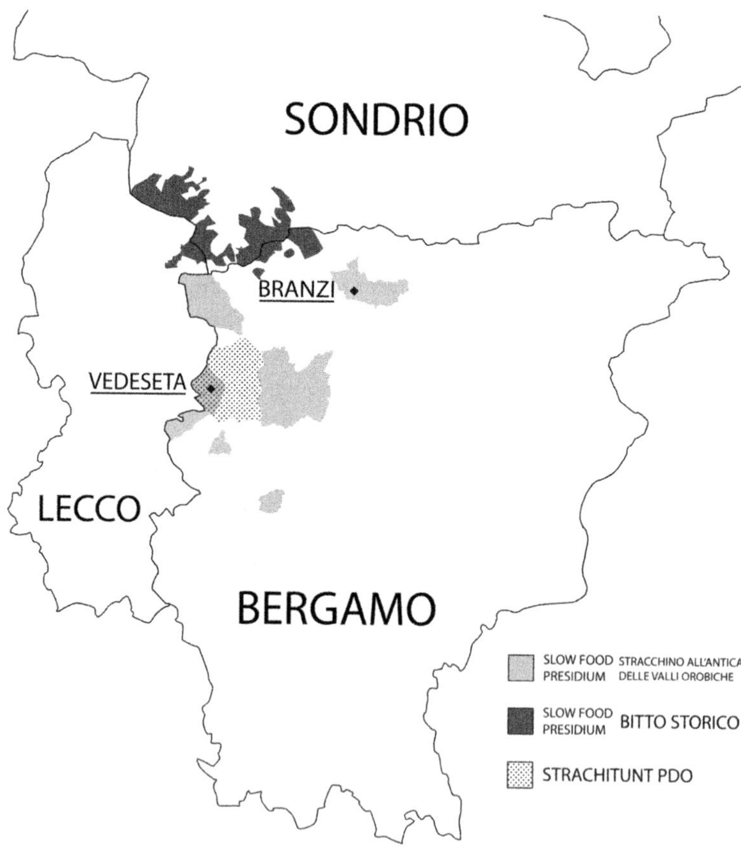

Map 3. Production area for Strachitunt PDO, Slow Food presidium Bitto Storico and Slow Food presidium Stracchino all'antica delle Valli Orobiche. Map produced by Federico De Musso.

between individual farming families and cheese-makers can be very real. One can only wonder at Antonio's diplomatic ability to introduce *two* new cheese names in an intensely fraught context without wreaking havoc on ever-fragile compromises and alliances, especially if one contemplates by comparison the turf war and consequent stalemate over the Branzi PDO request (see Part I). As Antonio himself put it:

> Think about it: Branzi could be the third PDO cheese in Valle Brembana *alone*, in good company with Strachitunt of Valtaleggio [which is a branch of Valle Brembana, my note] and Formai de Mut of the Upper Valle Brembana! (Antonio, a pseudonym, 20 August 2013)

Knowing that Valle Brembana is lucky enough to have two PDOs, Antonio supported instead a novel and broader alliance – cutting across PDOs and presidia, together with Branzi's dairy cooperative, to establish a truly local coalition of cheese denominations – six signature cheeses of the Bergamasque Mountains – the 'Princes of the Orobie Mountains' (Principi delle Orobie): the two new Slow Food presidia of Valle Brembana and Imagna (Agrì and Stracchino all'antica), the two PDOs of Valle Brembana and Valle Taleggio (Formai de Mut and Strachitunt), together with the unachieved PDO Branzi, allied with its twin rebel brother, Bitto Storico of course. Amidst the capricious landscape of cheese reinvention, the 'Princes of the Orobie' features as a political innovation: a commercial coalition – nothing more than an agreement, but 'laboriously underwritten' Antonio tells me – to jointly promote two community PDOs, two presidia, one presidium-but-not-PDO, and one neither.

Not even Antonio's Princes would be exempt from internal distinctions. For example, it was noted that the program presenting the project in November 2013 on national television (the popular newsreel *Striscia la Notizia*) only mentioned heritage Bitto. Further, the logo combining the outline of Pizzo dei Tre Signori (a mountain towering over the high pastures of northwestern Val Brembana) with the Bitto cauldron, the *calècc* risked overshadowing non-Bitto partners.[4] As for the Stracchino all'antica, the logic of territorial exception could once again clash with that of heritage distinction. Some producers were apparently trying to carve out their own geographical identity, in a presidium straddling a number of localities across Valle Imagna, Val Taleggio and Val Brembana (as in Map 3), in the name of their shared dairy excellence. To become privy to this last skirmish, we will need to sit and have lunch in the Bergamasque mountains, following a long-winded conversation, easing through many courses of *salame nostrano, polenta e osèi* and of course mountain cheese.

Deciphering a Meal

On 1 November 2013, Antonio and Battista (both pseudonyms), their respective families and I parked the car at a sparsely inhabited hillside borough, at an altitude of about 500 meters just above a sprawling village at the mouth of Valle Brembana. We began climbing a path up to arrive after about thirty minutes of steady pace to the pastures of Flowery Meadows (a pseudonym), enjoying a view of Mount Canto Alto and of the lower Valle Brembana. We were heading for an *agriturismo*, a farm offering meals prepared on site with homestead produce. The owner, Mario (a pseudonym), was well known to both Antonio and Battista because, now in his early forties, he is a well-respected cheese-maker and a recommended Slow Food provider.

I met Mario at the cheese-tasting course of 2006. Managing his farm with his father, he juggled the *alpeggio*, an ecotourism restaurant and the dairy farm. Antonio introduced him as one of the most charismatic cheese-makers in the area, proud to have hosted the Terra Madre Day here. Particularly appreciated is his stance on cows' nutrition: 'We are reasoning around the cows' diet, he is buying organic fodder, I introduced him to two producers, and he is trying them out both.'[5]

Flowery Meadows claims to be the first *agriturismo* acknowledged by the Lombardy regional government in 1979. To hikers and tourists seeking rustic accommodation, the farm's website announces: 'Our eco-tourist farm Flowery Meadows is in a mountainous area above XY. Don't be scared by the unavoidable hike: it's the best way to increase your appetite and prepare you to taste our menu: a complete meal from antipasto to dessert will offer you the best of our production: meat, *salumi* (cured meats), cheese and dairies that will surprise you for their genuine taste'. And for the price: €22 excluding wine. The family farm, run by two brothers who took over from their father, is traditionally organized around two stations: a low pasture near the village residence and an upper pasture for the summer with a *baita*. Here, at a relatively low altitude – 850 meters, practically a hill by Alpine standards – their father is known to keep at least part of the herd also in spring and fall. When I first heard of this family, at the cheese-tasting training course, Mario commented that his father 'practically comes down from the meadows for his Christmas meal. Then he goes up again after the Epiphany.'[6] We could appreciate the feasibility of such arrangement when we climbed to the meadows and were delighted to enjoy a sunny day on All Saints. However muddy, no snow was yet in sight on the hiking path, rather steep and certainly not wide enough for four wheels. As we were told, Mario goes up and down by motorbike when in a hurry, and relies on a lumberjack's ropeway to transport fuel, fodder, tools and supplies – sometimes riding it himself!

Given the unexpected warmth of the day, the inn keepers were overwhelmed with visitors. On wooden benches and tables outside the *baita*, Mario's wife and sister were serving wine and generous platters of homemade salami, lard, pancetta and ham to families waiting to be seated inside. In the meantime, everyone would rest and chat, and eat their antipasto under the grapevine. We had booked, but ended up waiting to be seated last out of courtesy to our host. He knew we came to talk business too – so there was no need to pack us away quickly.

We went full circle around the *baita*'s grounds, paid our respect to Mario's father, and returned to the inn, beginning to feel really hungry. Mario got it, and had us sit in the 'old kitchen' – practically a tool repository turned into a private parlour, in front of a fireplace whose chimney did not draft very well. My task quickly began one of keeping the wooden door just slightly ajar so as to allow cold air to be sucked in and drive the smoke away up the pipe, but judging when everyone's feet were so cold that we could cope with the smoke for a few minutes and shut the door. Around a wooden table marked by woodworm, simple planks or log stumps as seats, we made room amidst old pitchforks and shovels propped by the door and several cobweb-mantled implements on the window sill. There were seven of us among children, men and women, but the conversation had been driven by Antonio – occasionally Battista and me asking questions. Their wife and fiancé, though both educated young professionals and just as knowledgeable about the stories told, kept to a prudent second stage and left me – a woman, who all too often turned up without husband and kids – the risky role of the interlocutor.

We eased a bit around the table. When we had had our plentiful share of homemade pickles, *salame nostrano*, pancetta and lard, followed by polenta with poultry, pork ribs and beef roast, Mario turned up with donkey stew and cheesy polenta (*polenta taragna*) made with no ordinary cheese but his own – and we realized our mistake. The real meal – the one his wife had cooked especially *for us* – was just starting, and it would have been an affront to turn it away without an honest attempt at finishing it off, licking the pots. When he finally brought out *polenta e osèi* – polenta with roasted birds – namely thrushes (*tordi*)[7] that his father had shot in the woods nearby (legally they insisted, having had a license continuously for fifty-five years), we were dumbstruck. It had been Antonio's specific request for our lunch, but Mario caught us unprepared by serving it last, as if it was something that deserves being appreciated morsel by morsel, without hunger.

The dish epitomizes traditional Bergamasque cuisine and originates from the seasonal custom of hunting migratory birds with nets cast in woods – *this* technique is now outlawed, but still represents 'bird hunting' (which is not banned but regulated) in the local imaginary. A 1724 text printed in Bergamo describes the *roccolo* as a characteristic hunting building invented about 150 years before, when landowners entrusted sharecroppers with the added task of harvesting migratory birds on the hills and lower mountains (Angelini 1724). A three-storey building, the size of one single room, the *roccolo* is a hunting tower. Sometimes built entirely out of wood but more usually part wood and part stones, it is surrounded by concentric circles of alternately planted trees (variedly oak, elm, ash, sometimes combined with vines and juniper). On a slope, it would look like a turret in the middle of a green maze, beautifully geometric if the arboretum is well kept. Nowadays, it is not uncommon to find either abandoned *roccoli* amidst overgrown bush, or to recognize its original design in converted mountain chalets, with or more often without the tree plantation around. Now visible only to skilled eyes, this century-old hunting practice is still inscribed in the mountain landscape.

The feminist novelist Elena Gianini Belotti gives a heart-rendering description of bird hunting with nets in *Pimpì Oselì*, appropriately set in a remote and backward mountain village of the Bergamasque valleys in the 1930s. In the eyes of the author, the bloodshed and stench of the carnage well matched the uncouthness of the villagers and their archaic, guttural dialect as they brought up their children under the bigotry of the fascist regime, feeding them obscure and repetitive doggerels such as *Pimpì Oselì* (which is a nursery rhyme about counting birds). Now *polenta e osei* gives its name to a 'typical' dessert – a yellow cake with chocolate birds nesting atop, which 'real' *bergamaschi* ritually despise and would never dream eating, but take tourists to buy from expensive patisseries.

Probably because of long-lasting associations with illegal or bloody practices, the actual meat dish *polenta e osèi* is regularly presented and received, in my experience, with elaborate explanations of its legality ('It's in hunting season' or 'My father has a license' or 'We buy it from licensed hunters') or, on the other hand, with complicit nudges and winks. Either way, it stirs reactions, expectations and story-telling. In either words, it is a sure signpost for cultural intimacy (Herzfeld 2005), either to be protected from and justified to outsiders, or to be quietly shared. When I had *polenta e osèi* with my hosts in the upper pastures of Val Taleggio, it was cooked by an experienced woman of the family and after elaborate deliberations on how to serve them, we settled on 'drowning' them in fresh cream (after roasting them in butter and oil). It was the celebratory final meal after my prolonged second stay with this family on their upper pastures, living and sleeping and cooking and working with them for three months. No particular disclaimers were given then, and we dug in.

Almost as a way of excusing his nostalgic request, Antonio got Mario to tell us of when he offered *polenta e osèi* on the menu of the first Terra Madre day that Antonio organized for Slow Food. '*Madona me*!' ('Oh my Virgin Mary!') exclaimed Mario. The rest could only be a lamentation, suitably long, convoluted and intercalated with dialect expressions – mostly colourful and verging on foul. In short, the story went that Antonio received a number of infuriated phone calls from nondescript 'environmentalists', and Mario received an on-site investigation by public hygiene officers who 'practically strip-searched me' – and the farm, but could not find 'a grain of sand out of place'. The whole tale eloquently expressed the resentment for feeling under surveillance for simply being what one is: a peasant, a hunter, a meat-eater, a mountain man. Just out of time, and out of place at one's home. Mario resists the feeling of the ever-pervading encroachment of modernity by simply refusing to apply for a permit to dig a road up to his meadows. He keeps the path, a selective tool to filter in suitably humbled visitors, and keep out the bite-and-go tourists.

It is part of peasant culture to have festivals of plenitude, feasts, *sagre* or family banquets. Up until a generation ago, christenings, confirmations and weddings called for day-long banquets to which the extended family was invited – and no one should be forgotten. Parties of 100–200 people were the expected routine for weddings. Sitting and eating all day was a sure sign of abundance, social achievement and comfort. No one complained about cholesterol, and the portions were hearty and rich in fats and sugars. At Mario's, we could even choose between two versions of our *polenta e osèi*: one with butter, oil and sage or the other, drowned in fresh buttermilk cream. We relished it. And then Mario was ready to talk business.

'If food is treated as a code, the messages it encodes will be found in the pattern of social relations being expressed' is Mary Douglas's incipit of her famous essay *Deciphering a Meal* (1972). The code that Mario was serving us by the ladleful was one of intimacy and trust: everything from the uncustomary wait to the dusty spare room to the solicitous serving of a double meal (one for face, one for real) spoke of a slow but steady move into the realm of complicit trust. Mario was now sitting down and eating with us. His wife would serve us and occasionally joined us for a few minutes, then she was off again to tend to the paying guests. Family and friends must have patience and understanding; customers are not expected to. Trusted partners can take a ranting. We were in for one.

How come the well-known leader of a cheese cooperative was planning to hold a feast day dedicated to the *Principi delle Orobie*, right on the same day that Slow Food has committed full force to the Bitto day in the neighbouring Val Gerola? This clearly had to be rescheduled. How come one of the members of the newly born presidium is known to have used the logo on his own packaging, with no concertation with the other producers and, what's more, without consulting Mario – being the person in charge of it? How come the recent Sagra dello Stracchino was held without the official presence of the presidium but only of the local cooperative of producers? A *sagra* implies having many types of something: many types of wine, many types of potatoes . . . A Sagra dello Stracchino with just one *stracchino* producer is self-promotion, not a *sagra*!

Mario was only being encouraged. If one wants to join a network, rejoined Battista, one had to believe in it – it should not be exploited as a commercial opportunity alone. Despite the conviviality of the setting, criticisms and allegations were detailed and relentless – some notably similar to the issues regarding

Strachitunt – illustrating how a cheese-making technique can be operationalized into territorial boundaries. For example: 'It is not at all obvious to me *how* you can make *stracchino a munta calda* with milk coming from 10 kilometres away from the creamery! I bet they reheat it; I am tempted to just turn up one day at 6 am and say: I am here, show me how you make this cheese.'

Criticisms went back and forth and regarded both the new coalition of upland cheeses and the power balance within the presidium, since each of the family enterprises involved seemed to count on their own network of contacts and clients *first*, reluctant to share or coordinate with the others. An attractively designed carton box for *stracchini*, complete with logo and the name of the producers' cooperative, raised brows: 'So now they call themselves *Stracchino all'antica* of the valley such and such'. To differentiate themselves, 'they even ordered *their* own wrapping paper, with *our* logo'. While the practicalities were easy to smooth out – the exclusive wrapping paper and logo quickly disappeared even from the internet – it is clear that it takes the skill of a mediator and the authority of an ambassador to foster a sense of community among mountain cheese-makers, whom the very logic of heritage distinction as much as that of territorial exception drives apart.

The fate of Val Taleggio and its neighbours reinventing *stracchino* was a community of destiny, to use Edgar Morin's phrase: a common stake if not a common intent. Such stake includes the need to perform a sensorium in order to successfully position it on the market. In the case of Antonio, this performance was cultural and political, making full use of the language of taste and of Slow Food gastro-diplomacy. In the case of Val Taleggio, as we shall see next, it involved local entrepreneurs but also municipal administrations, in a cultural effort to portray the valley as a whole as an open-air, all-year-round exhibition of dairy excellence.

Performing Cheese Heritage

Tenaciously developed by two young mayors (a man and a woman) elected in 2006, the municipal administrations of Vedeseta and Taleggio pursued the project of establishing an ecomuseum in Val Taleggio. What an ecomuseum is, or should be, is a matter of debate among scholars and operators.[8] In brief, they are participatory projects that involve whatever a population determines as worthy of conservation and development: historical, artistic, natural or cultural heritage. In Lombardy, the first decade of the new century saw a proliferation of such institutions, variably interpreted and translated as open-air museums of specific anthropic landscapes – whether rural or industrial. Ecomuseums are institutional frameworks to 'add value' to local economies in the light of their cultural significance. For ecomuseums in Lombardy, economic and commercial considerations weigh heavily on the choice of name, of participatory over conservation projects, and on the profiling of certain practices and local foods over others. Metonyms for 'territory', they are treated as political and economic devices. The UNESCO convention for the safeguarding of Intangible Cultural Heritage of 2003, and the European Landscape Convention of 2004[9] are some of the institutional discourses inspiring the workings of public administrations to support and sustain processes of identification, documentation, protection, promotion and revitalization of cultural patrimonies – from traditional recipes to carnivals through eco-museums.

Despite the personal engagement of Hugues de Varine in Val Taleggio, and his recommendation as 'founding father' of French ecomuseums to develop participatory projects, few of the Lombard ecomuseums can be described as 'community museums' (de Varine 2012). Some specialize in postindustrial or postagrarian oral history;[10] some others focus on the landscape as a specific object of study and conservation.[11] Lobbied by active projects such as Val Taleggio's, the Lombardy regional government established a law in 2007 acknowledging existing and nascent ecomuseums. Regional law n. 13 of 12 July 2007, 'Acknowledgement of the ecomuseums to promote local cultures and traditions for environmental, cultural, tourist and economic objectives' was modelled on the existing experience of ecomuseums in Piedmont, giving access to dedicated funds for the promotion (*valorizzazione*) of specific products, traditions, or locations, in a wide interpretation of the meaning of 'heritage'.[12]

Local gossip pointed to political allegiances and personal ambitions, not too dissimilarly from the story of Formai de Mut twenty years earlier. Certainly some local events were dominated by the nascent ecomuseum, sometimes even overshadowing the PDO saga. For example, the Festa del Ritorno, newly established in 1999 to celebrate the descent of the herds from the upper pastures in coincidence with the local cattle fair every October, evolved from a very local affair, featuring folk bands and '*formaggi tipici della Val Taleggio*', to a mediatized event hosting speeches of renowned politicians (notably of the Lega Nord and Forza Italia – then ruling parties both at national and regional level). Fireworks, press and television announcements, and television comedians attracted crowds. In a crescendo of popularity, the mayor of Taleggio – then a single man – appeared on national television at a match-making program symbolically bringing a slab of Taleggio cheese to attract a bride! With a tinge of farce as opposed to the dignified predicament of the Bitto Rebels, publicity was nonetheless of some avail. For example, Val Taleggio cheese-makers appeared in 2009 on *Mela verde* (Green Apple), a television Sunday program devoted to agriculture, rural folklore and local cuisine. Led by a chef, it shared a similar format with *Linea Verde* – the state television program where farmer Guglielmo had appeared in 1997.[13]

Beyond actual appearances on television, the eco-museification of Valtaleggio derived from popular media culture a pervasive expectation of performance vis-à-vis rural culture and its culinary counterpart. This should not surprise, as media discourse about Italian rurality is historically characterized by condescension towards premodern economies and the concomitant celebration of the peasant as a pillar of traditional identity, as substantiated by Bindi's archive investigation in the National Television RAI since the establishment of national broadcasting via radio and then video (2005). Gastronomy and folklore often feature together in Sunday programs: an envoy from the city goes to the deepest countryside where the 'natives' welcome him and stage artisanal crafts and banquets of 'typical' foods. Follows a detailed explanation of some of the recipes and the reason of their *tipicità*, then visits to producers and local entrepreneurs.

The Ecomuseum perhaps lacked subtlety in its attempt at reaching a large audience, but certainly established a style of exploiting locality as a mediatized resource. The valley's pastured landscape was reconceptualised, from an unromantic economic production (transhumance, dairy-farming and cheese-making) to a receptacle of heritage – tangible and intangible. Culinary, cultural and environmental by-products of the material culture of the *alpeggio* came to include the architectural remains of the *baite*, the stone huts dotting the valley's pastures. *Tipicità* came the describe not just a foodstuff, but a whole locality: an ostensive patrimony that needs continuously exhibiting by producers and residents alike, in order to be promoted and *valorizzato*, namely given value.

The convergence between the Ecomuseum program and the cheese-development agenda became politically noticeable when the president of the Strachitunt consortium accepted the role of president of the Ecomuseum. The full name of the Ecomuseum of Val Taleggio became eventually Civiltà del Taleggio, dello Strachitunt e delle Baite tipiche, roughly translatable as 'Civilization' or 'Culture' of Taleggio cheese, of Strachitunt, and of typical mountain abodes. I participated in the brainstorming meeting of the Ecomuseum in 2006 that debated the initial idea: Civiltà del Taleggio. Strachitunt was far from obtaining its PDO, but the Ecomuseum management was far-sighted enough to comprehend that the battle against the Taleggio PDO consortium was lost, and bet on the new horse. Anchoring such 'intangible' cultural heritage as the Civilization of Taleggio to the *baite tipiche* provided an apt grounding of the ecomuseum in Val Taleggio's tangible rural architecture, characterized by cut stonemasons walls and stone roofs. Unfortunately, of the more than one thousand *baite* that lie scattered in the higher pastures of Val Taleggio, there were enough funds to do up only one. The Ecomuseum did it and opened it to tourists as a bold innovation: the '*Baita* & Breakfast'.

The logic of *tutela* (guardianship, custodianship), and the 'patrimonialization' logic of value-addition thus enforced each other: the *patrimonio* of Val Taleggio can only be saved if it is recognized as valuable. What can certify one's worth better than tele-visualization in the global hierarchy of value?[14] The reconceptualization of the valley itself as a form of open-air *but bordered* museum, population included, also played into the idea of turning the entire valley into heritage. Hence the apt choice of *Civiltà* as a self-description. In a cultural context traditionally biased for the monumental, artistic and literary forms of national heritage, to name a 'civilization' after cheeses and mountain huts could sound defiant, even ironic – when not comical.

In just a few years, textual self-representations had embraced the transition from a notion of Val Taleggio as a rural landscape per se to that of a rural landscape as patrimony in need of 'value addition' (*valorizzazione*). As Jaro Stacul observed of Carnia in northern Italy, this process followed a shift in policy discourse from a mere 'agricultural policy' to that of a multifunctional, tourist-oriented 'rural development policy' (Stacul 2010: 228; cf. Gray 2000). In the Ecomuseum project, the revaluation of local cheese went hand in hand with the idea of making available a multisensorial experience that would in one breath convey the lived experience of dairy farming (Gray 1999) but also 'sell' the Val Taleggio landscape – all in one package.

The refrain of the value of natural and cultural riches is ubiquitous in the Ecomuseum documentation: a bilingual tourist brochure that I picked up in 2007, the year in which the Ecomuseum was officially established, spells out its mission in English:

> Val Taleggio is an island of tranquillity in a sea of green. Over the last three years, with this inestimable wealth as a basis in the firm belief that the great natural, artistic and historical heritage of our valley will become a driving force for development, we have worked, and will continue to do so, to create the 'Val Taleggio Ecomuseum: the Culture of Taleggio, Strachitunt, and the Typical Local *Baite* [mountain refuges]. Day after day a precise identity is being established and the people, diligent and involved, are rediscovering their roots. Rebuilding and re-evaluation work is being carried out to rediscover ancient traditions, support business excellence and valorize the unspoilt countryside, for our valley and all those who love it and know how to appreciate it. (*Val Taleggio/Taleggio Valley. Ecomuseo/Ecomuseum. 5 Vie Tematiche/The 5 Routes*, no date, signed by the mayors of Taleggio and Vedeseta, p. 1)

This statement unequivocally establishes the ecomuseum as a tool to attract tourism and to support local businesses. The interpretation of heritage that is offered, however, is strongly patrimonial rather than communal. As noted, *patrimonio*, the Italian word for *heritage*, is something that is owned and can be handed down but also sold (or squandered). While it includes *priceless* resources such as natural, artistic and historical patrimony – including the uncontaminated environment and the anthropic landscape, with its indigenous knowledge and local practices, it is not envisaged as a *common* but rather as a 'civilization', a 'culture' that is 'owned' (Kaneff and King 2004). As part of adding value to local territory and products, the population is expected to 'diligently' engage in reappropriating, reconstructing, revaluing. Popular participation in the ecomuseum project was thus actively sought, but also tokenized.[15]

This is precisely the point where the conviction that place has taste, or rather that the cheeses of Val Taleggio are *tipici*, turns into territorial branding (Trubek 2008: 211). Just as maple syrup from Vermont is expected to 'deliver an experience', Strachitunt and the Taleggio of Val Taleggio were expected not only to embody the fragrance, the suasion and the moral pedestal of marginalized mountain people. They were expected to deliver the experience of *being* those people. In order to do so, the cheese of Val Taleggio had not only to be reinvented, but also performed.

For the Ecomuseum leadership, it was fundamental to rethink creatively how to showcase their assets. Both the practices of locality that make Val Taleggio what it is, and the reciprocal roles of producers and consumer had to be reconceptualized and performed. 'Defining landscape is tantamount to defining order', spells out Stacul (2010: 229), and certainly in the case of Val Taleggio the Ecomuseum project proposed a new symbolic, performative and eventually political order.[16] The hundreds of abandoned stone huts dotting the valley were considered *tipiche* like the cheese that used to be made in them. But at the same time they had to be recast in novel terms. The '*Baita* & Breakfast', complete with sauna, offered to tourists the experience of living in an ex cow-shed. A separate space would be devoted *not* to a predictable ethnographic exhibition but to an interactive sensorial experience of the *vaccanza* – a pun based on *vacca* (cow) + *vacanza* (holiday). The 'cowliday' is a video installation that reproduces the sounds of a real-life cowshed and invites the visitor to progressively uncover and smell, touch and watch significant samples of the sensorial experience of mountain dairy farming. Hidden in as many drawers of a treasure-hunt chest are hay to smell, wood to touch and a loop of photographs of the scenery, introduced and commented by the voice of a professional actor.

Similarly, *Tu, casaro!* (You, the cheese-maker!) is a video-installation of the Ecomuseum designed to accompany a cheese-making workshop for tourists. I attended it with about a dozen young families in August 2013, as part of the Festa del Fe', the Hay Fair, one of the new events inaugurated under the management of the Ecomuseum to animate the valley's summers. The program, congenially located at the cooperative dairy site, included a visit to the creamery, free peeking in the cow stable, a hand-milking competition, the installation itself, a banquet, and games for kids such as hay-bale races on the slope. Despite the capricious weather, which served us a foggy morning followed by an afternoon downpour, the feast was successful, with about two hundred paying customers queuing at the customary self-service banquet based on *formaggi tipici locali*: cold platter with polenta, polenta with melted Strachitunt, grilled cheese, ravioli and *stracchino*, etc.

An eloquent employee of the cooperative dairy guided us through a fifteen-minute visit, showing us the pasteurization machine (heating milk up to 72°C for ten seconds) but underlining how they don't use it anymore because their entire production is now raw milk only, *a latte crudo*. Five farmers confer two tons of milk a day, curdling Monday, Tuesday, Thursday and Friday. From the conferring area, the refrigerated milk reaches a cauldron where it is heated to a temperature ranging between 36 and 40°C for Branzi and Taleggio. Strachitunt is made instead *a munta calda*, straight after milking in the cow shed next door.

We were judiciously told that starting cultures are added to Branzi and Taleggio, not to Strachitunt, which is worked with rennet only. We were shown the tools to manually cut the curd: the *spino*, the *lira* (guitar) and the *basla* (*spannarola*). We were shown the PDO brand number 42 for the Taleggio made on site. The cheese-maker explained how their Taleggio sells to Australia, Japan and the United States. Someone from the audience remarked that a relative of his had gone to America and had eaten Strachitunt! To the question: 'Do you still make Salva?' the cheese-maker answered: 'Salva is now a PDO and we are not in the consortium; our production is very limited and it would cost us too much in membership. So we make it anyway and call it *magrèra* from the name of the *baita* just outside here' (14 August 2014, video-recorded guided tour of the Cooperativa Sant'Antonio di Vedeseta). He thus unwittingly confirmed that it was a ubiquitous matter of fact to continue to make cheese outside a PDO production area, usually in very similar ways but without the consortium's constraints, simply by renaming the product – a strategy that both Bitto Storico and Blutunt producers followed, when the former abandoned the Bitto PDO (Part I), and the latter was excluded from PDO Strachitunt (Part II).

The video installation *Tu, casaro!* consisted of a video projection of skilfully edited interviews with the valley's cheese-makers. The screen, a seemingly milky surface located inside a traditional copper cauldron, showed their talking heads. All around the cauldron, the audience was asked to make their own miniature cheese, each curdling freshly hand-pressed milk from the milking competition that had just taken place on the patio of the cooperative cow-shed. Rennet was added to miniature cauldrons with the help of a guide, then the installation would fill the time of the actual curdling process. The audience consisted of young families. Each child would cast their curd in a small plastic canister to take home – after having been judiciously advised *not* to eat the cheese because 'we cannot be 100 per cent sure that it is safe'.

The narrative, the photography, and the fresh irony in this enjoyable video installation evoke a sense of complicit collaboration with and between the cheese-makers – something that jars with the very real competition among local producers under the pressure of producing 'dairy excellence' (*eccellenza casearia*). Such performance is aimed not so much at participating, co-producing or allying with consumers, but rather to 'seduce' them (del Marmol et al. 2015).

Figure 7. *Tu, casaro!* (You, the cheese-maker!) interactive installation at the Ecomuseum of Val Taleggio, 14 August 2013. Photo by Cristina Grasseni.

The installation *You, the cheese-maker*! debuted at the Slow Food Salone del Gusto of 2010 and was part of the fortunate convergence of several projects: the Ecomuseum Val Taleggio working in concert with the Strachitunt consortium, as well as the first public appearance of Antonio's two new Slow Food presidia just established in the Bergamasque valleys: Agrì and Stracchino all'antica. So powerful was the game of reciprocal performance that it seduced the producers themselves! They so much enjoyed seeing themselves featured in the installation that they flocked to it – forgetting to *sell* their own cheese – and leaving me and Antonio to promote their cheese at the Slow Food stand.

As Trubek states, 'taste of place and brand are very distinct framing categories for preserving, protecting, and promoting farming and food, leading to very different long-term links between taste, place, people, and food' (Trubek 2008: 213). The Ecomuseum seemed to couple the project of adding value to local cheeses with one of relocalizing them, by identifying them with the landscape and the population of the valley as living testimony of a 'civilization' of cheese. Local cheese-makers welcomed the idea of increasing their on-site consumption, showcasing the valley's cheese in feasts, fairs, events, banquets and installations.

There is no doubt that the Strachitunt cause benefited – at least in terms of notoriety and press – from this comprehensive territorial rebranding. However, actual processes of transition towards sustainable local economies are difficult to trigger, and the Ecomuseum did not create new jobs in the valley. On the contrary, it required professional skills from outside in order to 'animate' it (including street-theatre performers, professional actors, video editors, and communication designers). *Animazione* is the ubiquitous word used by the Ecomuseum administrators to explain that the valley would not be museified/mummified but on the contrary enlivened/re-animated through professional performances. This certainly added to the scepticism of the residents, once it became apparent that the tourist infrastructure of the valley could not be revolutionized by a single '*Baita* & Breakfast', and that apart from organized events the Ecomuseum did not attract a reliable stream of visitors and customers.[17] While this effort of self-restyling was successful for a few competitive family businesses, it cannot be said to have impacted the valleys' economy in a diffused way. To substantiate this, I turn to an official report written by the municipality of Vedeseta in 2014, which conveys the picture of economic and demographic stagnation suffered over the last fifteen years.

The formal seat of the consortium for the protection of Strachitunt cheese is the municipality of Vedeseta. In his end of term report of 2014, the mayor of Vedeseta (a different mayor from the one that promoted the ecomuseum in 2006), wrote that his municipality now counts 216 residents and three employees, for a territory of about 20,000 square kilometres (over 7,600 square miles).[18] In the summer, the population swells to about 1,000 holiday residents, but in the national census of 2011, Vedeseta ranked as the municipality with the oldest average age. Sarcastically, the mayor observes that this is not because people live longer. It is because all the young move away. With only two resident couples still in their fertile years, Vedeseta does not have much of a chance to repopulate.

The mayor underlines the sorry state of the pastoral environment. He openly equates the woods encroaching the abandoned pastures to pests and laments the crumbling high-altitude hamlets. He suggests that the only hope is to attract new farming families. To promote this process, the municipality has acquired the dairy cooperative building, which includes two residential apartments. Able bodies and new blood could clear pastures and reclaim abandoned buildings. However, tourists' numbers are in sharp decrease as a result of the continuing recession. State taxes, underlines the outgoing mayor, are being exacted through municipal revenue in return for little or no coverage for local services. Despite this onerous mandate, the mayor was re-elected in 2014 with ninety-six votes. Vedeseta was one of the twenty-six mountain municipalities in the province of Bergamo where there was only one candidate.

In his brief, two-page-long comment to a twenty-eight-page report listing income and taxes levied for a total of €110,000, he suggests that the tourist economy should intercept the growing flux of foreign motor-bikers and (mostly local) mountain bikers who appreciate the uncontaminated landscape. However, he notes how the valley's ecomuseum project, launched eight years before, 'is complex and problematic because of the lack of conviction of the population'. In the same breath, the mayor acknowledges and thanks the local voluntary associations for the recreational, cultural and sportive events they organize, acting as 'veritable vital lymph for our valley from a social point of view'.

Published on 24 February 2014, no mention was made in this document of the recent acquisition of one of the longest-coveted geographical indications: the PDO for Strachitunt, produced in the dairy cooperative of Vedeseta. The final deliberation bestowing a protected designation of origin to Val Taleggio came only days after, on 7 March 2014. Post-rurality is the condition of Val Taleggio: its survival is dependent on the attractiveness of its rural ecosystem and on its dairy 'excellence', but neither of them seem to have played a sufficiently strong economic role to retain its population.

Notes

1. The series is downloadable from the Slow Food Lombardia Facebook page: https://www.facebook.com/media/set/?set=a.423359624410268.98503.246199312126301&type=3.
2. See the report of the visit, which I published on 27 July 2010 on the website of the Bassetti Foundation for Responsible Innovation: http://www.fondazionebassetti.org/it/grasseni/2010/09/il_cibo_come_innovazione_respo.htm.
3. 'Promozione di sistemi locali di produzione agro-alimentare di rilevante interesse', retrieved 20 August 2014 from http://www.consiglio.regione.lombardia.it/servizi/ricerchecommissioni.
4. Antonio, 13 November 2013. He was commenting on the press release circulated online on the blog of the Bitto rebels, retrieved 19 August 2014 from http://ribellidelbitto.blogspot.com/2013/11/progetto-vie-dei-principi-delle-orobie.html.

5. Antonio, 1 November 2013, field notes. All following quotes are reconstructed from the day's field notes.
6. 6 January, in the Catholic calendar, and a holiday in Italy.
7. In the fall it is legal to hunt turtledove (*Streptopelia turtur*), blackbird (*Turdus merula*), lark (*Alauda arvensis*) and various species of thrush: *cesena* (*Turdus pilaris*), *tordo bottaccio* (*Turdus philomelos*) and *tordo sassello* (*Turdus iliacus*).
8. See Davis (1999), de Barry et al. (1992), Clifford et al. (2006) on community maps and ecomuseums. Baldin (2006) distinguishes between ecomuseum and open-air museum. Garlandini (2010) sees ecomuseums as 'cultural infrastructure' for the Lombardy Region.
9. Retrieved 27 August 2016 from http://www.coe.int/t/dg4/cultureheritage/heritage/Landscape/default_en.asp; http://www.unesco.org/culture/ich/index.php?lg=en&pg=00006.
10. As in the case of the Ecomuseum of Nova Milanese, which developed out of a local cultural association for the safeguarding of the memory of Nova's rural past as it became engulfed in the urban growth of the Milanese metropolitan area.
11. As is the case of the Ecomuseum of the Province of Cremona, named 'the Territory as Ecomuseum', or as the 'Ecomuseum of the Landscape of Parabiago', a Milanese suburb that display a characteristic mix of postindustrial and postagrarian recession, as a number of local small and medium-sized factories closed down and the rural vocation of the landscape has been superseded by the urbanization of the area.
12. 'Riconoscimento degli ecomusei per la valorizzazione della cultura e delle tradizioni locali ai fini ambientali, paesaggistici, culturali, turistici ed economici'. The Ecomuseum of Val Taleggio was among the first 18 ecomuseums to be officially 'acknowledged' as such by the Lombardy regional government in 2008. Between 2009 and 2014, another 26 ecomuseums were formalized for a total of 44 in Lombardy alone.
13. On the persistence and repetitiveness of a distinctive visual rhetoric regarding radio and television programmes devoted to rurality and agriculture in Italy, see Bindi and Grasseni (2014).
14. I refer to Michael Herzfeld's work on value-addition as a ubiquitous process in urban planning, architecture and artisanship. The definition is found in his analysis of gentrification and museification of historical cities (specifically in Rethemnos, Rome and Bangkok); his critical study of value-addition through heritage discourse in Crete for example (1991) exposes how pedigree Venetian origins are claimed to value buildings, while claims of Turkish contamination dispenses from heritage-induced limitations to change or restore them.
15. The Ecomuseum initially invested in a community map effort that I was invited to lead, and developed in 2007–2008. However, since it was largely focused on ethnographic research of detailed local knowledge about, for example, local cheese-maturing techniques such as the *caselli*, the Ecomuseum leadership did not sustain it as it would have no immediate outcome in terms of tourism or advertising (Grasseni 2011). As a result, the online community map still exists, but maintenance of the site has been discontinued. My own collaboration with the Ecomuseum ceased when it became clear that there was no real interest in creating a centre of documentation about Val Taleggio's cheese-making tradition, but rather in investing on events and rural architecture.
16. The mayor of Taleggio elected in 2006 has been re-elected for his third mandate, being the only candidate. This will total twelve years of local government. In the meantime,

he became president of the Mountain Community for Valle Brembana, presiding over thirty-six municipalities.

17. Cf. Stacul (2010: 234–35) on a similar experiment of the Ecomuseum in Val Vanoi and its discontents. Oscar Biffi (2014) has studied comparatively two ecomuseums in Piedmont and Lombardy to assess their capacity to engender participation in a transition to sustainable economies. While in the Lombard case the participatory aspect proved cosmetic, and in fact grassroots associations for sustainable agriculture grew *outside* the Ecomuseum's institutional space, in the Piedmont case a sustained conversation among local administration, Mountain Community technicians and Ecomuseum promoters generated some economic return in the long run. The reintroduction of an autochthonous sheep breed (*pecora sambucana*) was however the result of personal synergies rather than of the Ecomuseum per se, and the tourist economy generated by the Ecomuseum would not suffice to keep the breeders in business.
18. *Relazione di fine mandato. Quinquiennio 2009–2014.* The report is a public document and can be consulted on the municipal website. Retrieved 26 May 2014 at http://www.comune.vedeseta.bg.it/.

Conclusion of Part III

Reinventing *strachì* was imperative for both the cheese-makers of Val Taleggio and their neighbours, and resulted in the reinvention of Strachitunt as well as the establishment of the Slow Food presidium Stracchino all'Antica delle Valli Orobiche. In both cases, the reinvention of *strachì* was a process of *calibration*, an adjustment and retargeting of local cheese production vis-à-vis a number of constraints and possibilities, one of which was the demand of dairy excellence from consumers, food activists and gourmands. In Part III, we revisited the Strachitunt strategy to relentlessly pursue a PDO on the basis of Val Taleggio's argument of territorial exception, explaining how it could not easily converge with a Slow Food agenda of dairy excellence, as was instead the case for the Bitto Rebels. We compared the Strachitunt strategy with Slow Food's alternative of reinventing *stracchino* itself on the basis of heritage distinction: dairy excellence being the unique criterion on the basis of which eleven producers were singled out by Antonio, the charismatic local Slow Food leader, to set up a presidium of Stracchino All'Antica delle Valli Orobiche. These choices entailed different discursive and practical strategies of relocalization even though they enrolled in some cases the very same actors.

Part and parcel of food reinvention is a matter of calibrating it to the market: packaging, serving and tasting cheese as a value-added commodity with apt language and imagery. Both in logistics and communication, calibrating means standardizing and packaging: certifying standards, physically wrapping and boxing. Issues of traceability, design and sheer marketability of a priced commodity are all implicated in the 'packaging' of reinvented foods (Shapin 2003). Strachitunt was difficult to calibrate because it was impossible to standardize: its natural moulds grant an extremely wide palette of tastes in one single slice, from creamy to spicy! Its unforeseeability (which to some means utter unpalatability) is the mark of its 'artisanship' and of its dairy 'excellence'.

To embrace a convincing argument of Slow Food's Piero Sardo, a 'complex' cheese *cannot* be 'typical', namely, literally repeatable according to a standard protocol (2003a). In this original twist on the very language of *tipicità*, Sardo accuses the very idea of *tipico* to equal that of a stamp: *fatto con lo stampino* in Italian means precisely mass-produced, stamped out in order to be identical to another specimen. While sameness 'ostensibly abolishes the specificities of time and place' (as Herzfeld argues in the case of 'iconic' craft tourism: 1992: 108), dairy excellence specifically transforms cheese from foodstuff into 'an item of cultural heritage' (*un bene culturale*: Sardo 2003b: 307). This is very much in line with Herzfeld's argument on artisanal skill and academic knowledge (2007): resistance to standardization is characteristic both of artisanal crafts (which are mistaken for idiosyncrasies or picturesqueness) and of embodied anthropological knowledge (which is under attack for its lack of 'applicability' and its 'unscientific' methodology). Moreover, as Herzfeld notices, the discourse of the 'traditional' with reference to skill and craft 'is doubly marginalizing, both through its implication of exclusion from modernity and in its appeal to a powerful form of localism' (2007: 101).

Precisely because difficult to market and very, very local, Strachitunt was almost lost. Its production was actively rescued, firstly by a Bergamo cheese merchant who began ordering consistent quantities from a Val Taleggio cheese-making family, then promoted by Slow Food, matured by the local cheese vendors, adopted by the valley's cheese-makers' cooperative, and finally bestowed a protected denomination of origin after eleven years of struggles.

In my earlier work I showed how alternative provisioning among critical consumers encompasses important aspects of social affect and political participation (Grasseni 2013). Similarly here, status, strategy and survival are the factors at stake from the point of view of the producers who sought Slow Food protection, or chose to enlist one's product in regional and national repertoires of traditional foodstuffs, or followed the even steeper path of filing for a European Protected Designation of Origin, as in the case of Strachitunt.

This meant repackaging the valley, attempting to identify it as a whole (cheese-making, rural architecture and landscape) with 'dairy excellence'. This meant finding and adopting a language of taste – a language that prescribed a 't' and not a 'd' in Strachitunt and much more: cheese-makers and refiners, in order to be recognized within a 'global hierarchy of value' (Herzfeld 2004: 3) must learn to articulate and market the full sensorium of their cheeses – aroma, taste, texture, including occasional 'clicks' under the tongue – and of course package it within a visual imaginary that is as pervasive as unfathomable. Reinvented cheese must be equipped with the correct logos, indications and quality certifications while looking as if serenely and 'naturally' emerging from a pristine and cohesive rural 'tradition': never lacking wood, foliage or straw in the background.

Elsewhere I have pointed to the 'packaging skills' required of alpine cheese-makers to match the expectation of a rural idyll (Grasseni 2003), which finds confirmation in the contested packaging paper of one of the producers of Stracchino all'Antica discussed over our alpine meal in Chapter 6. The Ecomuseum of Val Taleggio was swift to understand the equation, casting its own name in terms of Civiltà ('Civilization') del Taleggio, dello Strachitunt e delle Baite Tipiche: bearing the name of the valley's two most representative cheeses, and anchoring them in its rural landscape.

'Kings of a ghost valley' is the phrase I used to describe the undeniable success of one farming family in Val Taleggio and the concurrent demise of their socio-economic surroundings. A unique combination of human resources, division of labour and skills, entrepreneurial courage and media savviness make them qualify for current standards of 'excellence' under multiple points of view. As breeders, excellence meant adhering to an intensive model of dairy farming, investing in the productivity of their herd. Since its inception, the history of breed selection has privileged the intensification of production as a criterion for success: 'functional animal beauty' sums up this philosophy (Grasseni 2005a). Only with the current rethinking of the multifunctional vocation of mountain agriculture, planning documents now recognize 'the importance of mountain farms as providers of services for the public food, such as the safeguarding of the territory and conservation of the environment' but also underline that services such as milk quality monitoring, advice on cattle diet and artificial insemination 'are only economic for farms with an adequate number of cattle' (Galli and Oldrati 1993: 62). In the mountains, however, a farm of 150 cows has an environmental impact that one of fifteen cattle does not have, in particular in terms of how the very landscape becomes differently managed, to begin with disposing of liquid and solid manure (Bianchi et al. 2005). Bulky, clumsy and brittle, 'improved' cows would not fit in the Ecomuseum's *baite tipiche*. They are not made for climbing mountain paths to keep the tradition of the *alpeggio* alive, but rather they are literally moulded around machine-milking. The amount of locally made hay becomes insufficient to feed them.

As cheese-makers, alpine farmers could *also* perform dairy excellence for radical gourmands. But the request that they 'reconvert' to small and poorly productive animals after investing generational efforts into 'improving' their herd to Euro-American standards is the ironic mark of the schizophrenic re-invention of cheese. A beautifully selected herd of 'Super Browns', heralded as an example of entrepreneurship, community leadership and stewardship in animal husbandry, could not be discarded because these very animals, the product of intensive agriculture standards, need dietary supplements to sustain their more-than-doubled milk yield. PDOs and Slow Food presidia may well engender a 'politics of *terroir*' (Bingen 2012) that is substantively supportive of community economies. Nevertheless, they do so without challenging the premises of the commodity market and the fragile positioning of marginal economic actors within it.

The protagonists of the reinvention of Strachitunt are nowadays icons in the local and national press: cheese-maker, refiner, chef and merchant. However, their success consisted in harnessing the moral stance of an entire community behind them, as well as establishing functional if evanescent alliances – with Slow Food, the valley's Ecomuseum, the local press and the village dairy cooperative: ambivalent tectonics of alliance and competition. Competition is divisive and, over the last fifteen years, the rise in fortune of my host family was accompanied by undeniable conflict – as I noticed for example at the valley's cattle fair of 2006 and again 2010. Especially in small arenas, an intense exercise of staring takes place. For the adept, this incorporates the aesthetic appreciation of the cattle with the moral judgement of those who do not 'improve' their cows. But the social marginalization of the farmers who just do not make it to 'excellence' is resisted with scowling and muttering, venting anger at those who harnessed the right technical and political advice.

Increasingly successful in outracing their competitors, establishing their reputation as modern breeders *and* – culminating irony – *also* as the saviours of Strachitunt, my hosts could eloquently speak to two incommensurable and irreconcilable morals, one of 'improvement' and one of 'heritage'. Aronne was, in fact, 'a born Cicero' as he showed at the Turin event in 2004. Proud of their dynamic capacity to straddle tradition and innovation, my hosts initially resented Slow Food and its pretence to establish a presidium for Strachitunt as an *alpeggio* cheese *only*: produced exclusively in the summer, with no fodder, exclusively feeding cows on local pastures. All this seemed self-maiming in terms of quantity and primitivistic in its radicalness: 'Taliban', in fact. The Slow Food recipe for heritage Bitto seemed to work for its producers, carving an über-niche out of the *alpeggio* cheese *niche*, while providing a robust and vocal communication and commercial infrastructure. In the case of Val Taleggio, to portray the valley as both pristine and liminal (untouched and at risk of extinction) certainly added value to Strachitunt PDO as a scarce commodity. However, the strategic choice for a community PDO and a local consortium could only *hope* to attract new production forces to an enclave that is demographically imploding.

In Val Taleggio the reinvention of Strachitunt as a natural blue cheese came to coincide with the Ecomuseum's strategy to identify a locality – Val Taleggio – as a specific set of environmental and productive practices that can be identified and displayed. Mountain cheese is the embodiment of this heritage, the end product of careful 'balancing on an alp' (Netting 1981). Cheese-makers thus act as representatives of local heritage (ecological, historical and gastronomic). Historically, practices of sustainability in Italian mountain communities have diversely and creatively combined self-sustenance and seasonal migration of skilled practitioners, tapping into regional and even international flows of commodities and artisanal expertise (Viazzo 1989; Sanga 1979). Nowadays, forcibly compared against standard agriculture, 'improved' or 'culled', mountain herders and herds alike are being additionally asked to 'perform' their virtue of sustainable husbandry. Alpine cheese-makers in particular are increasingly expected not only to be skilled artisans but to take active part in communicating it, by posing in video-installations such as *Tu, casaro* or by featuring as testimonials at tourist feasts. For example farmer Guglielmo is now literally inscribed in the cheese-making landscape of Val Taleggio: he features on the dairy co-op van selling the valley's cheese (Figure 8). More than a living icon, he has become an 'immutable mobile' as Latour would call it – a circulating commodity that will survive his person.

The reinvention of *stracchino* was coined on an argument of heritage distinction based on Slow Food's criteria for dairy excellence rather than on territorial exclusiveness. In neighbouring Valle Imagna it fostered participatory projects such as another ecomuseum, a local cooperative and municipal backing. Cheesemakers teach visiting school children to make their own miniature cheese – following the Val Taleggio model of *Tu, casaro*, with or without interactive video installations. The restoration of mountain stone sheds for tourist use is now a common idea, encouraged among private owners as a way of developing 'diffused hotels' (*alberghi diffusi*), not dissimilarly from Val Taleggio's *Baita* & Breakfast.

Figure 8. Cooperativa Agricola S. Antonio, Vedeseta. 2012. Photo by Cristina Grasseni.

However, through the celebration of local agro-food systems as per se 'identity value-added', one does run the risk of using the language of place-based foods in ways that too easily become from locale-based to localist tout court. In published documents, interviews with local administrators and posters presented to the Italian 'territorialist' society, *stracchino* has been variously described as an 'identity marker', a tool for the 'renaissance of local community', a common heritage of a 'civilization of *stracchino* and stone', uncritically glossing over the complex political tactics and alliances underlying the making of community denominations and of relevant ecomuseums.[1]

Through these interwoven dynamics, a small number of actors – Slow Food activists, mountain smallholders, PDO consortia leaders and local administrators – recurrently take on overlapping roles, sometimes representing different products that are *both* competitors *and* allies: the large commercial PDO Taleggio, which sells internationally and covers an area of production the size of northern Italy; Strachitunt, a local 'reinvention' of a strictly territorial protocol, and finally the Stracchino all'Antica, a Slow Food 'reinvention' of raw-milk *stracchino* that insists more on the 'dairy excellence' of food heritage than on its territorial exception. This multiplies kaleidoscopically their capacity to position themselves in the heritage arena as competitive actors, without challenging the normative assumption that heritage cheese has added value because of its unique characteristics and not because of the social networks that sustain it. It is precisely these social networks – their fluidity, litigiousness and common stakes – that Part III has attempted to unpack.

Notes

1. Retrieved 20 August 2014 from www.ruralpini.it/Inforegioni27.01.11Agricoltura_multifunzionale_in_Valle_Imagna.htm and www.ruralpini.it/Inforegioni28.04.12-Casa-dello-stracchino.html.

Conclusion

Since my first visit to Val Taleggio in the summer of 1997, I have conversed with cheese-makers, mayors of remote mountain villages, ambitious politicians, village priests and community volunteers, local historians, restaurant owners and cheese retailers, tourists, school teachers, university professors, mountain hikers, dairy farmers, vets, hunters, leaders and consumers of 'alternative food networks', and many others. Each offered their view on *tipicità* and what makes it intrinsic to cheese in the Bergamasque mountains – more, to Bergamasque identity itself. Over the years, and with their help, I have witnessed the dynamic redefinition of a field of production, including the politics of denomination and localization of cheese in the province of Bergamo and beyond, keeping the region of Lombardy as my area of reference. All of these were implicated in the saga of Strachitunt. For the sake of this book, this drama opens on a Sunday in the fall of 2006 (Chapter 1), continues at the municipal hall of Vedeseta at the outset of winter 2009 (Chapter 4), and closes around the table of a mountain *baita* on All Saints of 2013 (Chapter 6). But the story began to unfold much earlier – at the end of the 1990s, or maybe even at the time of Pliny![1]

Reinventing Strachitunt in Val Taleggio was an effort in 're-imagining marginalized foods' (Finnis 2012) but also a defiant act of sovereignty, carried out at the edge of a nation by self-appointed economic leaders. They acted in the heritage arena, a quintessentially glocal scenario, exposed to the competitive dynamics of a potentially global market, but acted very much on the ground within the dialectics of local rivalries, the manoeuvring of fluid alliances and the harnessing of political visibility.

Tipicità is pivotal in generating a geography of competing cheese pedigrees, upheld by as many communities of practice, who skilfully engage in veritable 'cheese wars'. *Tipicità* is enrolled as a recognizable category for the purpose of advancing one's cause at many levels: economic, cultural and institutional. However, this skilful appropriation is not necessarily subservient to top-down 'heritage regimes' (Bendix et al. 2012) but rather creates diverse spaces for strategic claims to food heritage as a form of *patrimonio*. In the Alpine region, the reinvention of craft foods and cheese in particular is cast – and genuinely felt – as an expression of collective local cultures of 'resistance' (Grasseni 2012), as an act of cultural and economic sovereignty.

In my most recent work I showed how the relocalization of food provisioning is associated with *consumers*' increased awareness of collective responsibility for sustainable citizenship (Grasseni 2013). Buyers of local food see craft foods as resisting the standardized, uniformly tasting, cheaply priced, intensively farmed, heavily processed and globally distributed commodity foods – which are often produced at the cost of marginalizing family farming and community economies. Food relocalization is thus appropriated as an economic and political agenda by alternative consumers' networks that advocate more responsible production and consumption. There are many ways in which smallholders, traditional growers, family breeders and small and medium-sized manufacturers are marginalized *qua* producers in the current global food systems. Sometimes their crops fall victim to international dumping practices (as in the case of Mexican corn – see Castellanos and Bergstresser 2014). Or, marginalization can be the ironic effect of the rediscovery of certain peasant foods by gourmet restaurants and tourism, as is the case of the transformation of alpaca meat from an lowly indigenous foodway to 'Highland *haute cuisine*' in the Nuevo Andino culinary trend. This dramatically overpriced foodstuffs that were earlier despised and left to peasant indigenous communities, making them less accessible to their original consumers (Markowitz 2012).

In Val Taleggio, marginalization came from being a drop in the ocean of PDO Taleggio production: a Protected Designation of Origin whose area of production spans practically the entire plains of northern Italy, consolidated and dominated by large lowland concerns, whose market price is too low for small producers to compete with. For the dairy-farmers, cheese-makers and cheese-vendors of Val Taleggio, having control of the entire supply chain of one highly priced product that is identified with their valley – what I called an argument for territorial exception – was a question of resistance. Strachitunt was reinvented to be their patrimony.

Reinventing Strachitunt became part of a wider agenda to protect Val Taleggio's entire ecology of dairy production, including the livelihood of its farming families, the material culture of cheese-making (in turn historically tied to transhumance), as well as an anthropic landscape that is reverting to unkempt woods. Anchise's speech, which opens Chapter 1, could have come from many food activists. However, his expression 'patrimonio di una valle, patrimonio di una comunità' was used in lieu of a more radical notion of commons or commonwealth, which in the Alps historically describes the common holding and using of undivided resources such as pasture land, woods or springs. To be sure, Anchise's heritage claims to material and immaterial patrimony did not go as far as proposing the collective ownership of heritage. On the contrary, it set the ground for selling it at a higher price.

This book combines and compares the Strachitunt saga with the longitudinal ethnographic observation of more than a decade of this and similar processes of self-reinvention. Since I first portrayed the family economy of dairy-farming and cheese-making in the Bergamasque valleys in my film *Those Who Don't Work Don't Make Love* (1998), I have witnessed the bitter struggle to obtain a suitably denominated cheese for Val Taleggio, first in vain within the consortium for PDO Taleggio, then through a failed negotiation to establish a Slow Food presidium, and finally with the laborious reinvention of Strachitunt PDO. This achievement was earned amidst as many 'cheese wars': first, the 'mother of all battles': the rebellion of heritage Bitto makers to their larger PDO consortium; then, the refounding of a bankrupted and much gossiped community-wide PDO in neighbouring Valle Brembana (Formai de Mut). Finally, two brand new Slow Food presidia (the Stracchino all'Antica and the Agrì of Valtorta), involving among others producers of Formai de Mut and of Strachitunt. More recently then, the non-PDO, non-presidium Latteria Sociale di Branzi promoted the coalition of the six artisanal cheese of the Bergamasque valleys together with Slow Food: the Slow Food presidia Agrì of Valtorta and Stracchino all'Antica delle Valli Orobiche, the heritage (non-PDO) Bitto Storico, the PDOs Formai de Mut and Strachitunt, and Branzi itself (neither presidium nor PDO).

The reinvention of Strachitunt, contextualized among the diplomatic excogitations of these other cheeses, and countless other attempted or aborted reinventions (such as Erborinato Bergamasco and Taleggio della Val Taleggio) should illuminate what it means to turn cheese into heritage – which undoubtedly says something of the cheeses itself, of heritage foods more broadly and of heritage as a whole. Upland cheese is constantly *re*-invented *qua* patrimony of small or large communities of practitioners, consumers and estimators. Similarly to UNESCO's Intangible Cultural Heritage, heritage cheese needs both 'safeguarding' and 'promoting', including open calls on the part of producers and administrators, to their communities and populations, to take active part in a certain degree of performativity.

Reinvented cheese is not, however, an 'invented tradition' (Hobsbawm and Ranger 1983). There is something old-fashionably substantial to these craft mountain cheeses – whether friends, allies or enemies: 'typically' manufactured, locally sourced, traditionally aged and convivially consumed. It would be unfair to socially deconstruct away the generational transmission of a material culture that these dynamics underscore: specific tool use, processing environments and repeated techniques, as well as knowledge of the local landscape, milk quality and maturing conditions. Especially if compared with transnational examples of artisanship that are literally learnt from scratch, as documented, for example, in Paxson's historical and ethnographic analysis of American artisanal cheese

(2012), these cheeses smell of history – however reinvented, negotiated and performed. Harry West has provided a convincing overview of the intertwined dynamics of 'the social construction and contestation of place-named foods' through appellations and indications of origin (West 2013b). Defining American cheese-makers' entrepreneurialism as a form of heritage in itself, 'a tradition of invention' (Paxson 2014), helps us illuminate precisely the distinction of this conjuncture: a tradition of constant, laborious, conflictual reinvention.

I have explained and contextualized the sometimes divergent choices of neighbouring actors in a *post-transhumant* context. Ongoing interpretations of food as heritage coalesce on the ground into diverse forms of compromises and practices. I have argued that upland and lowland cheeses are adjusting their practices and rhetoric to the fact that the transhumant tradition from which they originate has perished. They are in effect *post-transhumant cheeses*.

The cheese-makers of Val Taleggio and Val Brembana share an indefatigable will to survive within an adverse socioeconomic context, which has led to the demographic implosion and the economic stagnation of their upland communities. Slow Food presidia, ecomuseums and no less than nine PDO denomination cheeses in a single province may be read as 'calibration' and 'packaging' strategies: marketing the sensorium of dairy excellence and performing the hyperlocality of mountain communities, but editing out their substantial failure to reproduce themselves socially. I insisted on the limits and potentials of doing 'PDO Italian style', namely, investing on extremely niche productions such as Strachitunt. Despite the fact that the unfettered struggle for a market niche did not, at least upon my relatively short-term observation, result in a visible resurgence of alpine dairy farming, I also provide a counterargument, one that does not come across easily in balance sheets or demographics, but seems to resonate deeply: the importance of naming cheese as an act of cultural and economic sovereignty.

The claim of a Protected Designation of Origin for Strachitunt of Val Taleggio was supported with the conviction and the ethical overtones of an entire 'people' claiming their right to cultural ownership (Kaneff and King 2004). For the protagonists, finding a cheese they can call their own had real-life impact: it meant that anyone *in the world* wishing to buy a cheese called Strachitunt would have to go to them, whether from Milan, Boston or San Francisco. Little did they know that it would have even further-reaching implications for imaginaries well beyond their trade. Even before obtaining its PDO, Strachitunt was internationally famed within connoisseurs' circles. For example, the Harvard mycologists who sampled European cheeses at the Slow Food Cheese fair in Bra in 2011 to carry out comparative analysis of their microbic genome with American craft cheeses – mentioned in Chapter 1 – picked Strachitunt among others.[2]

In the face of past transhumance and present transnational markets, we can appreciate the anachronism of the static political imaginary behind geographical indications, which reproduces what Lissa Malkki aptly called 'a metaphysics of sedentarism' (1992) in relation to notions of nationhood. We can appreciate the irony of current obsessions with locality and purity, while comprehending their validity and pertinence, not only to actual skills, but to the destiny of these people. The whole debate on *tipicità* reminds us that this is no idle distinction: the protagonists of this book strive to articulate, specify and monitor precisely *how* their cheeses are craft and artisanal. As alternatives to mass commodities, they are uniquely priced, idiosyncratically produced and sometimes require trained tasting to be appreciated. As such, they thrive in gourmet cultures and can be very expensive – or not, according to how successfully they have entered national and sometimes international circuits of media and marketing for niche commodities.

Strachitunt, as much as Bitto and Formai de Mut, made use of the *tipicità* argument in a territorial way, despite the mobility, hybridity and great dynamicity of the transhumant tradition that predated them. They are a prime example of how diverse, resourceful and polemic the age of global heritage can be (Grasseni 2011), and specifically of how local food cultures can be instrumental to what Aistara has aptly called 'authentic anachronism' in the case of the recycling of postsocialist material culture in 'heritage' Latvian bread-making (2014). In the case of post-transhumant cheese, the transhumant tradition of the Bergamini is both upheld as historical documentation of the rootedness of certain ways of cheese-making in the Bergamasque Alps, and positively overlooked when confronted with the competition of lowland cheese-makers who too claim ascendance to the 'authentic' recipes of alpine heritage cheese.

As Harry West puts it, 'little has been written about how heritage is discursively constructed – how various actors 'tell their stories' and how these narratives are read by others'.[3] With this book I have tried to do precisely that. I have explored those discourses conducting a critical analysis of *tipicità* and *patrimonio*. First I outlined the geography of opposites that pitches mountain makers against lowland dairies, unveiling the divergences and internal squabbles between upland cheeses that could easily claim transhumance as a common heritage. Then I focused on Val Taleggio as a particularly laborious case of finding a successful strategy for territorial uniqueness. Finally I elaborated on the articulate sensory expertise that contemporary cheese-makers need in order to showcase their product. The vitriolic meal about the reinvented '*stracchino* of the old days' provides a useful counterexample to the reinvented Strachitunt: it unveils the ubiquitous tactics of internal competition that go hand in hand with the vocal alliances against lowland competitors, rallying together with as many 'Princes of the Orobie'. It spelt out how arguments for territorial exceptions, such as the one upheld by PDO areas of production, can coexist and compete with arguments for heritage distinction that are based, in this case, uniquely on the dairy excellence (*eccellenza casearia*) of specific techniques and traditions – such as that of making cheese with raw milk *a munta calda*.

Is all this culinary 'postmodernism'? I use this expression referring to Laudan's definition of 'culinary modernism' (2004), namely the modernization of food systems at the turn of the previous century, and I suggest it is something more complex and multifaceted. The scenario I described is perhaps postmodern, because it has long lost the innocence of naturalization. We can certainly share Piero Sardo's provocation to think of mountain cheeses as 'exquisitely useless' in the big picture of food systems (Sardo 2003: 47), thus necessarily a luxury. However, partly because they will never generate the quantities of industrial dairies, partly because their economic returns will always be limited, their own existence is endangered when the communities of skilled practitioners they rely on fail to reproduce themselves. As historian Mauro Ambrosoli argues, 'natural' *alpeggio* cheese does not exist: 'the destiny of alpine cheeses has always been determined by local and national choices' (Ambrosoli 2003: 38).

As a political and cultural strategy, the Strachitunt makers certainly kept what they perceived as Slow Food's 'premodernism' at arm's length.[4] They initially accused Slow Food of exorbitant requests to reverse-engineer what was praised as a modern food chain – something to be proud of in the Bergamasque mountains – to return to 'Taliban' standards of animal husbandry that would actually be cruel to contemporary dairy cows, as they would 'starve' on 'just grass'. Such were the expressions used to counter the requests to purge fodder from cows diet (and thus to return to less productive, smaller-size dairy cows) as equal to an excess of puritan iconoclasm.

In the same breath, though, through its discourse and practice of relocalization, the Strachitunt spokespersons did embrace the 'reverse orientalism' that Ann Meneley (2007) rightly points out in the rhetoric around the 'naturalness' of Mediterranean olive oil. The argument for a mountain PDO claimed that Val Taleggio cannot be but the natural cradle of excellent Strachitunt because this is where Brown alpine cows thrive (regardless of what they eat) and this is where Strachitunt was traditionally and continuously made (regardless of the tradition of transhumant dairy farming). Ann Meneley is right to map the discourses and practices of induced 'economic revitalization' as a clear sign of cultural imperialism: in the case of olive oil, 'An explicit alterity between Northern Europe and the Mediterranean was posited, with the North seen as more advanced technologically and economically as opposed to the Mediterranean, which was lagging behind and stagnating (Meneley 2007: 681)'. While this held true of Central Italy in the eighteenth century, it still applies to the alpine backwaters in desperate need to sell *something*, especially after several years of economic crisis that have significantly shrunk the national industrial production.

The language and practice of dairy excellence refract on local level the major power imbalances of the market as well as the neoliberal moralization of the pervasive practice of competition: we can see them at work in the keen appropriation of territorial exceptionalism and of heritage distinction, extending the logic of free entrepreneurship to marginalized producers. In this competitive symbolic and economic framework, marketing the 'excellence' of a dairy system meant excluding some producers while celebrating others. Thus the Val Taleggio community-driven PDO did not necessarily instigate *collaboration* across a range of producers but rather competition. It did not produce commons, but rather a patrimony.

Administrative, municipal and production protocol boundaries are thus naturalized and risk becoming bounds of sense altogether, facilitating symbolic forms of localization of food systems: the 'civilizations' of Taleggio, of Strachitunt, or of *stracchino*. This aspect of the relocalization model, which is being hailed as a recipe for sustainable and participatory development, is often overlooked, especially in manifestos that insist on the local as the one dimension that allows to rescale trust, cooperation and transparency vis-à-vis global food systems.[5] Engagement, involvement and participation are the keywords by which a multisensory tourism of direct experience would sensitize the urban populations to the mountain patrimony they too should take care of. In a process of reciprocal modelling and mimicking, of competition and contamination, reinventions require performance.

However, heritage revaluation through autochthonous cultivars and reliance on the resilience of small farming communities adds to the 'the perils of belonging' that such insistence on autochthony brings along even in other world regions (Geschiere 2011). To avoid an all-too-easy localist short-circuit of the emerging need to refocus on local resources, a healthy response on the institutional side would consist of placing such social and cultural ferments within robust conversations on diversity and globalization. In my monograph on the solidarity economy movement in Italy (2013), I pointed out some of the ambivalences in the local food movement. Local provisioning through solidarity economy networks aims at shortening the food chain as a guarantee for trustworthy transactions, acting in 'solidarity' with local smallholders to counteract their marginalization. However, insistence on name-sovereignty and supporting local and regional economies seems to support further discourses of food autochthony and sovereignty. In other words, food activists can unwittingly connive in a discourse of the relocalization of food that does not spare parochial sentiments (Grasseni 2014b).

In this ethnography of producers, we saw how even within strategic coalitions that straddle parochial boundaries, competition and reciprocal suspicion can and do emerge. In fact, there is a diplomatic mistrust at work even among collaborating partners, who cooperate to survive, under the competitive framework of the global hierarchy of value. Performativity more than participation is expected of consumers, and elicited even in 'participated' projects such as those of eco-museums. An integrated social agricultural policy could ensure that sustain ability, economic revival and social participation do go hand in hand. This is nevertheless not happening yet. In fact this ethnography shows that it would be unfair to expect this from socioeconomic actors who ultimately pursue their own survival, by skilfully and dynamically positioning themselves in a heritage arena.

Notes

1. Pedigree historical documentation counts, and Taleggio claims its appearance in Pliny's Historia Naturalis (Book 3, Chapter 17) in its historical dossier for obtaining PDO designation: see http://ec.europa.eu/agriculture/quality/door/documentDisplay.html?chkDocument=3310_1_it. The source seems misquoted, as Chapter 17 of Book 3 of the Historia Naturalis focuses on the peoples of Central Italy. However, it is historically documented by local researchers that the 'well-matured cheese' of Val Taleggio features in tax tributes to the Dukedom of Milan in the fourteenth century (Arrigoni 2008: 52n202; Salvetti 1989: 94).
2. Many thanks to Benjamin Wolf for welcoming me at the Harvard FAS Center for Systems Biology and showing me the preliminary results of this cross-continental comparison of the biota living on cheese's rind. For an anthropological reading of the Dutton's laboratory developments, see Paxson and Helmreich (2014).
3. Food and Heritage: A Workshop to Underpin Future Research Collaboration, SOAS, London, 18 September 2014.
4. For a plea for 'culinary modernism' as opposed to Slow Food neo-rural celebration of the virtues of peasant traditions, see Laudan (2004).
5. See for instance the Manifesto of the Italian Territorialist Society, an influential circle of scholars and activists that fosters 'cultures of place' and of local landscapes against the deterritorialization and 'despatialization' of the global economy, retrieved 22 August 2014 from www.societadeiterritorialisti.it/images/DOCUMENTI/manifesto/110221b_draft.of.the.territorialists.society.manifesto.pdf.

Bibliography

Adell, N., R. Bendix, C. Bortolotto and M. Tauschek (eds). 2015. *Between Imagined Communities and Communities of Practice*. Göttingen: Universitätsverlag Göttingen.

Agnew, J. C. 2003. 'The Give and Take of Consumer Culture', in S. Strasser (ed.), *Commodifying Everything: Relationships of the Market*. New York: Taylor and Francis, pp. 11-39.

Aistara, G. 2014. 'Authentic Anachronisms', *Gastronomica. The Journal of Critical Food Studies* 14(4): 7–16.

Albera, D., and G. Lebaudy. 2001. *La Routo. Sulle vie della transumanza tra le Alpi e il mare*. Cuneo: Primalpe.

Angelini, G.B. 1724. *La Discrizione dell'Uccellare col Roccolo. Composta, e dedicata al genio de Bergomaschi, ed alla curiosità de Forestieri*. Bergamo: Stamperia Giovanni Santini.

Appadurai, A. 1981. 'Gastro-Politics in Hindu South Asia', *American Ethnologist* 8(3): 494–511.

———. 1986. 'Commodities and the Politics of Value', in A. Appadurai (ed.), *The Social Life of Things. Commodities in Cultural Perspective*. Cambridge: Cambridge University Press, pp. 3–63.

Arrigoni, A. (ed.). 1983. *Documenti sulla Valle Taleggio. Visita di San Carlo 1566. Stato d'Anime 1568. Testi Inediti a cura di Arrigo Arrigoni. Documenti dell'Archivio Arcivescovile di Milano*. Malnate: Tipografia La Grafica.

——— (ed.). 2008. *Documenti sulla Valle Taleggio. Giuseppe Locatelli, Cenni, ed Osservazioni sulla Vallata di Taleggio. Libri quattro in un sol' volume. Giorgio Maria Arrigoni. Memorie Storiche del Comune di Vedeseta nella Valle Taleggio Milanese. Due libri*. Città di Castello: GEAM.

Avogadri. A. (ed.). 1999. *Presente e futuro dei pascoli alpini in Europa*. Milan: Franco Angeli.

Baldin, L. 2006. 'Museo diffuso ed ecomuseo: analogie e differenze', in I. Testa (ed.), *Presente e futuro dell'ecomuseo. Strumenti per la comunità: ecomusei e musei etnografici. Atti del Seminario 21–22 Maggio 2004. Ecomuseo del Lago d'Orta e Mottarone*. Turin: Laboratorio Ecomusei Regione Piemonte, pp. 35–40.

Ballacchino, K., and A. Broccolini. 2009. 'La zappa, il fuoco e il lago. Cibo e identità intorno al Lago di Bolsena', *Culture della sostenibilità* 6: 102–33.

Bausinger, H. 1969. 'Zur Algebra der Kontinuität', in H. Bausinger and W. Brückner (eds), *Kontinuität? Geschichtlichkeit und Dauer als volkskundliches Problem*. Berlin: Erich Schmidt Verlag, pp. 9–30.

Belasco, W. 2006. *Appetite for Change: How the Counterculture Took on the Food Industry.* Ithaca: Cornell University Press (2nd. Edition).

Belotti, E. 2000. 'Ricerche su un formaggio tradizionale delle valli bergamasche: lo "Strachitund"', Ph.D. dissertation. Università degli Studi di Milano.

Bendix, R. 1997. *In Search of Authenticity: The Formation of Folklore Studies.* Madison: University of Wisconsin Press.

———. 2007. 'Kulturelles Erbe zwischen Wirtschaft und Politik. Ein Ausblick', in D. Hemme, M. Tauschek and R. Bendix (eds), *Prädikat 'Heritage'. Wertschöpfungen aus kulturellen Ressourcen.* Berlin: LIT-Verlag, pp. 337–56.

Bendix, R., A. Eggert and A. Peselmann. 2012. 'Introduction: Heritage Regimes and the State', in R. Bendix, A. Eggert and A. Peselmann (eds), *Heritage Regimes and the State.* Göttingen: Universitaetsverlag Göttingen, pp. 11–20.

Bendix, R., and V. Hafstein. 2009. 'Culture and Property. An Introduction', *Ethnologia Europaea* 39(2): 5–10.

Bendix, R., D. Hemme and M. Tauschek. 2007. 'Vorwort', in D. Hemme, M. Tauschek and R. Bendix (eds), *Prädikat 'Heritage'. Wertschöpfungen aus kulturellen Ressourcen.* Berlin: LIT-Verlag, pp. 1–19.

Bérard, L., and P. Marchenay. 1995. 'Lieux, temps et preuves. La construction sociale des produits de terroir', *Terrain* 24: 153–64.

Bertolotti, G., I. Melli, E. Minervini, G. Sanga, P. Sassu and I. Sordi. 1979. *Premana: ricerca su una comunità artigiana.* Milan: Silvana.

Bessière, J., and L. Tibère. 2011. 'Innovation et patrimoine alimentaire en Midi-Pyrénées', *Anthropology of Food* 8. Retrieved 29 June 2015 from http://aof.revues.org/6759.

Bestor, T. 2014. 'Most F(l)avored nation Status: The Gastrodiplomacy of Japan's Global Promotion of Cuisine', *Public Diplomacy* 11: 57–60.

Bianchi, C., M. Corti and G. de Ros. 2005. 'Il sistema zootecnico di una valle prealpina e le sue prospettive alla luce di criteri di sostenibilità', *Quaderni SoZooAlp* 2: 130–39.

Biffi, O. 2014. 'Sostenibilità e partecipazione in due aree rurali marginali: una comparazione di progetti di sviluppo locale', *EtnoAntropologia* 2(2): 47-68.

Bindi, L. 2005. *Bandiere, Antenne Campanili. Comunità Immaginate nello Specchio dei Media.* Rome: Meltemi.

———. 2012. 'Manger avec les yeux', in L. Fournier, D. Crozat,C. Bernié-Boissard and C. Chastagner (eds), *Patrimoine et valorisation des territoires.* Paris: Editions L'Harmattan, pp. 53–64.

Bindi, L., and C. Grasseni. 2014. 'Media Heritagization of Food', *Arxius de Ciències Socials* 30: 59–72.

Bingen, J. 2012. 'Labels of Origin for Food, the New Economy and Opportunities for Rural Development in the US', *Agriculture and Human Values* 29: 543-552.

Black, R. 2012. *Porta Palazzo. The Anthropology of an Italian Market.* Philadelphia: University of Pennsylvania Press.

Black, R., and R. Ulin (eds). 2013. *Wine and Culture. Vineyard to Glass.* New York: Bloomsbury Academic.

Bourdieu, P. 1993. *The Field of Cultural Production.* New York: Columbia University Press.

Bowen, S. 2011. 'The Importance of Place: Re-territorialising Embeddedness', *Sociologia Ruralis* 51(4): 325–48.

Braudel, F. 1995. *The Mediterranean at the Age of Philip II*. First published in French : *La Méditerranée et la Monde Méditerranéen à l'Époque de Philippe II*, 1949. Berkeley: University of California Press.

Brulotte, R., and A. Starkman. 2014. 'Caldo de Piedra and Claiming Pre-Hispanic Cuisine as Cultural Heritage', in R. Brulotte and M. DiGiovine (eds), *Edible Identities. Food as Cultural Heritage*. Dorchester: Ashgate, pp. 109–24.

Buijtin, C., J. van Ophem and G. Casimir (eds). 2013. *The Arena of Everyday Life*. Wageningen: Wageningen Academic Publishers.

Burigana, D. 2013. 'L'Italie, la France et les fromages « typiques » (1950–2009). Aux origines d'une politique étrangère europeènne?', in G. Ceccarelli, A. Grandi and S. Magagnoli, (eds), *La typicité dans l'histoire. Tradition, innovation et terroir/ Typicality in History. Tradition, Innovation, and Terroir*. Bruxelles: Peter Lang, pp. 239–62.

Carminati, A., and C. Locatelli (eds). 2004. *Bergamini. Ventun racconti di vita contadina della Valle Taleggio*. Sant'Omobono: Centro Studi Valle Imagna.

Castellanos, E., and S. Bergstresser. 2006. 'Food Fights at the EU Table: The Gastronomic Assertion of Italian Distinctiveness', *European Studies* 22: 179–202.

———. 2014. 'The Mexican and Transnational Lives of Corn: Technological, Political, Edible Object', in R. Brulotte and M. DiGiovine (eds), *Edible Identities. Food as Cultural Heritage*. Dorchester: Ashgate, pp. 201–18.

Cavanaugh, J. 2005. 'Lard', in D. Kulick and A. Meneley (eds), *Fat. The Anthropology of an Obsession*. New York: Penguin, pp. 139–51.

———. 2007. 'Making Salami, Producing Bergamo: The Transformation of Value', *Ethnos* 72(2): 149–72.

———. 2009. *Living Memory: The Social Aesthetics of Language in a Northern Italian Town*. Hoboken, NJ: Wiley Blackwell.

Ceccarelli, G., A. Grandi and S. Magagnoli (eds.) 2013. *La typicité dans l'histoire. Tradition, innovation et terroir/Typicality in History. Tradition, Innovation, and Terroir*. Bruxelles: Peter Lang.

Chastel, A., and J.P. Babelon. 1994 . *La notion du patrimoine*. Paris: Editions Liana Levi.

Chrzan, J. 2004. 'Slow Food: What, Why and to Where?', *Food, Culture and Society* 7(2): 117–32.

———. 2007. 'Dreaming of Tuscany. Pursuing the Anthropology of Culinary Tourism', *Expedition* 49(2): 21–27.

Clifford, S., M. Maggi and D. Murtas. 2006. *Genius Loci: perché, quando e come realizzare una Mappa di comunità*. Turin: IRES Piemonte.

Comunità Montana Valle Brembana. 2000. *Piano di sviluppo socio-economico. La qualità della vita in Valle Brembana*. Brescia: F.T. Service.

———. 2006. *Programma integrato di sviluppo locale*. DOCUP Obiettivo 2 Regione Lombardia (2000–2006). Allegato D, Delibera n. 8/37 del 09/12/2005. Retrieved 29 June 2015 from http://www.provincia.bergamo.it/provpordocs/Pisl%20Valle%20Brembana(1).pdf.

Consorzio Formaggio 'De Mut' Alta Valle Brembana. 1985. *Formai de Mut dell 'Alta Valle Brembana*. Piazza Brembana. Retrieved 6 August 2014 from http://www.politicheagricole.it/flex/cm/pages/ServeBLOB.php/L/IT/IDPagina/3340.

Consorzio Tutela 'Formai de Mut' dell'Alta Valle Brembana. 1995. *Integrazione dossier comunicato ai sensi del regolamento 2081/92*. Piazza Brembana. Retrieved 6 August 2014 from http://www.politicheagricole.it/flex/cm/pages/ServeBLOB.php/L/IT/IDPagina/3340.

Corti, M. 2004. '*Süssura de l' aalp.* Il sistema dell'alpeggio nelle Alpi lombarde', *Annali di San Michele* 17: 31–155.
———. 2006a. 'Bitto: una storia esemplare, una questione aperta', *Caseus. Arte e cultura del formaggio* 11(3): 19–30.
———. 2006b. 'I *bergamini*: un profilo dei protagonisti della transumanza bovina lombarda', *Studi sulla transumanza e l'alpeggio* 1: 1–49.
———. 2011. 'Il formaggio bitto, un re figlio delle Orobie', *Quaderni Brembani* 10: 85–123.
———. 2012. *I Ribelli del Bitto. Quando una tradizione casearia diventa eversiva.* Turin: Slow Food Editore.
Counihan, C. 2004. *Around the Tuscan Table. Food, Family and Gender in 20th Century Florence.* New York: Routledge.
Counihan, C., and V. Siniscalchi (eds). 2014. *Food Activism: Agency, Democracy and Economy.* New York: Bloomsbury.
Davis, P. 1999. *Ecomuseums. A Sense of Place.* London: Leicester University Press.
Da Lezze, G. 1596. (reprint 1988). *Descrizione di Bergamo e del suo territorio.* Bergamo: Provincia di Bergamo/Lucchetti Editore.
De Barry, M.O., A. Desvallées and F. Wasserman (eds). 1994. *Vagues, Une anthologie de la nouvelle muséologie,* vol. 2. Mâcon: Éditions W-M.N.E.S.
De Biasi, M., and G. Stecchi. 2004. *Racconti di Lombardia. Dalla terra alla tavola.* Regione Lombardia: Ezio Parma Editore.
De Martino, E. 1977. *La fine del mondo. Contributo all'analisi delle apocalissi culturali.* Turin: Einaudi.
Del Marmol, C., M. Morell and J. Chalcraft (eds). 2015. *The Making of Heritage. Seduction and Disenchantment.* London: Routledge.
Dematteo, L. 2007. *L'idiotie en politique. Subversion et néo-populisme en Italie.* Paris: Fondation Maison des sciences de l'homme.
———. 2009. *La Ruée des entrepreneurs italiens vers la Roumanie.* Paris: Notre Europe.
Desvallées, A. 1998. 'À l'origine du mot patrimoine', in D. Poulot (ed.), *Patrimoine et Modernité.* Paris: L'Harmattan, pp. 89–105.
De Varine, H. 2012. *As raízes do futuro: o patrimônio a serviço do desenvolvimento local.* Porto Alegre: Medianiz.
Di Giovine, M. 2009. *The Heritage-scape: UNESCO, World Heritage, and Tourism.* Lanham, MD: Lexington Books.
———. 2014. 'The Everyday as Extraordinary: Revitalization, Religion, and the Elevation of *Cucina Casareccia* to Heritage Cuisine in Pietrelcina, Italy', in R. Brulotte and M. DiGiovine (eds), *Edible Identities. Food as Cultural Heritage.* Dorchester: Ashgate, pp. 77–92.
Di Mambro, A. 2009. 'Quando la Dop all'Italiana rischia il flop', *DNews*, 7 July.
Disciplinare di Produzione della Denominazione di Origine Protetta 'Bitto'. No date. Retrieved 6 August 2014 from http://www.politicheagricole.it/flex/cm/pages/ServeBLOB.php/L/IT/IDPagina/3340.
Douglas, M. 1972 'Deciphering a Meal', *Daedalus. Journal of the American Academy of Arts and Sciences,* 101(1): 61-81.
Ferrario, D. 1990. *Lontano da Roma.* Rome: RAI, Radio Televisione Italiana.
Finnis, E. (ed.). 2012. *Re-imagining Marginalized Foods.* Tucson: University of Arizona Press.

Fournier, L., D. Crozat, C. Bernié-Boissard and C. Chastagner (eds). 2012. *Patrimoine et désirs d'identité.* Paris: Editions L'Harmattan.
GAL (Gruppo di Azione Locale) Valle Brembana. 1998. *Piano di Azione Locale.* Bergamo: Corponove Editrice.
Galli, A., and G. Oldrati. 1993. *L'assistenza tecnica in agricoltura: quale futuro?* Bergamo: Amministrazione Provinciale Settore Agricoltura.
Gambera, A. and Surra, E. 2003. *Le forme del latte.* Bra: Slow Food Editore.
Garlandini, A. 2010. 'Ecomusei e musei per la valorizzazione del patrimonio culturale immateriale. Nuovi istituti culturali per nuove missioni', in C. Grasseni (ed.), *Ecomuseologie.* Rimini: Guaraldi, pp. 19–32.
Geschiere, P. 2011. *The Perils of Belonging. Autochthony, Citizenship, and Exclusion in Africa and Europe.* Chicago: University of Chicago Press.
Gherardi, S., and G. Oldrati (eds). 1997. *Alpeggi in Provincia di Bergamo.* Clusone: Ferrari Editrice.
Ghezzi, A. 2013. 'Blutunt. Così Taddei rilancia l'Erborinato della Tradizione', *Affari di Gola* n. 8 June 2013. Supplemento al n. 24 de 'La Rassegna', 20 June 2013. Retrieved 17 June 2016 from https://issuu.com/affaridigola/docs/affari_di_gola_-_giugno_2013
Gieser, T. 2014. 'Enskillment inhibited: 'industrial gardening' in Britain', *Journal of the Royal Anthropological Institute* 20: 131-149.
Gilberti, L. 2005. 'Alpeggi e Affari, la guerra del Bitto', *Corriere della Sera*, 14 October 2005, p. 12.
Grasseni, C. 2003. 'Packaging Skills: Calibrating Italian Cheese to the Global Market', in S. Strasser (ed.), *Commodifying Everything: Relationships of the Market.* New York: Routledge, pp. 341–81.
———. 2004. 'Skilled Vision. An Apprenticeship in Breeding Aesthetics' *Social Anthropology* 12(1): 1–15.
———. 2005a 'Designer Cows: The Practice of Cattle Breeding between Skill and Standardization', *Society and Animals* 13(1): 33–50.
———. 2005b. 'Disciplining Vision in Animal Biotechnology', *Anthropology in Action* 12(2): 44–55.
———. 2007a. *La reinvenzione del Cibo. Culture del gusto fra tradizione e globalizzazione ai piedi delle Alpi.* Verona: Qui Edit.
———. (ed.) 2007b. *Skilled Visions. Between Apprenticeship and Standards.* Oxford: Berghahn.
———. 2007c. 'Managing Cows: An Ethnography of Breeding Practices and Reproductive Technology in Contemporary Dairy Farming', *Studies in the History and Philosophy of Biological and Biomedical Sciences* 38(2): 488–510.
———. 2009. *Developing Skill, Developing Vision. Practices of Locality at the Foot of the Alps.* Oxford: Berghahn.
———. 2011. 'Re-inventing Food: Alpine Cheese in the Age of Global Heritage', *Anthropology of Food* 8. Retrieved 29 June 2015 from http://aof.revues.org/index6819.html.
———. 2012. 'Resisting Cheese. Boundaries, Conflict and Distinction at the Foot of the Alps', *Food Culture and Society* 15(1): 23–29.
———. 2013. *Beyond Alternative Food Networks. Italy's Solidarity Purchase Groups.* London: Bloomsbury Academic.
———. 2014a. 'Relocalizing Milk and Cheese', *Gastronomica. Journal of Critical Food Studies* 14(4): 34–43.

Grasseni, C. 2014b. 'Family Farmers between Re-localisation and Co-production', *Anthropological Notebooks* 20(3): 49–66.

———. 2015. 'Seductions and Disenchantments in the Making of an Ecomuseum', in C. del Marmol, M. Morell and J. Chalcraft (eds.), *The Making of Heritage. Seduction and Disenchantment.* New York: Routledge, pp. 59-78.

Grasseni, C., and H. Paxson (eds.). 2014. 'Introducing a Special Issue on the Reinvention of Food: Connection and Mediation', *Gastronomica* 14(4): 1–6.

Gray, J. 1999. 'Open Spaces, Dwelling Places. Being at Home on Hill Farms in the Scottish Borders', *American Ethnologist* 26(2): 440–60.

———. 2000. 'The Common Agricultural Policy and the Re-Invention of the Rural in the European Community', *Sociologia Ruralis* 40(1): 30–52.

Halbertsma, M. 2011. 'Introduction', in M. Halbertsma, A. van Stipriaan and P. van Ulzen (eds), *The Heritage Theatre: Globalisation and Cultural Heritage.* Newcastle: Cambridge Scholars, pp. 1–30.

Handler, R. 1985. 'On Having a Culture: Nationalism and the Preservation of Quebec's *Patrimoine*', in G. Stocking (ed.), *Objects and Others. Essays on Museums and Material Culture.* Madison: University of Wisconsin Press, pp. 192–217.

Harper, D., and P. Faccioli. 2010. *The Italian Way. Food and Social Life.* Chicago: University of Chicago Press.

Harrison, R. (ed.) 2010. *Understanding the politics of heritage.* Manchester: Manchester University Press.

Hausschild, T. 2005. 'A Short Cultural History of Puking', in I. Zimprich (ed.), *Relocated Identities Part II. Relocating Products and People.* Amsterdam: Public Space With A Roof, www.pswar.org.

Heady, P. 1999. *The Hard People. Rivalry, Sympathy and Social Structure in an Alpine Valley.* Amsterdam: Harwood Academic Publishers.

Herzfeld, M. 1986. *Ours Once More. Folklore, Ideology, and the Making of Modern Greece.* New York: Pella.

———. 1991. *A Place in History: Social and Monumental Time in a Cretan Town.* Princeton, NJ: Princeton University Press.

———. 1992. *The Social Production of Indifference. Exploring the Symbolic Roots of Western Bureaucracy.* Chicago: University of Chicago Press.

———. 2004. *The Body Impolitic: Artisans and Artifice in the Global Hierarchy of Value.* Chicago: University of Chicago Press.

———. 2005. *Cultural Intimacy: Social Poetics in the Nation-State*, 2nd edn. New York: Routledge.

———. 2007. 'Deskilling, 'Dumbing Down' and the Auditing of Knowledge in the Practical Mastery of Artisans and Academics: An Ethnographer's Response to a Global Problem', in M. Harris (ed.), *Ways of Knowing. Anthropological Approaches to Crafting Experience and Knowledge.* Oxford: Berghahn Books, pp. 91–110.

———. 2009. *Evicted From Eternity: The Restructuring of Modern Rome.* Chicago: University of Chicago Press.

Hobsbawm, E., and T. Ranger. 1983. *The Invention of Tradition.* Cambridge: Cambridge University Press.

Huseby, K. 2012. *The Taste of Mountain Grass.* Video. Tromsø: Visual Cultural Studies Unit, University of Tromsø.

Igoe, J. 2010. 'The Spectacle of Nature in the Global Economy of Appearances: Anthropological Engagements with the Spectacular Mediations of Transnational Conservation', *Critique of Anthropology* 30(4): 375–97.

Jacini, S. 1882. *Atti della Giunta per la Inchiesta Agraria e sulle condizioni della classe agricola. Volume VI, Tomo I, Fasc. I. Relazione del Commissario Conte Stefano Jacini, Senatore del Regno, sulla DECIMA CIRCOSCRIZIONE (provincie di Pavia – meno i circondari di Voghera e Bòbbio – Milano, Cremona, Mantova, Como, Sondrio, Bergamo e Brescia).* Rome: Forzani e C., Tipografi del Senato.

Jasanoff, S., and S.H. Kim. 2009. 'Containing the Atom: Sociotechnical Imaginaries and Nuclear Power in the United States and South Korea', *Minerva* 47: 119–46.

Jones, S. 2005. 'Transhumance Re-examined', *Journal of the Royal Anthropological Institute* 11(2): 357–59.

Kah, S., and N. Weixlbaumer, 2013. 'Walser's Pride. A Mountain Cheese as Part of Regional Identity and Regional Development Strategies in the Biosphere Reserve *Großes Walsertal*, Austria', in G. Ceccarelli, A. Grandi and S. Magagnoli, (eds), *La typicité dans l'histoire. Tradition, innovation et terroir/Typicality in History. Tradition, Innovation, and Terroir.* Bruxelles: Peter Lang, pp. 177–88.

Kalb, D. 2004. 'Editorial. Danse Macabre', *Focaal* 44: v–vii.

Kaneff, D., and A. King. 2004. 'Introduction. Owning Culture'. *Focaal* 44: 3–19.

Karpik, L. 2007. *L'économie des singularités.* Paris, Gallimard.

Kim, C.-H. 2012. 'From Kimchi to Infinity. The Spicy Fermented Cabbage Prepares for Its Moment in the Spotlight', *Hyphen. Asian American Unabridged* 25. Retrieved 29 June 2015 from http://www.hyphenmagazine.com/magazine/issue-25-generation/kimchi-infinity.

Kirshenblatt-Gimblett, B. 1995. 'Theorizing Heritage', *Ethnomusicology* 39(3): 368–80.

———. 2004. 'Intangible Heritage as Metacultural Production', *Museum International* 56(1–2): 52–65.

Kulick, D., and A. Meneley (eds). 2005. *Fat. The Anthropology of an Obsession.* New York: Penguin.

Latour, B. 1988. *The Pasteurization of France.* Cambridge, Mass.: Harvard University Press.

Laudan, R. 2004. 'Slow Food: The French Terroir Strategy, and Culinary Modernism', *Food, Culture and Society* 7(2): 134–44.

Leitch, A. 2003. 'Slow Food and the Politics of Pork Fat: Italian Food and European Identity', *Ethnos* 68(4): 437–62.

Lions Club Valle Brembana (ed.). 1980. *Statuti Antichi di Valle Taleggio e Averara. Monumenta Bergomensia.* Gorle: Grafica Gutenberg.

Long, L.M. 2004. 'Introduction', in L. Long (ed.), *Culinary Tourism.* Louisville: University of Kentucky Press, pp. 1–19.

Malkki, L. 1992. 'National Geographic: The Rooting of Peoples and the Territorialization of National Identity among Scholars and Refugees', *Cultural Anthropology* 7(1): 24–44.

Markowitz, L. 2012. 'Highland Haute Cuisine. The Transformation of Alpaca Meat', in E. Finnis (ed.), *Redefining Marginalized Foods. Global Processes, Local Places.* Tucson: University of Arizona Press, pp. 34–48.

Masoni, T. 1990. *Lontano da Roma. Il cinema di Ermanno Olmi.* Lucca: La Casa Usher.

May, S. 2013. 'Cheese, Commons and Commerce. On the Politics and Practices of Branding Regional Food', *Ethnologia Europaea* 43(2): 62–77.

Meneley, A. 2007. 'Like an Extra Virgin', *American Anthropologist* 109(4): 678–87.
———. 2011. 'Blood, Sweat and Tears in a Bottle of Palestinian Extra-Virgin Olive Oil', *Food, Culture and Society* 14(2): 275–92.
———. 2014. 'Resistance Is Fertile', *Gastronomica. The Journal of Critical Food Studies* 14(4): 70–79.
Messina, P. 2006. 'Culture politiche locali e comparazione per contesti: un approccio ecologico all'analisi dei sistemi politici locali', in C. Grasseni (ed.), *Antropologia ed epistemologia per lo studio della contemporaneità*. Rimini: Guaraldi, pp. 77–96.
Milano, S., and R. Ponzio (eds). 2004. 'Le pagine gialle dei presidi Slow Food', *I Quaderni di Micromega*, supplement to n. 5: 167–222.
Mitterpacher, L. 1784. *Elementi d'agricoltura di Lodovico Mitterpacher, pubblicati per ordine del Regio Governo*, Milan: Imperial Monistero di S. Ambrogio Maggiore.
Mocarelli, L. 2013. 'The Long Struggle for the Chianti Denomination. Quality versus Quantity', in G. Ceccarelli, A. Grandi and S. Magagnoli, (eds), *La typicité dans l'histoire. Tradition, innovation et terroir/Typicality in History. Tradition, Innovation, and Terroir.* Bruxelles: Peter Lang, pp. 323–40.
Netting, R. McC. 1981. *Balancing on an Alp. Ecological Change and Continuity in a Swiss Mountain Community.* Cambridge: Cambridge University Press.
Oriani, R. 2014. 'Il Supermercato del Futuro', *Wired Magazine*, April 2014, pp. 27-29.
Papa, C. (ed.). 1992. *Il pane: antropologia e storia dell'alimentazione.* Perugia: Electa Editori Umbri.
———. 1999. *Antropologia dell'impresa.* Milano: Guerini.
———. 2002. 'Il prodotto tipico come ossimoro: il caso dell'olio extravergine di oliva umbro', in V. Siniscalchi (ed.), *Frammenti di economie. Ricerche di antropologia economica in Italia.* Cosenza: Luigi Pellegrini Editore.
Paxson, H. 2008. 'Post-Pasteurian Cultures: The Microbiopolitics of Raw-Milk Cheese in the United States', *Cultural Anthropology* 23(1): 15–47.
———. 2010. 'Cheese Cultures: Transforming American Tastes and Traditions', *Gastronomica* 10(4): 35–47.
———. 2012. *The Life of Cheese: Crafting Food and Value in America.* Berkeley: University of California Press.
———. 2014. 'Re-Inventing a Tradition of Invention: Entrepreneurialism as Heritage in American Artisan Cheesemaking', in R. Brulotte and M. Di Giovine (eds), *Edible Identities – Food as Cultural Heritage.* Dorchester: Ashgate, pp. 29–38.
Paxson, H., and S. Helmreich. 2014. 'The Perils and Promises of Microbial Abundance: Novel Natures and Model Ecosystems, from Artisanal Cheese to Alien Seas', *Social Studies of Science* 44: 165–93.
Paxson, H., and H. West (eds). 2012. *Naming Cheese: Essays by the Cheese Scholars Collective,* Special issue of *Food Culture and Society* 15(1).
Pesenti, E. 2002. "La produzione d'alpeggio e di latteria di un formaggio tradizionale: lo 'Strachitund'". Ph.D. dissertation, Università degli Studi di Milano.
Peters, J.D. 1997. 'Seeing Bifocally: Media Place Culture,' in A. Gupta and J. Ferguson (eds), *Culture, Power, Place: Explorations in Critical Anthropology.* Durham, NC: Duke University Press, pp. 75–92.
Petrini, C. 2007. *Slow Food Nation: Why Our Food Should Be Good, Clean, And Fair.* New York: Rizzoli Ex Libris.

Petridou, E. 2012. 'What's in a Place Name? Branding and Labeling Cheese in Greece', *Food Culture and Society* 15(1): 29–34.
Revelli, N. 1977. *Il mondo dei vinti. Testimonianze di vita contadina*. Turin: Einaudi.
Roigé, X., and J. Frigolé (eds). 2012. *Constructing Cultural and Natural Heritage. Parks, Museums and Rural Heritage*. Barcelona: Documenta.
Sage, C. 2011. 'Conventions of Quality and Governance of Artisan Food: Revealing the Tyranny of 'Sound Science' in the Regulation of Irish Raw Milk Cheese', in P. O'Mahony (ed.), *Irish Environmental Politics: The Communicative Turn*. Manchester: Manchester University Press, pp. 117–39.
Salvetti, S. 1989. *Taleggio: la terra la storia*. Clusone: Edizioni Villadiseriane.
Sanga, G. 1979. 'La colonia in patria. La funzione della cultura tradizionale nella costruzione dell'ideologia premanese', in G. Bertolotti, I. Melli, E. Minervini, G. Sanga, P. Sassu, I. Sordi, *Premana: ricerca su una comunità artigiana*. Milano: Silvana, pp. 271-528.
Sardo, P. 2003a. 'La squisita inutilità dei formaggi di montagna', *L'Alpe* 9: 46–49.
———. 2003b. 'Tipico?', in A. Gambera and E. Surra (eds), *Le forme del latte*. Bra: Slow Food Editore, pp. 305–7.
———. 2004. 'Dall'Arca del Gusto ai presidi', *I Quaderni di Micromega*, supplement to n. 5: 159–66.
Schneider, J. (ed.). 1998. *Italy's 'Southern Question'. Orientalism in One Country*. London: Berg.
Scholliers, P., and A. Geyzen. 2010. 'Upgrading the Local. Belgian Cuisine in Global Waves', *Gastronomica. The Journal of Food and Culture* 10(2): 49–54.
Shapin, S. 2003. 'Cheese and Late Modernity. Review of *Camembert, A National Myth* by Pierre Boisard', *London Review of Books* (11): 11–15, 20 November.
Sibum, O. 1995. 'Reworking the Mechanical Value of Heat: Instruments of Precision and Gestures of Ac-curacy in Early Victorian England', *Studies in the History and Philosophy of Science* (26): 73-106.
Silverman, S. 1975. *Three Bells of Civilization. The Life of an Italian Hill Town*. New York: Columbia University Press.
Siniscalchi, V. 2009. 'I processi di tipicizzazione tra singolarità e ripetizione', *Culture della sostenibilità* 6: 51–66.
Smith, L.J. 2006. *The Uses of Heritage*. London and New York: Routledge.
Smith, L.J., and N. Akagawa. (eds.). 2009. *Intangible Heritage*. London and New York: Routledge.
Stacul, J. 2003. *The Bounded Field. Localism and Local Identity in an Italian Alpine Valley*. Oxford: Berghahn.
———. 2010. 'Contesting Consumption: Changing Meanings of Landscape in Northern Italy', in P. Stewart and A. Strathern (eds), *Landscape, Heritage, and Conservation: Farming Issues in the European Union*. Durham, NC: Carolina Academic Press, pp. 227–43.
Strathern, M. (ed.). 2000. *Audit Cultures*. London: Routledge.
Stefanelli, G. 1998. *Formaggi della Valle Brembana*. Bergamo: Comunità Montana Valle Brembana/ Corponove Editrice.
Sutton, D. 2006. 'Cooking skills, the senses, and memory: The fate of practical knowledge', in C. Counihan and P. Van Esterik (eds), *Food and Culture*. New York: Routledge, Third Edition, pp. 299-317.
Terrio, S. 2000. *Crafting the Culture and History of French Chocolate*. Berkeley: University of California Press.

Trubek, A. 2008. *The Taste of Place. A Cultural Journey into Terroir.* Berkeley: University of California Press.

Ulin, R. 1996. *Vintages and Traditions: An Ethnohistory of Southwest French Wine Cooperatives.* Washington, DC: Smithsonian Institution Press.

UNESCO (United Nations Educational, Scientific and Cultural Organization). 2010. *Traditional Mexican Cuisine—Ancestral, Ongoing Community Culture, the Michoacán Paradigm.* Nomination File no. 00400 for Inscription on the Representative List of the Intangible Cultural Heritage in 2010. Retrieved 11 August 2012 from http://www.unesco.org/culture/ich/index.php?lg=en&pg=00011&RL=00400.

Vaccaro, I. and Beltran, O. 2007. 'Consuming space, nature and culture: patrimonial discussions in the hyper-modern era', *Journal of Tourism Geographies* 9(3): 254-274.

Viazzo, P.P. 1989. *Upland Communities: Environment, Population, and Social Structure in the Alps since the Sixteenth Century.* Cambridge: Cambridge University Press.

Viazzo, P., and S. Woolf (eds). 2002. *Formaggi e mercati. Economie d'alpeggio in Valle d'Aosta e Haute-Savoie.* Aosta: Le Chateau.

Vitali, R. 2011. 'Guerra Fredda tra Consorzi. Per il Branzi la DOP resta lontana', *Primo Piano* 19 July. Retrieved 3 April 2014 from http://www.italiaatavola.net/articolo.aspx?id=21875.

Vitrolles, D. 2011. 'When Geographical Indication Conflicts with Food Heritage Protection. The Case of Serrano Cheese from Rio Grande do Sul, Brazil', *Anthropology of Food* 8. Retrieved 29 June 2015 from http://aof.revues.org/6809.

Weiss, B. 2011. 'Making Pigs Local: Discerning the Sensory Character of Place', *Cultural Anthropology* 26: 438-461.

West, H. 2012. 'Je m'appelle . . . Cheese', *Food Culture and Society* 15(1): 8–12.

———. 2013a. 'Thinking Like a Cheese: Towards an Ecological Understanding of the Reproduction of Knowledge in Contemporary Artisan Cheesemaking', in R. Ellen, S. Lycett and S.E. Johns (eds), *Understanding Cultural Transmission in Anthropology: A Critical Synthesis.* Oxford: Berghahn, pp. 320–45.

———. 2013b. 'Appellations and Indications of Origin, Terroir, and Social Construction', in A. Murcott, W. Belasco and P. Jackson (eds), *Handbook of Food Research.* New York: Bloomsbury, pp. 209–28.

West, H., and N. Domingos. 2012. 'Gourmandizing Poverty Food: The Serpa Cheese Slow Food Presidium', *Journal of Agrarian Change* 12(1): 120–43.

Zannoni, M., B. Morara and L. Berozzi. 2004. *La degustazione dei formaggi.* Grinzane Cavour: ONAF. Organizzazione Nazionale Assaggiatori di Formaggi.

Index